$49.95

W9-CKI-791

Culture and Customs of Portugal

Map of Portugal. (Cartography by Bookcomp, Inc.)

Culture and Customs of Portugal

CARLOS A. CUNHA AND RHONDA CUNHA

Culture and Customs of Europe

 GREENWOOD

AN IMPRINT OF ABC-CLIO, LLC
Santa Barbara, California • Denver, Colorado • Oxford, England

Library of Congress Cataloging-in-Publication Data

Cunha, Carlos.
    Culture and customs of Portugal / Carlos A. Cunha and Rhonda Cunha.
      p. cm. — (Culture and customs of Europe)
    Includes bibliographical references and index.
      ISBN 978–0–313–33440–5 (hard copy : alk. paper) — ISBN 978–0–313–04946–0 (ebook)
1. Portugal—Social life and customs—21st century. 2. Etiquette—Portugal. 3. National
characteristics, Portuguese. I. Cunha, Rhonda. II. Title.
DP533.C85   2010
946.9—dc22   2010002237

ISBN: 978–0–313–33440–5
EISBN: 978–0–313–04946–0

14 13 12 11 10   1 2 3 4 5

This book is also available on the World Wide Web as an eBook.
Visit www.abc-clio.com for details.

Greenwood
An Imprint of ABC-CLIO, LLC

ABC-CLIO, LLC
130 Cremona Drive, P.O. Box 1911
Santa Barbara, California 93116-1911

This book is printed on acid-free paper ∞

Manufactured in the United States of America

Dedicada à nossa querida filha, Cátia Sofia,
com raízes em dois mundos.

Contents

CONTENTS

Series Foreword

THE OLD WORLD and the New World have maintained a fluid exchange of people, ideas, innovations, and styles. Even though the United States became the de facto world leader and economic superpower in the wake of a devastated Europe in World War II, Europe has remained for many the standard-bearer of Western culture.

Millions of Americans can trace their ancestors to Europe. The United States as we know it was built on waves of European immigration, starting with the English, who braved the seas to found the Jamestown Colony in 1607. Bosnian and Albanian immigrants are some of the latest new Americans. In the Gilded Age of one of our great expatriates, the novelist Henry James, the Grand Tour of Europe was de rigueur for young American men of means to prepare them for a life of refinement and taste. In the more recent democratic age, scores of American college students have Eurorailed their way across Great Britain and the Continent, sampling the fabled capitals and bergs in a mad, great adventure, or have benefited from a semester abroad. For other American tourists and culture vultures, Europe is the prime destination. What is the new post-Cold War, post-Berlin Wall Europe in the new millennium? Even with the different languages, rhythms, and rituals, Europeans have much in common: They are largely well-educated, prosperous, and worldly. They also share similar goals, face common threats, and form alliances. With the advent of the European Union, the open borders, and the Euro, and considering globalization and the prospect of a homogenized Europe, an updated survey of the region is warranted.

Culture and Customs of Europe features individual volumes on the countries most studied for which fresh information is in demand from students and other readers. The Series casts a wide net, including not only the expected countries, such as Spain, France, England, and Germany, but also countries that lie outside Western Europe proper, such as Poland and Greece. Each volume is written by a country specialist who has intimate knowledge of the contemporary dynamics of a people and culture. Sustained narrative chapters cover the land, the people, and the country's brief history; they also discuss religion, social customs, gender roles, family, marriage, literature and media, performing arts and cinema, and art and architecture. The national character and ongoing popular traditions of each country are framed in a historical context and are celebrated, along with the latest trends and major cultural figures. A country map, a chronology, a glossary, and evocative photos enhance the text.

The storied and enlightened Europeans will continue to fascinate Americans. Our futures are strongly linked politically, economically, and culturally.

Preface

PORTUGAL has had a strong national identity, and for about a millennium the country has been a homogeneous nation regarding language, religion, culture, and ethnicity. Indeed, its borders have remained basically unchanged since the thirteenth century. Although the Portuguese people are culturally unified, a definitive divide exists between the rural and urban populations in terms of attitudes, lifestyles, and traditions. The gap is pronounced enough that it is difficult to make generalizations about the Portuguese people without marking the distinction between urban and rural citizens, and at times it may seem like two separate worlds are being discussed. Portugal's two largest metropolitan areas, Lisbon and Porto, have a population of approximately 6.3 million people combined, leaving the remaining 4.4 million citizens spread throughout other smaller cities and in the countryside. Urban or rural, the 10.7 million Portuguese also refer to themselves as Lusitanians, which harkens back to the name the early Romans gave to the local residents.

Despite Portugal's small size, regional diversity exists and has a strong influence on the nation's politics. The south has a long history of radicalism when compared to the conservative north, partially a result of the landless status of lower-class southerners.

António Salazar's and Marcello Caetano's dictatorship—from 1932 to 1974—did little to remedy the plight of the nation's peasants. Because Salazar realized that much of his support lay with the uneducated, conservative peasants, he had little interest in educating the rural population and thus risking an unwanted side effect: disaffection with the regime and class consciousness. Salazar believed strongly in the "traditional" model of organizing an economy and society based on birth. He believed that God had given the peasant "the privilege of being poor" and that "education, health, and economic reform 'would not create happiness.'"[1]

When compared to the rest of Europe, industrialization during Salazar's leadership progressed at a snail's pace. As a result, by the 1960s and 1970s the social structure continued relatively unchanged. The upper class comprised only 1 percent of the population, while the middle class comprised 15 percent to 25 percent. The vast majority of Portuguese people were still at the bottom layer of society, but they lacked a mutual bond or a collective class consciousness to bind them together. Industrialization contributed to an increasing urban proletariat, but the major change occurred during the emergence of a large class of clerks, low-level civil servants, and others who lived just above the poverty line.[2]

In the years leading up to the revolution of 1974 that ended the dictatorship, the very small elitist class recognized the potential threat to its interests from the rising lower middle class and working class. It tightened the grip on its exclusive social position through intra-class marriages, so that by 1974 the elites were the largest landowners and held positions as directors and owners of the largest industries. They also held positions as high-ranking government officials, leading financiers, superior military officials, members of the Catholic Church hierarchy, senior university professors, and professional elites, such as top lawyers and medical professionals. Eighty percent of the economy was controlled by only eight of these elite families. Upward mobility was almost impossible except through education, which was virtually inaccessible to the lower classes.[3]

The result was mass exodus. Prior to the early 1970s Portugal lost a large part of its citizenry to emigration. More than 1.5 million Portuguese emigrated between 1960 and 1973, leading to a negative population growth rate. As a result, the second-largest "Portuguese" city after Lisbon became Paris rather than Porto. Portugal regulated and encouraged some types of emigration to meet its own requirements, such as labor for its colonies or to fulfill foreign currency needs, but about 36 percent of emigration was illegal. Northerners were more likely to emigrate externally—which was more expensive—while southerners migrated internally to the cities, adding to the radicalism of the domestic labor force. Most emigrants—whether legal or illegal—were young, single males. Reverse migration, as emigrants returned to Portugal, did not contribute substantially to economic development. Lacking transferable skills, returning emigrants did not want the same menial jobs they were willing to take abroad, and their savings generally went toward consumption rather than productive investments.[4]

One of the most dramatic changes seen in Portugal during the last few decades is that the country has shifted from a place people had to leave in order to seek their dreams of greater prosperity to a place where the standard of living and public services now attract immigrants and returning Portuguese retirees. By the mid-1990s, legal foreign residents accounted for close to 2 percent of the population. Since then, the inflow of East Europeans has inched this figure closer to 4 percent.[5]

As explained in this brief introduction, the varied aspects of the Lusitanian people and their culture are dynamic and in many ways unique, and they will be examined in detail in the following chapters. The discussion will unveil one of the oldest cultures in Western Europe. The tenacity, pragmatism, and adaptability of the Portuguese have no doubt played a hand in the nation's stubborn durability.

The authors are blessed to be a part of Portuguese communities in the United States and in Portugal. This work has benefited from the support of the Dowling College Travel and Research Funds and its Release Time Program. In addition, the Center for Sociological Study and Research at the Lisbon University Institute has provided generous assistance. Special thanks to Luísa Vasconcelos, who read and provided advice as the manuscript evolved, and André Freire in Portugal. In the United States, Maria dos Anjos Cunha and Maria Veludo provided valuable insights into rural Portuguese customs, past and present. The authors would like to express their deepest appreciation and affection for our friends and family in Fronhas, Portugal, the "home of our hearts," and to the Portuguese community of Peabody, Massachusetts for keeping the old traditions alive. The generosity of these friends and scholars has led to a study that is as free of error as possible. The authors take full responsibility for any inaccuracies that may remain.

Notes

1. Eugene K. Keefe et al., *Area Handbook for Portugal* (Washington, DC: U.S. Government Printing Office, 1977), 119.

2. Ibid., 119–120, 125–126.

3. Ibid., 119–123.

4. Maria Ioannis B. Baganha, "Portuguese Emigration After World War II," in António Costa Pinto, ed., *Contemporary Portugal: Politics, Society and Culture* (Boulder, CO: Social Science Monographs, 2003), 139–158.

5. António Barreto, "Social Change in Portugal: 1960–2000," in Ibid., Chapter 7.

Chronology

15,000–3,000 B.C.	Paleolithic cultures develop in Western Portugal.
400–200 B.C.	Greek and Carthaginian trade settlements appear on the coast.
202 B.C.	Roman armies invade ancient Lusitania.
410 A.D.	Germanic tribes Suevi and Visigoths begin their conquest of Roman Lusitania and Galicia.
714–716	Muslims begin their conquest of Visigothic Lusitania.
1034	The Christian re-conquest reaches Mondego River.
1139	Portugal is founded with Afonso Henriques as its first king.
1250	Last Muslim city, Silves, is captured by the Portuguese army.
1308	University of Coimbra is established.
1385	Castilian invaders are defeated in the Battle of Aljubarrota.
1415	Overseas expansion begins as Portugal captures the Moroccan city of Ceuta.
1418–19	Maritime expansion begins under the guidance of Prince Henry, the Navigator. Madeira is discovered.
1427–52	Azores is discovered.

1470	São Tomé and Príncipe islands are colonized.
1488	Bartolomeu Dias rounds Cape of Good Hope, South Africa, and finds a route to the Indian Ocean.
1494	The Treaty of Tordesillas between Portugal and Spain gives explorations up to 370 leagues west of Cape Verde Islands to Portugal.
1497–99	Vasco da Gama conducts sea voyages to west India.
1500	Pedro Álvares Cabral claims the coast of Brazil for Portugal.
1510	Afonso de Albuquerque conquers Goa, India, to begin the Portuguese hegemony of south Asia.
1543	The Portuguese arrive in Japan.
1557	Portuguese merchants are granted the Chinese territory of Macau as a trading base.
1572	Luís de Camões publishes "Os Lusíadas," a national epic poem.
1578	Moroccan forces defeat the army of King Sebastião of Portugal.
1580	King Philip II of Spain conquers Portugal.
1640	The Portuguese overthrow Spanish rule.
1661	An Anglo-Portuguese alliance treaty is signed.
1750	Pombal becomes chief minister of King José I.
1755	Earthquake occurs and the reconstruction of Lisbon begins.
1807–11	Napolean conquers Portugal.
1822	First Portuguese Constitution is created under Dom João VI. Brazil proclaims its independence.
1867	Capital punishment is abolished.
1900	Eça de Queiroz, one of the greatest Portuguese authors of the nineteenth century, dies in Paris at age 55.
1910	Revolution ends the Monarchy and creates the First Republic.
1916	Portugal enters World War I.
May 13, 1917	Three shepherd children, Francisco, Jacinta, and Lúcia, claim that the Virgin Mary appeared to them at Fátima.

1922	The first crossing of the South Atlantic by airplane is completed by Gago Coutinho and Sacadura Cabral.
1925	The first Portuguese radio broadcasts are emitted in Lisbon.
1926	A military coup overthrows the First Republic and replaces it with a right-wing military dictatorship.
1928	António de Oliveira Salazar becomes Minister of Finance.
1932	Salazar becomes prime minister (dictator).
1933	Corporatist Constitution is adopted.
1935	Fernando Pessoa, possibly the greatest Portuguese poet of the century, dies in Lisbon at age 47.
1936	The Spanish Civil War begins.
1939	Portugal announces its neutrality in impending World War II.
1940	The Portuguese World Exposition is held in Lisbon.
1946	Transportes Aéreos Portugueses (Air Portugal) is founded.
1948	Americans are installed at Lajes (Terceira), Azores, air base.
1949	Portugal becomes a founding member of the North Atlantic Treaty Organization.
	António Egas Moniz becomes the first Portuguese Nobel Prize winner (in Medicine).
1955	Portugal becomes a member of the United Nations.
1957	The first television transmissions under the responsibility of the Portuguese Broadcasting Network (RDP) begin.
1959	The SS *Santa Maria* is highjacked on the high seas by an opposition political group.
1961	The National Liberation war begins in Angola.
	The Indian army invades Goa.
1963	The National Liberation war begins in Portuguese Guinea.
1964	According to UNESCO, Portugal's percentage of school-age children attending school represents only 47 percent of that sector of the population.
	The National Liberation war begins in Mozambique.

1966	The Salazar Bridge (Now Ponte 25 de Abril), crossing the Tejo River, is inaugurated.
1968	Salazar collapses from a blood clot to the brain. Marcelo Caetano is named prime minister.
July 27, 1970	Salazar dies in Lisbon.
April 25, 1974	A Military coup ushers in the Portuguese Revolution, which ends the 48-year dictatorship and restores democracy.
1974–1975	Revolutionary period continues in Portugal.
1975	First democratic elections to new Constituent Assembly are held.
	African decolonization begins.
1976	Portugal adopts a democratic constitution after 43 years of dictatorship.
	Mario Soares becomes Portugal's first democratically elected prime minister in half a century.
1979	Maria de Lourdes Pintasilgo becomes Portugal's prime minister, the first woman ever to hold that post in the Iberian Peninsula.
1980	Carlos Lopes wins the Olympic Marathon in Los Angeles. Rosa Mota finishes third among women and wins bronze medal.
1984	Rosa Mota wins the Olympics Marathon at Seoul, Korea.
1985	Portugal's great runner, Carlos Lopes, sets World Marathon record at age 42.
1986	Portugal joins the European Economic Community.
1987	Rosa Mota is the first Portuguese woman ever to win the Boston Marathon, a victory she repeats in 1988 and 1990.
1988	The historic commercial and cultural area of Chiado, Lisbon, is destroyed by an arsonist's fire.
1992	First commercial and private television is broadcast.
1998	The Expo98 World's Fair is held in Lisbon.
	The Vasco da Gama Bridge is inaugurated to supplement the previously-built 25 of April Bridge.
	José Saramago wins the Nobel Prize in Literature.

1999	Amália Rodrigues, Portugal's most recognized Fado singer, dies.
	The last overseas territory, Macau, is handed over to Chinese.
January 2002	The Euro replaces the escudo.

1

The Portuguese: Land, People, and History

CONTEMPORARY PORTUGAL is an outward-looking, modern, democratic, and European state, but with a legacy of a relatively recent traditional, colonial, and often inward-looking past that continues to shape and influence its development in the twenty-first century. The country's modernity is evident in its new highways, apartment buildings, hypermarkets, and mobile phones. (There are more active cell phones than people in Portugal.) What was until the 1970s a traditional society increasingly conformed to a model of an advanced European state in economic structure, democratic political traditions, social organization, welfare services, and the aspirations and expectations of its citizens. Socioeconomic indicators show a rapid convergence with European norms in diet, electoral turnout, and demographic characteristics. Because Portugal took half the time (i.e., two to three decades) to make these changes compared to most other Western European nations, current social and economic conditions are more fragile and vulnerable. For example, significant gaps still exist between Portugal and the rest of Europe in terms of the diversity and strength of the economy, the citizens' levels of education and training, and the quality and efficiency of public services. "Old country" traditions persist in that the dominant political elites have survived and traditional lifestyles endure in the countryside. With modernization comes a new set of tensions and paradoxes such that a dichotomy is created between traditional and modern forms of production, consumption, and social reproduction. These new demands and maturity have forced the Portuguese to confront many of the problems of advanced western nations, including a decrease in electoral turnout, immigration, drug abuse, and increased crime.[1]

Portugal has always had a strong national identity, and it has been a homogeneous nation with regard to language, religion, culture, and ethnicity. Military conscription for the colonial wars, national television broadcasts, the expansion of health care and social security, schooling, and postal and banking networks have spread throughout the nation to make it an even more tightly knit society.

Still, the nation has changed drastically since the 1974 revolution in ways that have affected its customs and culture. Alterations to its colonial empire, increased involvement in international relations, and new patterns of emigration have caused Portugal to adopt a broader global vision. Additionally, social change, democratic consolidation, integration into the European Union and the accompanying economic development, national identity, and the changing character of contemporary literature and art have had an enormous impact in diversifying perspectives in Portugal. To best understand these most recent changes and their influence on the customs and culture of Portugal, one needs to delve into the historical context of this ancient nation-state. This chapter briefly examines the regional, social, historical, economic, and political conditions that have molded the Portuguese nation. Subgroups (social groups or classes such as the landed elite, military, and church) that play or have played an important role in Portugal are also discussed.

REGIONAL DIVERSITY

Any discussion of regional diversity should be prefaced by the existing dualism between rural and urban society. The largest city in Portugal is the capital Lisbon, and if the suburbs are included, about 10 percent of all Portuguese live and work in this metropolitan area. The rural-urban dichotomy is evident in all cities and even towns. While the rural areas have modernized somewhat in the last 30 years as electrification and improved roadways have spread throughout the nation, there is still a significant cultural difference between traditional, rural life and more modern, urban culture.

Since 1875 there have been many maps of Portugal based on varied criteria. A preferred geographic division sees the nation as follows: Noreoeste Cismontano, Alto Portugal, Nordeste Transmontano, Beira Douro, Beira Alta, Beira Litoral, Beira Serra, Beira Baixa, Estremadura, Sado e Ribatejo, Alentejo, Algarve,[2] and the two autonomous Atlantic Ocean archipelagos Açores (Azores) and Madeira.

To the west and south, Portugal faces the Atlantic Ocean with a 523-mile coastline. To the north (for 210 miles) and east (for 540 miles) lies Spain.

The Noroeste Cismontano lies south of the Rio (river) Minho (which forms the border with Spain), east of the Atlantic Ocean, north of the Rio Douro, and generally west of the Serra (mountain) do Gerês chain. The coastal plain is only about five miles wide before rising steeply to 1,000 to 2,000 feet above sea level. Plenty of rain and a favorable climate makes mini-fundio (small-scale, intensive farming) the norm. The area is densely populated and hosts Porto, Viana do Castelo, and Braga as major cities. The first two cities support significant fishing activities, and all three also have considerable industry.[3]

Alto Portugal descends south of the Spanish border from the Serra do Penedo, heads east encompassing the Serra do Gerês, and then north along Serra do Mogueira to Serra do Montesinho on the Spanish border. The main city of the region is Chaves. The high mountains force precipitation down in the Alto Cismontano, leaving Alto Portugal as arid, chinook country. This is one of the poorest regions of the nation, and it is where cereal production and animal grazing dominate. It is sparsely populated, and one of the few places where snow falls.[4]

To the west, sandwiched in between Alto Portugal and Spain (to the north and east), lies Nordeste Transmontano. These two regions as well as most of Beira Douro make up the area that many Portuguese call Trás-os-Montes. The Nordeste Transmontano's main city is Bragança. This area is generally less mountainous than Alto Portugal.

The Beira Douro region lies to the north of the Rio Douro surrounded by Alto Portugal to the north, the Noroeste Cismontano to the west, Nordeste Transmontano to the east, and Beira Alta south of the Rio Douro. In all of these regions granite and schist dominate. The Beira Douro is best known for the grapes used to make port wine (grown on terraced, steep slopes rising above the deep Douro valley). Vila Real is the main city of the region.

Beira Alta heads south from the Rio Douro to form an upside-down triangular shape with Beira Litoral to the west and Beira Serra to the east. The main city is Viseu, although Lamego is also a sizeable town. This is a densely populated region with terraced slopes producing varied vegetables, including corn and kale.

To the west lies Beira Litoral, a coastal plain about 30 miles wide made up of marshes, alluvial deposits, and sand dunes, where sandstone, limestone, and volcanic rock dominate. It is a fertile region producing rice, corn, grapes, and forestry products. Coimbra (the third-largest cultural center) and Aveiro are the major cities.[5]

To the east of Beira Alta lies Beira Serra, a mountainous region. Its focal point is Serra da Estrela, the highest mountain in continental Portugal (at 6,532 feet). The western terraced slopes provide a variety of agricultural products and the mountains themselves have summer pastures for sheep and goat herding. The famous Queijo (cheese) da Serra (available in a soft, mild variety as well as an aged, stronger-tasting type) comes from these mountains. Forestry products and textiles are also important economic activities, although the latter is suffering from Asian competition. The eastern slopes are less populated and more arid. The largest city is Guarda.[6]

Southwest of Beira Serra is Beira Baixa. It is similar to the Noroeste Transmontano in its windiness, aridity, and lower population density. It is an extension of the Spanish plateau system. Mining, stock raising, and cereal cultivation are all important economic activities. The main city is Castelo Branco.[7]

To the west lies Estremadura's boomerang shape, sandwiched between the northern shores of the Rio Tejo (Tagus) and the Atlantic Ocean. The major cities are Leiria, Santarem, and Lisbon. This is a fertile agricultural region with a dense population. Lisbon and its environs comprise the most important industrial and commercial center of the country, and the Tejo estuary forms one of the world's largest, natural harbors. There is an important glass and plastic mold-making industry in Marinha Grande.

South of the Tejo lies the Sado and Ribatejo region, where the largest and most industrial city is Setúbal. Orange groves are also abundant around the area. Northern Ribatejo is known for horse and cattle breeding.

The Alentejo lies to the east between Sado and Ribatejo and Spain. The region has gently rolling hills flowing south of the city of Portalegre, past Évora and Beja. Large landed estates are the norm (latifundios) owned by absentee landlords. Wheat, rye, olive groves, and cork oak dominate agriculturally, and the raising of pigs and cattle is also important. The region is sparsely populated.[8]

South of the Sado and Ribatejo, as well as Alentejo's Monchique and Caldeirão mountain ranges, is the Algarve. Vestiges of Moorish influence are strongest in this region. The coastal areas are fertile and densely populated. Almonds, carob, figs, oranges, pomegranates, olives, and cork are produced in the abundant sunshine. The region is also a major destination for northern European tourists, especially British and German, and Americans. The major city is Faro.[9]

Along the Atlantic coasts of all these regions fishing contributes to the economy. The traditional industries of canned fish, textiles, wine, and cork have diversified into machinery, transport equipment, pulp and paper, clothing and footwear, as well as chemicals.

The Açores are located about 800 miles west of continental Portugal. There are nine inhabited islands and the uninhabited islets Formiga Rocks. Corvo is the smallest island and São Miguel the largest. (The others are Flores,

Graciosa, São Jorge, Faial, Pico, Santa Maria, and Terceira.) With the exception of Santa Maria, the islands are volcanic. Pico's peak reaches a height of 7,615 feet above sea level. The volcanic soil is especially fertile and is used mainly for self-sufficient, intensive farming, with excesses exported to the mainland. Cereals, vegetables, pineapples, sugarcane, tobacco, and wine grapes are all grown. Fishing is important in all of the islands, although the whaling industry has declined over time. The United States operates a strategically important air base in Lajes, Terceira. Islanders live mainly in small villages, although there are three small cities (Horta, Faial; Angra do Heroismo, Terceira; and Ponta Delgada, São Miguel).[10] The inhabitants of each island speak Portuguese with their own distinctive accent, and there is a good-natured rivalry between Açoreanos and the "mainlanders," with each group using the other as the punch line of demeaning humor.

The other Atlantic archipelago is Madeira, located about 600 miles southwest of Lisbon. There are two major inhabited islands, Madeira and Porto Santo, and several minor uninhabited islands, including Ilhas Desertas. As in the Açores, the volcanic soils are fertile and rugged. The climate is semi-tropical, allowing for the cultivation of bananas, citrus, vegetables, and wine grapes. (Madeira wine is a major export.) Fishing, tourism, and crafts such as embroidery and wicker furniture are important economic activities.[11]

The continental northern and central regions (those listed above except Estremadura, Sado e Ribatejo, Alentejo, and Algarve) are among the most populated of Portugal. Low standards of living are prevalent in the north as in the south, but at least most peasants own their own plots of land, no matter how small, from which they can farm a self-sufficient living. (Seventy-eight percent of the farms are less than four hectares.) The self-sufficiency and strong Catholicism are major factors contributing to the conservatism of the north and islands. In the north, the lower classes are generally "equally" poor.[12]

While land distribution in the north has centered on small plots since Swabian (Germanic tribes) settlement, the latifundios—large estates of the south, comprising up to 1,000 acres and often owned by absentee landlords—can be traced to the Roman conquests. Although the 1974 revolution ushered in a partial land reform that transformed some of the larger estates into cooperatives, much of the reform has since been rolled back. Most of the inhabitants of the southern region are landless and earn their living as agricultural laborers.[13]

Despite Portugal's small size, regional diversity exists and has a strong influence on politics. The south has a long history of radicalism when compared to the conservative north. This is partially a result of the landless status of lower-class southerners. Most are totally dependent on the local landowner for their existence and would have very little to lose if radical change was initiated. Every day they work for the local latifundista reminds them of the uneven distribution of wealth. Even within their own class, the southern poor have an established hierarchy. Those who own some land have the highest prestige, followed by the sharecroppers, and at the bottom are the landless laborers.[14]

SOCIAL STRUCTURE

Social Class

At the turn of the twentieth century the working class was still relatively small. With the addition of many nouveau riche elements and the fall from grace of the clergy and aristocracy, the elitist classes comprised about 1 percent of the total population while the middle class increased to 15 percent. The majority of the population was still poor peasants.[15]

António Salazar's dictatorship did little to remedy the plight of the peasants. Because he realized that much of his support lay with the uneducated, conservative peasants, he had little interest in educating the rural population and risking an unwanted side effect: disaffection with the regime and a class consciousness. Salazar believed strongly in the "traditional" model of organizing an economy and society based on birth. He believed that God had given the peasant "the privilege of being poor" and that "education, health, and economic reform 'would not create happiness.'"[16]

The industrial pace under Salazar's leadership was much slower compared to the rest of Europe's. As a result, by the 1960s and 1970s the social structure continued relatively unchanged. The upper class still comprised 1 percent of the population, while the middle class comprised 15–25 percent. The majority of the Portuguese were still at the bottom layer of society, but they lacked a mutual bond or class consciousness to bind them together. Industrialization contributed to an increasing urban working class, but the major change was in the emergence of a large class of clerks, low-level civil servants, and others who lived just above the poverty line.[17]

In the years prior to the revolution, the very small elitist class recognized the potential threat to its interests from the rising lower middle class and working class. It tightened the grip on its exclusive social position through intra-class marriages. By 1974 the elites were the largest landowners, directors, and owners of the largest industries, and they also held positions as high-ranking government officials, leading financiers, superior military officials, members of the Catholic church hierarchy, senior university professors, and professional elites, such as lawyers and medical professionals. Eighty percent of the economy was controlled by only eight of these elite families. Upward mobility was almost impossible except through education, which was virtually inaccessible to the lower classes.[18]

The middle class was difficult to define and describe. Compared to the middle class in other nations, it was small and encompassed a wide range of income groups if defined broadly. In the mid-1800s, it comprised approximately 15 percent of the population. The traditional middle class was made up of small-scale entrepreneurs, those in the professions, and university teachers below the level of full professor. On the whole this class was better off than the mass of the population, and its interests aligned more closely with the upper classes. Beginning with the industrialization and urbanization of the 1960s and 1970s, a lower-middle class began to emerge. This new class was composed primarily of skilled technicians, clerks, and employees in the service sector, mid-level business executives, school teachers, lower-to-mid-level civil servants, small businessmen, and medium-sized landowners.[19]

Emigration and Immigration

Prior to the early 1970s Portugal lost a large part of its citizens to emigration. Northerners were more likely to emigrate externally, which was more expensive, while southerners migrated internally to the cities, adding to the radicalism in the domestic labor force. Between 1960 and 1973 more than 1.5 million Portuguese emigrated, leaving the nation with a negative population growth rate. As a result, after Lisbon the second largest "Portuguese" city became Paris rather than Porto. Until the 1950s, 80 percent of emigrants departed for Brazil, declining afterwards to 50 percent. From 1966 to 1973 many left for Northern Europe to labor in the "dirty" jobs—construction, janitorial services, and farm laborers—that the locals did not want. After 1973, increased restrictions in the north made emigration more difficult. Portugal regulated and encouraged some types of emigration to meet its own requirements, such as labor for the colonies or to fulfill foreign currency needs, but about 36 percent of emigration was also illegal. Most emigrants, whether legal or illegal, were male, single, and young. Reverse migration as emigrants returned to Portugal after making their "fortunes" abroad did not result in much internal economic development. Returnees did not have many transferable skills, did not want the same jobs, and their savings generally went toward consumption rather than productive investments.[20]

In terms of the United States, from 1950 to 1988 approximately 193,000 Portuguese (14% of total emigrants during that period) chose to seek a better life across the Atlantic and become Lusitanian-Americans (Luso-Americans). If these official figures are corrected to include illegal immigration, the United States received only 9 percent of the emigrants given the greater difficulty in terms of cost and distance to reach the destination illegally. The United States was an especially favored home from 1965 to 1969 after it amended its immigration policy to allow family reunification and revised the national origin quota system. Açoreano emigration to the United States has generally made up a disproportionately large total of the flow.[21] Most Portuguese have chosen to settle in communities on the eastern (mid-Atlantic to New England) or western (California) coasts. The largest concentration lives in Newark, New Jersey, with pockets flowing northward to Lowell and Gloucester, Massachusetts. Most Portuguese have bypassed the interior and have headed for the California coast, including San José, San Diego, and San Clemente. Their preferred occupations have been in fisheries or industry from leather tanning to textiles and plastics. Subsequent generations have assimilated and become Americanized, but always on their own terms. Portuguese folk culture and customs have been kept alive through clubs, schools, soccer teams, festivals, dance troupes, cable or satellite television carrying Radio Televisão Portuguesa (RTP), and regular trips to Portugal to visit friends and family. The Luso-Americans are extremely proud of their culture to the point of preserving habits that have already faded in their homelands.

One of the most dramatic changes in Portugal during the last few decades is that the nation has become a destination for immigrants. By the mid-1990s legal foreign residents accounted for close to 2 percent of the population. Since then the inflow of East Europeans has increased this figure to close to 4 percent.[22] At the turn of the twenty-first century, Cape Verdeans made up the biggest group (23%), with Brazilians next (11%), Angolans (9%), and Guinea-Bissauans (7%). Many of the African immigrants are employed in non-skilled labor such as the construction industry,[23] but these trends can change quickly. As of 2005, Brazilians made up the largest group of immigrants, with Ukranians second, and Cape Verdeans slipping to third place.[24]

HISTORICAL BACKGROUND

Early History

Portugal is one of the oldest and geographically most stable nations in Europe. Its 800-year history as a nation-state has led to a high degree of cultural unity. With one of the world's most stable frontiers, there has been hardly any change to its continental boundaries since it became an Iberian nation in the thirteenth century. Formally, the borders are based on treaties signed with Spain in 1864 and 1906.[25]

Until the Roman invasions around 200 B.C., the Lusitanians (the Roman name for the local residents) continued to dominate the western part of the peninsula. Even after the invasions, Roman settlers preferred southern Lusitania to the northern regions. Latifundios, or large estates, became abundant in the Alentejo and the Algarve, while few Roman settlers ventured up into northern Portugal. With the fall of the Roman Empire in the fifth century A.D., the Swabians, a Germanic tribe, created a kingdom in Western Iberia. Perhaps their major legacy to Portugal was the system of agriculture they left in the north—dispersed, single, small holdings that became ever smaller from generation to generation as the land was further divided among heirs. To this day, this pattern of small landholding remains a main factor in the politically conservative nature of the northern and central Portuguese peasant. Title to even limited amounts of property, combined with a strong allegiance to the church, leads the peasant toward conservatism. The south continued to consist of small "nucleated villages" and large estates farmed by landless agricultural workers of the Alentejo and the Algarve regions.[26]

In 1128 Portugal emerged as an independent nation under the rule of Afonso Henrique, Portugal's first king. By 1249 Afonso III captured the Algarve region from the Moors, which established the present boundaries of Portugal, with the exception of languishing skirmishes with Castille (Spain) that stabilized in 1295.[27] Nevertheless, four centuries of Moorish rule left its mark on Portuguese customs and culture. Agricultural advances, such as irrigated orchards, were introduced. Southern Portugal still showcases the architecturally distinctive white housing and place names beginning with "al," such as Algarve, Alentejo, Alenquer, and Alfama. The carpet weaving craft from Arroiolos to Portalegre is another vestige of this influence, as is the use of tile throughout the nation.

During the Moorish occupation of Lusitania the landholding patterns of the north and south continued. Portugal's expulsion of the Moors did not alter the basic agricultural structures. In the south the crown and the church merely redistributed the vast latifundios to aristocrats in return for services rendered during the conquests. "The land was tilled by sharecroppers, by peasants contracted to the land (though dependent serfdom appears to have been rare), and, most numerously, by wretched masses of itinerant rural laborers who worked without the protection of a lord or a manorial contract that would have regulated their status and assured them of minimal rights."[28]

By the fifteenth century, much earlier than other major European powers, Portugal was already enjoying a strong sense of national unity. It was relatively free of civil strife, and it was governed by a strong, institutionalized, monarchical government. Since Portugal had firm territorial boundaries, its militaristic aristocracy turned its attention to the sea. The focus became one of exploration, maritime trade, and colonization.[29] Even today, this tie to the sea is evidenced everywhere in the country from the fierce pride the Portuguese have in their exploration of trade routes and discovery of new lands and peoples to the very symbol of Lisbon, which is that of a crow atop a "caravela," the sailing ships used by the great Portuguese navigators, including Gil Eanes, Diogo Cão, Vasco da Gama, Pedro Alvares da Cabral, and Bartolomeu Dias, who slowly opened routes to the Orient and brought great prosperity to Portugal. Everywhere one looks in Lisbon and in the coastal towns, the sidewalks are decorated with cobblestones arranged in patterns of flowing water, fish, and caravelas. Prince Henry the Navigator was a much beloved monarch for his adventurous spirit and support of the Discoveries.

Because the sea-going ventures were state run—and very lucrative with returns of at least 100 percent and often reaching between 400 percent and 600 percent—the profits went into state coffers and were used by the elite for extravagant lifestyles. This was a major reason why the industrial revolution did not flourish in Portugal. Whereas the Netherlands' and England's industrialization was primarily financed by the middle or entrepreneurial classes, in Portugal significant capital was never accumulated by these ranks. It remained instead in the hands of the elite, who used the wealth to build expensive churches and to purchase luxuries. They preferred to import these goods rather than invest in their domestic production. By the sixteenth century Portugal began to see a fall of profits from the colonies. The combination of a series of weak kings, such as Sebastião from 1557 to 1578 and Cardinal Henrique from 1578 to 1580, and the decrease in revenues led to serious foreign debt problems. The 60-year Spanish rule that followed the end of the Aviz dynasty did not help matters.[30]

The Methuen Treaty of 1703 with England was a clear hindrance to Portugal's industrial development by favoring British woolen imports. The end result was the "old country's" transformation into a giant sieve through which Brazilian gold passed to help England finance its industrial revolution, leaving Portugal on the sidelines well into the twentieth century. Even during the Marquis of Pombal's restoration period—he governed the nation for King José from 1750 to 1777, as the ruler wanted power but not the responsibility of governing—little attention was devoted to Portuguese development. Through his authoritarian, highly centralized government, Pombal introduced the Enlightenment (i.e., rationalism) to Portugal, but even these conditions did not produce the middle class Portugal needed to one day take its place alongside the industrial nations.[31]

The Liberal Era

Until the nineteenth century, Portugal remained free of the anti-monarchical civil unrest and coups occurring in many other nations. From the 1820s on, however, ever since the crown's flight to Brazil during the Napoleonic invasions and its reluctance to return to Portugal after Napoleon's defeat, the upper-middle class and military elements assumed a broader role in Portuguese politics. Increasingly, liberal ideas such as democracy, equality, and popular sovereignty began to influence these nascent political groups.

While the crown remained in Brazil, the English General William Beresford ruled the nation. His resistance against these progressive ideas undermined the credibility of the regime since it was foreign as well as reactionary. As a result, liberals were able to muster wide-ranging support since their opposition was not only ideological but also patriotic. Civil strife led by the upper-middle class and military officers in 1820 succeeded in driving Beresford out of the country and marked the beginning of Portugal's modern political evolution.[32]

The new power groups created a constitution in 1822 that limited royal power, abolished the Inquisition (which was not significant by this time), and expanded the suffrage to all but the illiterate 90 percent of the population, women, and friars in the biennial election for a parliament independent of the crown. The drafters of the new constitution wanted to limit the power of the crown, create a representative system, ensure individual rights, and "create a rational, unified legal system." The liberal changes should not be mistaken for a restructuring of Portuguese society to its roots. The constitution succeeded in compromising with the traditional forces by maintaining a monarchy that reigned—yet did not rule—and "preserving the religious and economic interests of the church, and not imposing social and economic reform of the landholders."[33]

The compromise failed in 1832 as civil war broke out between the traditional forces—martial, rural, Catholic—and the liberals who won in 1834. One consequence of the war was the seizure of large southern land holdings, another bastion of conservative strength. A decision was made to auction the property to help pay the enormous debt incurred during the war. The result was a missed opportunity to implement a radical land reform. Instead, as is so often the case in Latin societies, the latifundios of the old church and noble elites were transferred to the liberal upper and upper-middle classes, mainly to successful merchants or industrialists, making them a new landed elite. The reform did not alter the squalid existence of the landless peasants, nor did it help to eliminate the debt as intended because the land was purchased by only 623 families at below market prices, with 60 percent of the cost covered by state credits. The urban liberal class, therefore, was to become an avid supporter of the new regime since it was responsible for its newly found elitist position.[34]

Although industry was beginning to emerge (as well as the first Portuguese millionaires), the Portuguese economy still lacked domestic capital, skilled labor, and the raw materials necessary to fully industrialize the nation. Agriculture, which continues to be underdeveloped to this day, had already been causing problems for some time, such as balance-of-payment problems that were a result of grain and food imports. The rural areas suffered from poverty, capital shortages, lack of chemical fertilizers and irrigation, emigration, primitive techniques, and alarmingly low yields. Plots were too small in the north (minifundios) to improve production through modern techniques. The latifundios of the south, where modern techniques would have worked best, were usually poorly run because their owners had little interest in investing to improve production, having acquired the land as status symbols.[35]

Republicanism, or a belief in representative democracy, began to make inroads through teachers, journalists, small businessmen, clerks, and artisans. By 1896, rather late for a European nation, these new political groups were attracting between 15 percent and 20 percent of the population. The Portuguese Republicans' proposals included "complete political freedom and equality, guarantees for the rights to associate and strike, separation of church and state, and the elimination of most indirect, regressive taxes." Elitist solidarity began to weaken in the 1890s in the face of political change.[36]

King Carlos I and his eldest son were assassinated in 1908 by radical Republicans, leaving the monarchy on shaky ground. In 1910, a revolution led by the Republicans with the support of urban intellectuals and the lower-middle class created the first republic in Portugal and the third in Europe, following the French and Swiss. The republic was installed with little opposition due to the gradual transformation that had been occurring within the Portuguese system. The hierarchy in the military was neither republican nor authoritarian and allowed events to unfold. The landed elite were not very concerned because land reform was not a republican goal. In short, because the revolution that overthrew the monarchy was not a radical revolution, the elite in Portugal were not overly concerned with its consequences.[37]

The instability that existed prior to 1910 continued into the newly formed republic. In a nation where personalism was a dominant characteristic of the political system, no strong leader emerged to head the victorious Portuguese Republican Party (PRP). As with many other revolutions, the coalition of forces that helped bring the Republicans to power in 1910 quickly began to drift apart. Parliament was dominated by intellectual classes rather than by business, worker, or farmer groups. In addition, the government under the 1911 constitution rejected a strong executive branch and decentralization of power and opted instead for a strong legislative branch. Because the parties were plagued with divisions and disagreements, focusing power on Parliament only exacerbated the political system's instability, leading in time to extremely unstable governments. The economic and social underdevelopment did not help the situation either.[38]

The continued instability that plagued the nation, compounded by the PRP's treatment of the military, eventually led to a coup in 1917 under Major Bernardino Sidónio Pais. He sought to usher in a semi-authoritarian system, with the parliament subordinate to the executive. He made the PRP illegal and increased the role of the monarchist, religious, and business groups. It was a conservative, but not a traditionalist, regime that maintained many of the trappings of the republic. The new regime was integral, traditional, and strongly opposed to liberalism, individualism, socialism, and other doctrines that denied God, the family, and other traditional concepts. The integralist movement that was founded in 1910 was one of the first signs of a right-wing backlash against republicanism.[39]

Pais's assassination in 1918 by a radical corporal was followed by the second republican regime that lasted until 1926. This was an extremely fragile political system, perhaps even more so than the first republican regime that Pais replaced. Even though the Democratic Party continued to be the largest party during the republican era, it was plagued with internal divisions that prevented it from governing effectively. Frustrated by their inability to alter the floundering political system by legal means, rival republican parties increasingly turned to violence and unlawful measures to resolve the dilemma. Assassinations became common, especially by secret societies such as the Carbonaria. That Portugal had four governments in 1919 and nine in 1920 are good indicators of the instability that affected the political system. By the 1920s even urban professional and middle-class elements were abandoning the parliamentary system. Abstentions in parliamentary elections became increasingly common as voters tired of the political deadlock and extra-parliamentary violence.[40]

The response was the emergence of several progressive governments after 1923 that led to a rise in conservative opposition. Whereas previous governments only fought over the spoils of government, the new progressive governments actually contemplated the implementation of broad-reaching reforms of the agricultural sector, education, the banking system, the tax structure, and social welfare. The Seara Nova group and the Leftist Democratic Party especially exemplified the model of a progressive party, committed to ideology and not merely groups of individuals more interested in their own personal motivations. These parties, however committed, lacked the parliamentary majorities that were necessary to implement their programs. Instead, they provided the fragmentary counter-revolutionary forces with the common foe needed to fuse them.[41]

The new radical rhetoric lost republicans the support of conservative groups—clergy, capitalists, landowners, and a portion of the middle class—who regarded the proposed transformation as too rapid. They also lost the support of radical intellectuals and workers who saw the evolution as too slow. They wanted more action and less talk. Upper and mid-ranking civil servants, including the military, were displeased with post-World War I inflation that had decreased their real salaries by 50 percent. Bankers, merchants, and industrialists were displeased with high taxes, economic crises, and the emergence of socialism and anarchism. The clergy favored a regime that would reinstate its lost influence. The conservative intellectuals became disenchanted with Republicanism and looked instead to Fascism. Even the middle and lower classes of Lisbon and Porto, the Democrats' greatest basis of support, were tiring of the constant coup attempts, street violence, and interruptions of daily life. Neither could the Democrats expect support from the peasants or the women, for while they comprised two-thirds of the Portuguese population they were extremely conservative, under the influence of the conservative church and beyond the PRP's reach.[42]

As has been seen, the 16 years of Republican rule were as unstable as the final years of the constitutional monarchy. Strikes were legalized and became common affairs as workers attempted to keep their wages on par with inflation, which increased 2,800 percent from 1911 to 1923.[43] Governments under the republic were short-lived, averaging one every four months. (Forty-five governments, seven parliamentary elections, and eight presidential elections were held during this period.) Political violence, involvement in World War I, budget deficits, bread shortages, capital flight, a backward agricultural sector, and currency devaluation added to the instability and to increasing unhappiness with the republican regime. As time progressed, the regime became increasingly unable to deal with the precariousness and became isolated. By 1926 a general unhappiness with the Democrats began to infiltrate all sectors of society, and the majority of Portuguese acquiesced to the need for a right-wing, non-republican solution. Up to this time the Right had not been able to unify because of the monarchist question. Once the regeneration of the monarchy was dropped as a goal, even the middle classes were attracted to the Right.

The decrease in liberal democratic values was accompanied by an increase in the formation of anti-parliamentary groups, most of which succeeded in recruiting the young and drew heavily from French rightist ideas. The upper-bourgeois youth and the military were especially drawn to authoritarian and integralist solutions. Even the press began attacking liberal democracy and gave favorable coverage to the Italian and German solutions. Calls for a military coup became ever more popular. After one failed in 1925, a second attempt in 1926 successfully ended Portugal's experiment in liberal democracy.[44]

Salazar's "New State"

The coup, as in the 1910 and 1974 revolutions, was a bloodless one because the military had such broad support across most social sectors, including Republicans, monarchists, integralists, Catholics, and nationalists. As liberal measures were eliminated, the military regime led by General Oscar Carmona became more repressive. Initial support came from the public at large, which hoped that authoritarianism would lead to stability and economic recovery. However, the new leaders seized the reins of power from the middle classes and returned them to the upper-class conservatives. Not since the early 1800s had the upper classes amassed so much power.[45]

In 1926, political parties that were involved in an attempted military coup were banned. In addition, the right to strike was withdrawn. The economy in Portugal deteriorated to the point where many compared the crisis to the worst periods of the republic because the military was not experienced in economic management. By providing Professor António de Oliveira Salazar, an economics professor at the University of Coimbra, with broad budgetary powers, the military was able to recruit him to manage the economy. His solution was to trim the budget by cutting benefits to the lower-class and middle-class groups. The level of military spending remained untouched despite bureaucratic waste and a 23.42 percent share of the budget.[46]

By 1930 the military and Salazar succeeded in returning political stability to the nation. That same year Salazar proclaimed the formation of the National Union party, which became part of his "new state." Corporatism replaced the political parties, trade unions, a free press, and other organizations. Power was focused on the executive, and the values of God, family, and the nation were given the highest priority. Change was controlled, partly through the use of a secret police apparatus used for political surveillance. Corporatism was to be the Portuguese solution to alien radical transformations such as socialism, liberalism, or communism.

In theory, social unrest would end because the "corporation" would represent the clergy, military, students, workers, employers, and all other groups equally. The central government would guarantee a harmonious coexistence to all. In reality, the government was biased toward the employers and traditional elements at the expense of the lower classes. As a result, the Portuguese solution to harness, tame, and manipulate radical change failed because the lower classes realized the government was not mediating between contending classes but was instead using corporatism to favor the upper classes.[47]

Most of Salazar's support in the early years came from the Church and other groups that had the most to gain under the new regime. His opposition came primarily from the middle and lower classes. In 1933, Salazar quickly began to set up the formal structure of his "new state" by creating a new constitution. Although basic civil rights were included, they were nullified by a clause allowing the state to restrict them when necessary for the "common good."

In 1933, the government banned all remaining parties, including the conservative Catholic Center party. Because parties were blamed as the source of Portugal's past ills, even the government's National Union was considered more of a civic association or movement than a party. Elections were also deemphasized, with only 7.8 percent of the population allowed to vote in the 1945 elections. Women were not granted the right to vote until 1968, and even then there were still many restrictions imposed on both sexes.

A comparison of Salazar's dictatorship with German or Italian fascism shows that Portugal was not a fascist state. Despite Salazar's sharing views with Adolf Hitler and Benito Mussolini on authoritarianism, anti-communism, and hierarchy, Portugal's dictatorship was not as harsh or violent.[48]

In the early 1900s, Portugal was just beginning to develop the communist and other radical parties that had existed much earlier in other parliamentary systems. Because the parties were mainly city oriented, it was easy for Salazar to dispose of them. Any political instigators that remained were from the Right and were eventually co-opted into the system as members of elite conservative groups. Therefore, intervention at all levels of society was not necessary, allowing for a low-key, authoritarian regime without a mass-based, fascist party.[49]

Salazar's reign must be categorized as a "clerical-conservative" or "corporatist-authoritarian" one "of personal rulership." Salazar purposefully sought to keep Portugal underdeveloped. He used press censorship, controls on foreign investment, and other measures to prevent foreign influences from infiltrating Portuguese society. In this manner he hoped to prevent change, or at least retard it to a pace that he could manage.[50]

By the late 1950s and early 1960s, economic and political factors, such as the African wars of independence, led Salazar to initiate measures that conflicted with his "isolationist" policies. By allowing an increase in foreign investment and joining the European Free Trade Association and the General Agreement on Tariffs and Trade he was planting the "seeds of change" that would help bring about the inevitable transformations he had hoped to avoid.[51]

In 1968, Salazar suffered an incapacitating stroke and was succeeded by the scholar Marcello Caetano, who was thought to be somewhat more liberal. Changes were expected to bring Portugal closer to the rest of the European community as it shifted from its dependence on a colonial empire. With time the "seeds" that Salazar had planted began to sprout. The increase in foreign investment from 1.5 percent in 1960 to 27 percent in 1970 made Portugal more sensitive to changes in the world economy. Inflation reached the double digits by the early 1970s, with unionization and labor unrest rising as well. Emigration, which for years had solved the government's inability to deal with underemployment and unemployment, began to have unwanted reper-cussions. While the emigrants returned with the desperately needed foreign currency, they also brought undesired foreign ideas and values that spawned a desire for change. Because the change that had been expected of Caetano never took place, the tension mounted.[52]

In 1974, a military coup was carried out by mid-level officers reflecting their own grievances. Given the widespread dissatisfaction with the Salazar-Caetano dictatorship, popular support soon transformed the coup into a revolution. A brief summary of the resulting major changes would include the following:

1. The breakup of the colonial empire
2. The government's increased involvement in the economy
3. The emergence of political parties
4. An increase in labor rights and Portuguese Communist Party domination of unions
5. A reorganization of local governments
6. A limited agrarian reform[53]

Portuguese Revolution, 1974–1976

After the Armed Forces Movement overthrew the dictatorship in 1974, its major goals were democratization, decolonization, and development. During these two years there was a prolonged national debate on what new form of government and social organization the country should adopt. After six provisional governments, three elections, and two failed coups, the Portuguese settled on a West European-style democracy. However, even then the 1976 constitution gave the military's Council of Revolution oversight in the new system. The military had always played a strong role in Portuguese politics and was continuing to do so. The ultimate democratization goal was to ease the military back into the barracks, which was achieved from 1976 to 1982.

Contemporary Portugal

After the arduous two-year transition period, Portugal inaugurated its new democratic regime on July 23, 1976. The fragile democracy was seriously challenged politically, economically, and militarily over the next 15 years. Begun with a weak national assembly, faced with governmental instability and persistent economic problems, the consolidation of the new regime was imperiled to the point where the national assembly asserted its authority over the military, until continued governmental stability and economic recovery became the order of the day.[54] Despite a social revolution, poorly developed civil society, and political instability, Portugal was able to navigate the stormy waters caused by its decolonization and simultaneous democratization. While the nation's standard of living is lower than the European average, public satisfaction is generally higher.[55] Portugal is now an outward-looking, modern, democratic, and European state, but the legacy of the recent traditional, colonial, and often inward-looking past continues to shape and influence development in the twenty-first century.

ECONOMY

Portugal's economy experienced very slow growth over the centuries. The problems persisted in the 1970s because of the colonial wars, oligarchic control, the widening gap between the rich and the poor, and the inefficient agricultural sector that produced some of the lowest yields in Western Europe. One of the few bright spots in the economic picture was that Salazar's frugal monetary policies had resulted in large gold and foreign exchange reserves. Largely because of its development aid to the colonies, the International Monetary Fund and the World Bank labeled Portugal a developed country. By most other standards, Portugal rated behind Spain and Greece, which were considered developing countries by these bodies in 1975.[56] In 2004 the nation still remained at the bottom of the 15 western European Union members, surpassed even by the new member Slovenia and averaging only 75 percent of the European Union's average in standard of living.

In many ways the colonial empire actually harmed Portugal's economic development more than it helped. The nation's diversion of increasing amounts of its budget to fight the independence movements in the colonies had a significant negative impact on the economy by neglecting education and infrastructure developments on the continent. Even before the colonial wars that began in the 1960s, however, Portugal suffered negative effects because of its colonies. Its wealth led to economic dependence on export/import trade with the colonies at the expense of domestic economic development. Neglect of internal development had also been encouraged by its long alliance with Britain that preferred the exchange of manufactured goods for wine and agricultural products. Economic development was limited to infrastructure modernization and was financed primarily by the poor, who paid the brunt of the excise taxes.

Portugal was a late developer. By 1910 only 20 percent of the workforce was employed in the industrial sector, of which a mere 20 percent worked in firms that employed 10 workers or more. Industrialization was still at the rudimentary stages, centering in leather goods, textiles, and cork and wine processing. More than 60 percent of the workforce was still engaged in farming and fishing. The Republicans were not devoted to economic development, and the economy deteriorated as severe inflation reduced the currency in 1926 to only one-thirtieth of its 1910 value. Bank failures, labor unrest, budget deficits, and chronic balance-of-trade problems exacerbated the situation.

The economic crisis had a significant role in bringing down the Republican experiment.[57]

After the coup of 1926, the military found itself unable to handle the same economic problems that had contributed to the Republicans' downfall. In 1928 Salazar took over total control of the economy. He was a strong believer in:

> balanced budgets and fiscal solvency and of corporate free enterprise within the limits of strict state control. His faith in the gold standard and in a stable currency backed by gold and substantial foreign exchange reserves was unshaken even in the worst days of the worldwide depression and war during the 1930s and 1940s. These policies were apparently effective in bringing the country through the depression with only moderate disruption of its stable, albeit static, economy. At the end of 1933, for example, when the rest of the world was suffering from widespread unemployment, registered unemployment in Portugal was less than 1 percent.[58]

Portugal emerged from World War II unscathed and in excellent condition in relation to the rest of Europe. Had Portugal pursued the appropriate economic measures it could have become a developed nation along with its European neighbors. Because of Salazar's economic policies, however, it was left behind as its neighbors became more industrialized. "His insistence on a stable currency, a positive balance of payments, and a balanced budget and his suspicion of foreign aid and foreign investment outweighed the arguments of those who would have preferred a more dynamic attack on the low living standards and static economic development." His critics argue that Salazar did not exploit foreign aid to its maximum potential.[59]

Although the Portuguese economy did remarkably well in the 1960s with a 6.2 percent average gross national product increase, this number reflects primarily the industrial and service sectors of the urban areas. Agriculture grew at only 1.3 percent while industry grew at 9 percent, construction at 8.1 percent, and services at 5.9 percent. The colonial wars sapped the economy of manpower and capital. Despite Salazar's 40-year rule as "economist-dictator," Portugal continued to be Europe's poorest nation.[60]

Caetano recognized that Portugal had to initiate changes to deal with the economic problems and he implemented limited liberal policies. Wages were allowed to improve at a faster rate, and foreign investment was encouraged. The increase in world oil prices as well as the onslaught of a worldwide inflationary spiral complicated Caetano's attempts to upgrade the economy. Inflation in 1973 rose to 30 percent.[61]

Portugal's economic policy changed drastically after 1974, and the slow growth that resulted is generally blamed on the nationalizations and land reforms of 1975 and other side effects of the revolution. The elected governments were challenged to balance economic recovery with social fairness. These attempts were complicated by the provisional governments' costly decisions, such as the rapid increase in wages and public spending and the short-term care and integration of 650,000 retornados (Portuguese citizens living in the African colonies that were expelled after independence in 1975). The measures led to budget deficits exacerbated by a drop in tourism, the decline of emigrant remittances, the loss of colonial markets and resources, and a global economic recession. From 1974 to 1976 per capita income and capital investment declined, and inflation as well as unemployment increased. In 1977, concern about the unstable economy led to the implementation of an International Monetary Fund austerity program. By 1979 Portugal faced an overvalued escudo and large budget deficits. The privatizations that began in 1982 and entry into the European Union in 1986 are credited with turning the economy in a favorable direction. The influx of European Union funds led to massive infrastructure developments throughout Portugal. A nation that had one major international, single-lane road connecting via the Spanish border to the rest of Europe quickly developed a complex system of multi-lane highways throughout the nation. Building projects have not seemed to stop ever since. Overall, however, 1974 to 1990 was a period of low growth rates in industry and agriculture and a period of high inflation and unemployment.[62]

While the primary sector was the largest, at 43.6 percent, until the 1960s, it is now the smallest with 7 percent or 8 percent of the workforce in 2000. The secondary sector, at 28.9 percent in the 1960s and between 34 percent and 36 percent in 2002, was never the main one, but the tertiary sector, at 27.5 percent in 1960s and about 55 percent in 2002, jumped from last place to first place, especially in the areas of tourism, finance, retail, telecommunications, and media services. Tourism has blossomed, providing an alternative to agrarian work in the coastal areas. After adjusting for inflation, the national minimum wage for industry and services is slightly lower at the beginning of the twenty-first century than it was in the 1970s. Overall, the economy has experienced tertiarization, coastalization, and urbanization.[63]

A decade of full membership in the European Union was good for the Portuguese. The result was an age of consumerism with citizens purchasing goods from vehicles and apartments to kitchen appliances and cell phones. (Cell phone ownership was the fourth highest in Europe in 2000.) Average savings declined from 16.4 percent of earnings in 1990 to only 9.5 percent in 1999, and indebtedness increased from less than 20 percent of earnings in 1990 to almost 80 percent in 1999. The Portuguese embraced leisure, with more vacationing or frequenting bars as they saw their incomes double from 1990 to 1995.

Likewise, the government spent lavishly on infrastructure, transportation, culture, and leisure with European Union funds. During this period the government stabilized with centralist politics. Much of the public sector was privatized during the decade, and this move was partially responsible for the economy being the seventh most globalized of the world in 2000. In 1987 Portugal's Gross National Product was only 50 percent of the European Union average, but by 1999 it had improved to 75 percent.

Seeing Portugal today, with its vibrant economy (although less vibrant than in the early 1990s), large middle class, progressive commitment to technological development, and the value placed on its cultural heritage, it is hard to believe that only 35 years ago the Portuguese were living under a repressive, insular dictatorship. Despite its relatively slow embrace of development, it is closing the gap with lightening speed. One has only to look around to see the Portuguese people enjoy a sophisticated style of living, with cultural activities made available to the general public at very low cost. One example is the construction of sites like Expo 98 that, in its initial planning, was forward thinking and sensitive to the way the Portuguese socialize. Expo incorporated interesting eateries, bars, shopping centers, residential apartments, and broad esplanades along the Tejo river that provide a wonderful backdrop for families and friends to gather long after the world exposition ended.

NOTES

1. Stephen Syrett, ed., *Contemporary Portugal: Dimensions of Economic and Political Change* (Aldershot, UK: Ashgate Publishing, 2002), 1–3.

2. J. Pina Manique e Albuquerque, "Regiões Naturais. Caracterização eco-fisionómica," in *Portugal Atlas do Ambiente* (1984) and www.tuvalkin.web.pt/terravista/guincho/1421/bandeira/pt(otr.htm#nat.

3. Eugene K. Keefe et al., *Area Handbook for Portugal* (Washington, DC: U.S. Government Printing Office, 1977), 65.

4. Ibid.

5. Ibid., 65–66.

6. Ibid., 66.

7. Op. cit.

8. Ibid., 67.

9. Ibid.

10. Ibid., 75–78.

11. Ibid., 78.

12. Thomas C. Bruneau, *Politics and Nationhood* (New York: Praeger Press, 1984), 18, and Keefe et al., *Area Handbook for Portugal*, 5–6.

13. Ibid., 66–67.

14. Keefe et al., *Area Handbook for Portugal*, 6, 116, 126–127.

15. Ibid., 118.

16. Ibid., 119.

17. Ibid., 119–120, 125–126.

18. Ibid., 119–123.

19. Ibid., 123–125.

20. Maria Ioannis B. Baganha, "Portuguese Emigration After World War II," in António Costa Pinto, ed., *Contemporary Portugal: Politics, Society and Culture* (Boulder, CO: Social Science Monographs, 2003), 139–158.

21. Ibid.

22. António Barreto, "Social Change in Portugal: 1960–2000," in Ibid., 159–182.

23. Martin Eaton, "International Population Mobility, Immigration and Labor Market Change in Portugal," in Syrett, *Contemporary Portugal*, 116.

24. Dulce Pereira comment at presentation of "O Português e os crioulos. Políticas da língua (séculos XIX e XX)," University of Lisbon, November 9, 2005.

25. Tom Gallagher, *Portugal: A Twentieth Century Interpretation* (Manchester: Manchester University Press, 1983), 1; and Keefe et al., *Area Handbook for Portugal*, 1, 60.

26. Gallagher, *Portugal*, 1–2; and Keefe et al., *Area Handbook for Portugal*, 14–17.

27. Gallagher, *Portugal*, 2–3; and Keefe et al., *Area Handbook for Portugal*, 17–22.

28. Keefe et al., *Area Handbook for Portugal*, 26.

29. Gallagher, *Portugal*, 4.

30. Stanley G. Payne, *Spain and Portugal* (Madison: University of Wisconsin Press, 1973), vol. 1, 198; Douglas L. Wheeler, *Historical Dictionary of Portugal* (Lanham, MD: Scarecrow Press, 1993), 10–14; Gallagher, *Portugal: A Twentieth Century Interpretation*, 6–8; and Keefe et al., *Area Handbook for Portugal*, 35–37.

31. Gallagher, *Portugal*, 9–10.

32. A. H. de Oliveira Marques, *History of Portugal* (New York: Columbia University Press, 1972), vol. 2, 54; and Gallagher, *Portugal*, 12–13.

33. Marques, *History of Portugal*, 30, 41–44; and Payne, *Spain and Portugal*, 518.

34. Gallagher, *Portugal*, 14.

35. Marques, *History of Portugal*, 2–5; and Payne, *Spain and Portugal*, 537–539.

36. Payne, *Spain and Portugal*, 550; and Gallagher, *Portugal*, 17.

37. Marques, *History of Portugal*, 74–75; and Gallagher, *Portugal*, 18.

38. Marques, *History of Portugal*, 129–134, 150–153; and Payne, *Spain and Portugal*, 559–561.

39. Gallagher, *Portugal*, 25.

40. Ibid., 29.

41. Payne, *Spain and Portugal*, 572.

42. Marques, *History of Portugal*, 174–175.

43. Payne, op. cit., 571.

44. Gallagher, *Portugal*, 31.

45. Ibid., 43.

46. Ibid., 48.

47. Howard J. Wiarda, "The Corporatist Tradition and the Corporative System in Portugal: Structured, Evolving, Transcended, Persistent," in Lawrence S. Graham

and Harry M. Makler, eds., *Contemporary Portugal* (Austin: University of Texas Press, 1979), 93–100.

48. Pinto, "Twentieth Century Portugal: An Introduction," in Pinto, *Contemporary Portugal*, 19–22, 41–43.

49. Gallagher, *Portugal*, 96–97.

50. Bruneau, *Politics and Nationhood*, 18.

51. Ibid., 20.

52. Ibid., 21–26.

53. Ibid., 64–67.

54. Paul Christopher Manuel, *The Challenges of Democratic Consolidation: Political, Economic, and Military Issues, 1976–1991* (Westport, CT: Praeger, 1996).

55. Nancy Bermeo, "Learning from the Portuguese Experience: Some Quick Conclusions About Some Long Processes" in *Modern Portugal*, ed. António Costa Pinto (Palo Alto, CA: The Society for the Promotion of Science and Scholarship, 1998), 270–274.

56. Bruneau, *Politics and Nationhood*, 311.

57. Ibid., 313–314.

58. Ibid., 315.

59. Ibid., 315.

60. Ibid., 314–316.

61. Ibid., 318.

62. Pedro Lains, "The Portuguese Economy in the 20th Century: Growth and Structural Change," in *Contemporary Portugal*, ed. Pinto; and Manuel, *The Challenges of Democratic Consolidation*.

63. António Barreto, "Social Change in Portugal: 1960–2000," in *Contemporary Portugal*, ed. Pinto.

SELECTED READINGS

Bermeo, Nancy. "Learning from the Portuguese Experience: Some Quick Conclusions About Some Long Processes." In *Modern Portugal*, edited by António Costa Pinto. Palo Alto, CA: The Society for the Promotion of Science and Scholarship, 1998.

Bruneau, Thomas C. *Politics and Nationhood*. New York: Praeger Press, 1984.

Costa Pinto, António, ed. *Contemporary Portugal: Politics, Society and Culture*. Boulder, CO: Social Science Monographs, 2003.

Gallagher, Tom. *Portugal: A Twentieth Century Interpretation*. Manchester, England: Manchester University Press, 1983.

Keefe, Eugene et al. *Area Handbook for Portugal*. Washington, DC: U.S. Government Printing Office, 1977.

Manique e Albuquerque, and J. Pina. "Regiões Naturais. Caracterização eco-fisionómica," in *Portugal Atlas do Ambiente*, 1984.

Manuel, Paul Christopher. *The Challenges of Democratic Consolidation: Political, Economic, and Military Issues, 1976–1991*. Westport, CT: Praeger, 1996.

Oliveira Marques, A. H. de. *History of Portugal.* 2 Vols. New York: Columbia University Press, 1972.

Payne, Stanley G. *Spain and Portugal.* 2 Vols. Madison: University of Wisconsin Press, 1973.

Syrett, Stephen, ed. *Contemporary Portugal: Dimensions of Economic and Political Change.* Aldershot, UK: Ashgate Publishing, 2002.

Wheeler, Douglas L. *Historical Dictionary of Portugal.* Lanham, MD: Scarecrow Press, 1993.

Wiarda, Howard J. "The Corporatist Tradition and the Corporative System in Portugal: Structured, Evolving, Transcended, Persistent." In *Contemporary Portugal*, edited by Lawrence S. Graham and Harry M. Makler. Austin: University of Texas Press, 1979.

www.tuvalkin.web.pt/terravista/guincho/1421/bandeira/pt(otr.htm#nat.

2

Religion and Thought

RELIGION

Portugal is predominantly a Roman Catholic country, partly as a result of the forced conversions of non-Catholics when the Moors were defeated and the Inquisition's persecution of Jews, Moors, and Protestants. The Portuguese Inquisition's roots began under King Manuel I, who reigned from 1492 to 1521. In 1494, the king formed an alliance with the Spanish monarchs Ferdinand and Isabella, which required the expulsion of any Jews in Portugal that refused to become Christians and the implementation of purity-of-blood regulations to restrict those who did. Manuel did not aggressively enforce these laws, but public anti-Semitism made life difficult for the Jews (New Christians). The Inquisition initiated by João III, who reigned from 1521 to 1557, began in 1531 and was formalized in 1536, eventually resulted in the burning of more than 1,000 Jews in the sixteenth century. This led to the flight of many Jews to Northern Europe and colonial Brazil. The Inquisition included book censure and prosecution of divination, witchcraft, and bigamy. It contributed to the slow Portuguese absorption of innovations beyond Iberia by preventing, for example, the integration of Enlightenment ideals.

The Pyrenees insulated the Iberian Peninsula from the protestant reformation that swept Europe north of the mountain range. Until 1910, Catholicism was seen as the religion of the monarchical reign. After 1910, under the first republic, state secularization was begun as the liberals embraced science and positivism, leading to anti-clericalism and a lay society. During the Salazar-Caetano dictatorship that ruled from 1933 to 1974, Catholicism was again designated the official state religion and integrated into public school curriculum. After the 1974 Portuguese revolution, a new constitution emphasized religious pluralism. Today, Jehovah Witnesses, Mormons, Evangelicals, and other religious groups have a minor presence; but Catholicism and its influence still dominate.

The piousness of the Portuguese has historically been imbued with a certain degree of magical or even pagan rituals. The clerical hierarchy has unsuccessfully struggled for centuries to stifle these aspects. Sanctuaries or saints are often associated with certain mystical activities, such as holy baths, miraculous fountains, and supernatural plants, trees, or even rock formations. São Torcato, for example, is believed to sweat through his coffin, which the devout wipe up with handkerchiefs and take home as holy relics and good luck charms. Individuals routinely pray to particular saints to help them or others recover from an illness, disability, or other misfortune, such as accidents, love and marriage problems, loss or theft of objects, and recovery from devastation by natural disasters. These prayers are often accompanied by tokens pinned onto the saint's robes or placed at the foot of the statue. Years ago, this act involved significant monetary sacrifice, for the little charms were fashioned from gold. However, frequent theft caused the gold to be replaced with wax objects, in a larger scale; now arms, legs, eyes, and hearts can often be seen placed at the foot of the statue. Sometimes there are pictures of lost or ill relatives or paintings showing the sick parent or child with the request for help painted in the margins. Some of the requests involve proactive demands for protection or good luck in forthcoming events, such as trips, exams, commerce, or harvests. In exchange, promised contributions range from monetary and gold jewelry donations, the offering of masses, gifts of animals and produce, fogaças (meals that are auctioned during the religious festival called "romaria"), or pilgrimages to a particular sanctuary. In the fifteenth and sixteenth centuries, monasteries and churches were constructed as payment for blessings of victory in battle or safe passage during the Discoveries. It is common to see pilgrims hiking long distances to the Fátima shrine—especially in May, the anniversary of the appearance of the Virgin Mary in 1917 to three shepherd children—to fulfill their promises, sleeping where they can find shelter. In many cases the last kilometer of the voyage is traversed on one's knees while reciting the rosary, often resulting in a painful, bloody visit to a hospital emergency ward. Wiser pilgrims fashion knee pads of cut tire or cotton padding to avoid injury.

The links between religion and culture are very strong. Religious holidays are numerous, including Easter, Assumption, and Christmas, as are festivals.

Bawdy humor ridiculing the human failings of priests is virtually a national pastime. Yet, the public at large also appears to turn a blind eye to their priests' occasional mistresses and illegitimate children. Perhaps they recognize that one's personal behavior and piety are not mutually exclusive. Sometimes the most crass person in the village, or the worst gossip, can also be the staunchest and most generous supporter of the church, giving selflessly of his or her time and meager funds to the village chapel and romaria. The man who always gets drunk at the festa at night could be the very man who led the religious procession through the streets earlier in the day. What matters most is one's personal commitment to God. Religious references such as "graças a Deus" (thanks be to God) or "se Deus quiser" (God willing) are frequently used in the most casual of conversations: "Next week, se Deus quiser, I will go visit my children."

Historically the church has had considerable influence in the political realm. Its origins can be traced to at least the mid-third century A.D. when Roman Catholicism appeared in the territory, making it older than the nation itself. The church dominated all public and private life prior to the rise of a central government because it was solely responsible for providing education, hospitals, and charity. From the earliest days during the national conquest of territory and battles against the Moors, the church played a significant role, whether in supporting the king's divine right to the throne or accompanying and blessing the battles against the infidels. It was common for warriors, from the lowest soldier to the ruling king, to ask for God's guidance toward victory and survival in exchange for a specific promise. Batalha, central Portugal's fantastic Gothic cathedral, was built to fulfill such a pledge after victory in the battle of Aljubarrota against the Castilians in 1385. The Church accompanied Portuguese sailing vessels during the Descobrimentos (Discoveries) as they traveled throughout the world claiming territories and peoples for the crown. By 1700 the institution owned one-third of the national territory.

The Church's control, however, did not go uncontested. The first major onslaughts came during Marquis de Pombal's tutelage from 1750 to 1777, which included the expulsion of the Jesuits. Tensions eased after Pombal's departure but returned with the Liberalism and secularism of post-1820 governments. In 1834 the property of religious orders was confiscated, and the agrarian reforms of the 1830 and 1840s seized and sold much of the Church's land. By the end of the century its influence had returned, only to suffer again under the initial seven years of the First Republic, which ruled from 1910 to 1927. The apparitions of Our Lady of Fátima in 1917, in which it was alleged that the Virgin Mary appeared and spoke a message to three peasant children, breathed new life into the Catholic Church. The Salazar dictatorship's espousal of conservative values meant the Church regained its sway and role in public education. Today the Church voices its views through many venues, including the Catholic University, newspapers and magazines, and Radio Renasença, the country's most popular radio station. While it is illegal, the clergy does not shy away from preaching politics at the pulpit, and many priests will boldly instruct their congregations as to how they should vote on issues of concern to the church, such as abortion or gay marriage.

At the turn of the twenty-first century, Portuguese attitudes toward religion are open-minded, pragmatic, and personal. The demographics of the most conservative Catholic adherents—the 43 percent of the population labeled Ritualistic Catholics—is an older, less-educated female, living in the rural areas of northern and central Portugal. These Catholics tend to have puritanical views of sexuality, family life, and bioethics (i.e., euthanasia, abortion, cloning). Nominal Catholics make up 46 percent of the population, and they tend to be individualist in their practices and tolerant of others' approaches to religion. They do not consider themselves "practicing" Catholics. While they have not rejected religion, they do not follow Catholicism's teachings. About 3 percent of the remaining population are affiliated with a non-Catholic religion, 2 percent of which are Protestant or related groups, and 7 percent who consider themselves non-religious.

THOUGHT

Philosophically, scholasticism and positivism have had the greatest impact on Portugal. Scholasticism in the eighteenth century and earlier focused on technical derivatives, such as summaries, commentaries, and scholarly manuals in the presentation of classics such as St. Thomas, Plato, or Aristotle. Nineteenth-century positivism emphasized that only scientific knowledge could be authentic as measured by strict method.

Liberalism

Until the nineteenth century, Portugal remained free of the anti-monarchical civil unrest and coups occurring in many other nations. From the 1820s on, however, ever since the crowns' flight to Brazil during the Napoleonic invasions and its reluctance to return to Portugal after Napoleon's defeat, the upper-middle class and military elements assumed a broader role in Portuguese politics. Increasingly, liberal ideas such as democracy, equality, and popular sovereignty began to influence these nascent political groups. While the crown remained in Brazil, the English General William Beresford ruled the nation. His resistance against these progressive ideas undermined the credibility of the regime since it was foreign as well as reactionary. As a result, liberals were able to muster wide-ranging support since their opposition was not only ideological but also patriotic. A revolution in 1820 succeeded in driving Beresford out of the country and marked the beginning of Portugal's modern political evolution.

These new power groups created a constitution in 1822 that limited royal power, abolished the Inquisition, and expanded the suffrage to all but the illiterate (about 90% of the population), women, and friars in the biennial election for a parliament independent of the crown. The drafters of the new constitution wanted to limit the power of the crown, create a representative system, ensure individual rights, and "create a rational, unified legal system." The liberal changes should not be mistaken for a restructuring of Portuguese society to its roots. The constitution succeeded in compromising with the traditional forces by maintaining a monarchy that reigned (yet did not rule) and "preserving the religious and economic interests of the church, and not imposing social and economic reform of the landholders."[1] In more concrete terms, the sweeping ideological changes had little effect on a peasant's life.

At this time, however, the liberal, urban, middle class still provided a very small base from which to increase its powers. Liberalism was imperiled in Portugal for three reasons. First, it represented only 9 percent of the Portuguese population; second, the cities were the centers of liberal strength (and Porto and Lisbon were just about the only cities that existed); third, the flood of British imports continued to undermine domestic commerce, the mainstay of liberal strength. The conditions that could lead to the emergence of a class of "economically independent, prosperous townsmen" who could support a new democracy simply did not exist. These conditions were compounded by divisions among the liberal groups, exacerbated by their disagreements on how to react to Brazil's declaration of independence in 1822.

Republicanism

Republicanism began to make inroads through teachers, journalists, small businessmen, clerks, and artisans. By 1896, rather late for a European nation, these new political groups were attracting between 15 percent and 20 percent of the population. The PRP's proposals included "complete political freedom and equality, guarantees for the rights to associate and strike, separation of church and state, and the elimination of most indirect, regressive taxes."[2]

The instability that dominated the nation, compounded by the PRP's treatment of the military, eventually led to a coup in 1917 under Major Bernardino Sidónio Pais. The new regime was integralist, traditional, and strongly opposed to liberalism, individualism, and socialism.

Integralism

The integralist movement was founded in 1910 and was influenced by the French writer Charles Maurras. Among the Lusitanian Integralists' goals were the restoration of the Portuguese monarchy and an emphasis on God, the family, and other traditional concepts. Along with corporatism and fascism, integralism formed the basis for authoritarian rule following the overthrow of the First Republic in 1926.

Socialism

When the Russian revolution occurred in 1917, Portugal had already developed a lively labor movement and a political atmosphere that was unique. The working class was represented by diverse parties and movements that were engaged in an old debate concerning workers' exploitation by capitalists. By the time the Portuguese Communist Party was formed in 1921, the continuous debates concerning the labor movement's pursuit of a revolutionary path were no longer novel. Since 1913, anarchists and syndicalists had debated whether syndicalism alone could end the capitalist exploitation of workers. Although many concluded that syndicalism was not the correct method to succeed in the overthrow of capitalism, they felt it was a good approach to confront it. Today, Portuguese trade unions, especially public servants and teachers, remain strong, although the decline of heavy industries has also led to less unionization.

Porto School

A major philosophical development in twentieth-century Portugal was what is labeled the Portuguese Renaissance, or the Porto School, from 1910 to 1932. It primarily contested foreign domination of, or influence on, Portuguese ideas that led to the denigration of all things Portuguese. The Porto School sought to answer the question: "What is the essential purity of the Lusitanian spirit?" They argued that the Portuguese should be actively involved in fulfilling their civilizing destiny. One goal was to give a national and spiritual content to the new republican regime and liberate it from the ideals of positivism, evolutionism, scientism, utilitarianism, rationalism, and intellectualism, which, they argued, squeezed feelings and desire (spirit) out of life in favor of reason. While positivists focused on objectivity and science, the Portuguese Renaissance looked at subjectivity and the integral element of spirit in contrast to external forces. Science was not opposed, but the limits and value of scientific knowledge were questioned in favor of qualitative values and intuition. Renaissance themes could be seen in the writings of Teixeira de Pascoaes, Guerra Junqueiro, Sampaio Bruno, Fernando Pessoa, Leonardo

Coimbra, and Jaime Cortesão. They did not contest that the Portuguese had fallen behind much of European philosophical developments (the Portuguese "unease"), but they did not want the Portuguese point of view to be ignored as intellectuals tried to close the gap with Europe.

Foreign political ideas such as liberalism, republicanism, anarchism, anarcho-syndicalism, socialism, communism, corporatism, fascism, and integralism influenced the educated elite and middle classes in Portugal. Through them, many of these views metamorphosed into Portuguese variants that were then used to mobilize or influence the masses. As liberalism and republicanism took root in the urban areas in the nineteenth and early twentieth century, the urban masses were often attracted to their competitors, such as anarchism, anarcho-syndicalism, socialism, and communism. In reaction, conservative forces, especially in the central and northern rural areas, were drawn to corporatism, fascism, and integralism.

Corporatism

Corporatism (or corporativism) was based upon social hierarchy and elitism as well as Catholic doctrines. One goal was to diffuse antagonism among the varied social groups (i.e., employers, industrial workers, agrarian laborers, clergy, nobility, military orders, universities, municipalities, and so forth) by empowering the state to arbitrate for the good of the society as a whole. If the government considered it to be in the best interests of the Portuguese nation that its working class be paid higher wages, for example, it could mandate that employers do so. In reality, however, Salazar's government tended to side with the elites.

By 1930 the military and Salazar had succeeded in returning political stability to the nation. That same year Salazar proclaimed the formation of the National Union party, which would become part of his "Estado Novo" (new state). Corporatism would replace the political parties, trade unions, a free press, and other organizations. Power was to be focused on the executive, and the values of God, family, and the nation would be given the highest priority. Change would be controlled. Corporatism would be the Portuguese solution to alien radical transformations such as socialism, liberalism, or communism.[3]

In theory, social unrest would end because the "corporation" would represent the clergy, military, students, workers, employers, and all other groups equally. The central government would guarantee a harmonious coexistence to all. In reality, the government was biased toward the employers and traditional elements at the expense of the lower classes. Salazar believed that God had given the peasant "the privilege of being poor" and that "education, health, and economic reform 'would not create happiness.' " As a result, the Portuguese solution to harness, tame, and manipulate radical change failed because the lower classes realized the government was not mediating between contending classes but was instead using corporatism to favor the upper classes.[4]

A comparison of Salazar's dictatorship with German or Italian fascism shows that Portugal was not a true fascist state. Despite Salazar's sharing views with Adolf Hitler and Benito Mussolini on authoritarianism, anti-communism, and hierarchy, Portugal's dictatorship was not as harsh or violent.

Portuguese philosophy in the twentieth century also explored phenomenology, existentialism (especially Raul Brandão), philosophy of law, philosophy of education, political philosophy (like the nationalism of Lusitanian integralism), the New State ideology of Salazar, and Marxism (in the works of Vasco de Magalhães-Vilhena), logic, theory of knowledge, and philosophy of science.

Popular Thought

Despite national unity and identity, the Portuguese today, especially the younger generation, are quickly being assimilated into globalized world culture, due mainly to the influence of foreign, especially American, cinema and music. The young in rural and urban areas are more likely to travel abroad in search of employment and return with new experiences as well as new dissatisfactions with their Portuguese way of life. The Lusitanian uniqueness of the past may not endure in the future.

The Portuguese people are a study in paradoxes. Piety and mysticism are not diametrically opposing beliefs. They are just as likely to pray as they are to consult the zodiac. While they are a hard-working people, they are economically peripheral in Western Europe. The Portuguese often have a fatalistic perspective on life, accepting the cards they have been dealt in life rather than trying to change their destiny. Fittingly, this attitude is reflected in Portugal's national music called "fado," with its plaintive and melancholic songs of lost love and life's hardships. This fatalistic perspective contradicts the adventurousness of the fifteenth- and sixteenth-century explorers and twentieth-century emigrants. Their inherent melancholy does not alter their ability to enjoy themselves while facing their difficulties, and many take comfort in simply being surrounded by family and friends. In the summer months when villages and towns celebrate the festivals of their patron saints, the Portuguese make merry at dances and *romarias* nearly every weekend. They love music, and unless they are mourning a death in the family, they actively participate in playing, singing, or dancing.

The Portuguese are a people proud of their culture and accomplishments, yet they also see themselves as developmentally inferior to the people in North America or Northern Europe. They are fiercely proud of their history, but do not cling to it. They readily embrace new technologies, continue to make important and cutting-edge contributions to architecture, create innovative social programs, and show a strong commitment to cultural enhancement.

Notes

1. A. H. de Oliveira Marques, *History of Portugal* (New York: Columbia University Press, 1972), vol. 2, 30.

2. Stanley G. Payne, *Spain and Portugal* (Madison: University of Wisconsin Press, 1973), 2 Vols, 550.

3. Howard J. Wiarda, "The Corporatist Tradition and the Corporative System in Portugal: Structured, Evolving, Transcended, Persistent," *Contemporary Portugal*, eds. Lawrence S. Graham and Harry M. Makler (Austin: University of Texas Press, 1979), 93–100.

4. Thomas C. Bruneau, *Politics and Nationhood* (New York: Praeger Press, 1984), 120.

Selected Readings

Bruneau, Thomas C. *Politics and Nationhood*. New York: Praeger Press, 1984.

Calafate, Pedro, ed. *História do Pensamento Filosófico Português: Volume 1—Idade Média*. Lisbon: Editorial Caminho, 1999.

———. *História do Pensamento Filosófico Português: Volume II—Renascimento e Contra-Reforma*. Lisbon: Circulo de Leitores, 2002.

———. *História do Pensamento Filosófico Português: Volume 5—O Século XX— Tomo 1*. Lisbon: Editorial Caminho, 2000.

———. *História do Pensamento Filosófico Português: Volume 5—O Século XX— Tomo 2*. Lisbon: Editorial Caminho, 2000.

Marques, A. H. de Oliveira. *History of Portugal*. New York: Columbia University Press, 1972. vol. 2.

Pais, José Machado, Manuel Vilaverde Cabral, and Jorge Vala, eds. *Religião e Bioética*. Lisbon: Imprensa de Ciências Sociais, 2001.

Payne, Stanley G. *Spain and Portugal*. 2 Vols. Madison: University of Wisconsin Press, 1973.

Sanchis, Pierre. *Arraial: Festa de um Povo, as Romarias Portuguesas*. Lisboa: Pulicações Dom Quixote, 1983.

Wiarda, Howard J. "The Corporatist Tradition and the Corporative System in Portugal: Structured, Evolving, Transcended, Persistent." In *Contemporary Portugal*, edited by Lawrence S. Graham and Harry M. Makler. Austin: University of Texas Press, 1979.

3

Family, Marriage, Gender, and Education

FAMILY

After the United Kingdom, Portugal has the highest rate of marriage in Europe. Most children live with their parents until they wed, typically between the ages of 20 and 30. If the significance of family allegiance has been mentioned 20 times elsewhere in this book it will serve to underline this most essential aspect of Portuguese cultural identity. After marriage the newlyweds are integrated into the new, extended family network, spending most of their free time in the company of their families. Newlyweds are generally pressured from all sides to get busy making babies right away. The Portuguese are crazy for children. As in the United States and other post-industrialized nations, Portuguese women are increasingly postponing motherhood until their careers are more established. This is considered downright unexplainable to the more traditional older generation. "After all," they would argue, "isn't that what marriage is for?" In spite of social pressures, in 2007 the majority of children were born to mothers aged 30 to 34. Children are seen everywhere, loved and appreciated even by strangers. In parks and at cultural events they run and shriek among the crowds of adults, and their noise and boisterousness are not only tolerated but smiled upon. Young children and babies are especially irresistible, and there is always a loving hand reaching out to pet and fuss over them. Even the most jaded teenagers are happy to play with and entertain their small cousins at family gatherings or outings.

The well-known saying, "It takes a village to raise a child," is an apt one for the Portuguese approach to raising their children; and in the country or the city there are watchful, loving eyes everywhere, looking out for all the children's safety. As courtship age approaches, this watchfulness is less appreciated by the young, though tolerated as a reality of village life.

The birth of a child is a serious affair, with great importance placed on choosing the best possible godparent. It is an honor to be asked to serve in this position. The parents of the child and the chosen godparents become *compadres* (and share a special tie, almost like a brother or sister). If the godparents are not already part of the family, they become members by association. The position is taken very seriously, as godparents play an important role throughout the life of the child and take an almost parental pride in all of their godchild's achievements. Godparents are frequently chosen for their potential ability to assist and improve a godchild's chances of economic success or social standing. Baptism is generally performed within a year of birth and is celebrated lavishly.

With modernization and urbanization, the extended family has been replaced by the nuclear family. Prior to the 1970s families were large to ensure against the high infant mortality rate. (In 1975 there were 40 deaths per 1,000 births in the first year of life, whereas in 2006 mortality had declined to only 3.5 deaths per 1,000 births.) Many children meant more hands to help with the farming and housework, and later in life they provided care-giving to their aging parents, who in turn assisted with raising the next generation. Economic and mobility factors have contributed to changes in the traditional family structure. Childbearing has decreased—1.36 children per woman of childbearing age—as the cost of raising large families has increased, especially for the urban middle classes. While the extended family still maintains its importance as a social support system, and aging parents often live with their adult children, young adults are more likely to leave their home villages in search of work. A shift from the past is that the number of households where more than two generations live has decreased. As social norms broadened, so too has the public perception of family: common-law marriage, single-parent families, and households of just one person have risen. In 2001, 5.5 percent of the population, or 572,372 Portuguese, lived alone, 3.7 percent of them women and 1.8 percent of them men. Of these, 8.4 percent were under the age of 30. Most are widowed, single, or retired. The divorce rate rose to 25 percent, and second marriages also increased.

Devotion to one's village is second only to devotion to one's family. No matter where Portuguese meet (in Lisbon, Paris, or New York) the first question asked is usually, "Onde é sua terra?" (Where is your home?)—meaning, "What village are you from?" A child may be born in Lisbon or Porto, or even

France or the United States, but whatever connection the parents hold to the *aldeia* (village) is adopted by the child as well. Even though there has been a huge exodus of youth from the economic dead end of the village, no matter what direction life takes them, Portuguese are bound by their love for their roots and the place of their birth. Even the most erudite city dweller will head for the *aldeia* on weekends if possible, and always for at least a part of the long five-week summer holiday each worker is entitled to by law. Today, weekend warriors bring their cell phones and portable laptops with them, and it is an amusing juxtaposition to see them typing madly away in the nearly primitive setting of a small village that may have only had electricity and plumbing since the early 1980s.

MARRIAGE

Physical courtship in Portugal is rather more public than in the United States, and it is a common sight to find most benches in public parks occupied with embracing couples. On any given weekend, most secluded niches or seating in any of the public parks, gardens, and castles will have its requisite romancing couple, who are accepted with matter-of-fact calm by any who happen to blunder into their chosen spot. It would not be unusual to see, on the very same bench, a black-clad widow feeding pigeons, not in the least put out by the goings-on right next to her. Nor would the busy couple feel that their space or privacy had been invaded. Courtship is truly a part of the public domain. In an overwhelmingly Catholic country it can seem surprising that public, physical displays of affection would be so casually supported, but logical when one remembers that most children live at home until they marry between the ages of 20 and 30. Is it any wonder that courting couples would choose the public arena among strangers as an alternative to courtship at home under the watchful eyes of their parents?

Times are changing, and attitudes have become more liberal in the last 30 years, but the rural areas tend to be more conservative regarding courtship. In the countryside, couples frequently meet and develop their relationships during the summertime weekly religious festivals (*romarias*) that always include a public dance of some kind. As people travel some distance to attend these festivals, the same boy and girl can see each other frequently, though they may be from distant villages. On the dance floor they are free to get close, but not too close, under the hawk-like eyes of the older generation, the row of village widows and elders that line the perimeter of the plaza, a vigilant fixture at all country dances. An errant couple can be sure their behavior will be enthusiastically reported and discussed to any and all concerned. Nowadays, there seems to be little more anyone can do about it besides wag their tongues and gossip, and as the statistics will illustrate, there is plenty that goes on beyond the watchful eyes of the village elders.

Even so, some villages still preserve the old traditions during their *festas*, which provide other charmingly old-fashioned ways a country boy can impress his intended, such as during the special waltz (usually to the tune of the *Midnight Waltz*) called the *Dança do Ramo* in which a girl, all alone on the sidelines, is given a bouquet that allows her to choose her partner. They join the dance floor for a few seconds prior to being approached by the master of ceremonies (MC), who asks into the microphone "*Quanto vale o ramo?*" (How much is the bouquet worth?) For the privilege of dancing with her, the chosen boy must publicly announce his donation to the *festa* (repeated into the microphone by the MC for all to hear). If the donation is unusually large, the MC makes a big public show, demonstrating the boy's monetary contribution on behalf of the girl that chose him. While the boy pays, the girl then passes the *ramo* off to another girl who goes in search of her own partner. As the dance goes on, and more and more couples pay their way on to the dance floor, donations become competitive as each boy tries to top the previous donation. This serves to impress the girl in two ways. It demonstrates to her the boy's generosity and relative "wealth," and lets her know—albeit in the most literal sense—her value to him. In the case of the *Dança do Ramo*, not only is the courtship providing entertainment for the onlookers, but it also has economic benefits to the village as well. Such customs are fast disappearing and are rarely seen today as the young people abandon the villages and the older generation fades away, taking their traditions with them.

In spite of the vigilant surveillance of young couples that village life enables, the amorously inclined are still able to find ways to be alone. Most women were in stable relationships when they had their first sexual relationships and found the experience positive. Although the population is about 90 percent Catholic and doctrine forbids premarital relations or the use of contraceptives, the statistics speak of a more pragmatic approach to religion and sex as they intersect with real life. A dozen years ago only 20 percent of women were using contraceptives, although 30 percent had had sex before 17 years of age, 43 percent between the ages of 17 and 18, and 92 percent before the age of 20. Childbirth out of wedlock has climbed to 25 percent. Until April 2007, abortion was allowed only in cases of rape, fetal malformation, or threat to the mother's health or life. As a result of a referendum in February 2007 in which 59 percent voted to legalize abortion, the procedure is now available on demand within the first 10 weeks of pregnancy.

Today, women are more likely to initiate a relationship than in the past, but if a woman appears too forward she is still often dismissed by men. While men's roles are increasingly more progressive, a certain amount of machismo prevails. Portuguese men do not expect their partners to be submissive, but neither do they wish to relinquish control.

The status of widows before the 1974 revolution was dismal from a cultural, financial, and legal perspective. Prior to 1974, the autonomy of all women was suppressed, and legally they were seen as minors before the law and needed their husband's permission to travel, among other restrictions. With the reforms in the Civil Code in 1966 women gained some basic rights, but they were not considered full citizens with equal rights until the new constitution in 1974, revised in 1989. Post-revolution social transformations such as increased medical care, fewer deaths in childbirth, and such have changed mortality patterns, with life expectancy for women at 80.5 years, and at 73.8 for men, as rated in 2002. Additionally, there is less likelihood of being widowed than in the past. Nevertheless, there are a disproportionate number of widows in Portugal due to dangerous occupations (especially deep-sea fishing), the colonial wars, and large age differences between men and women at marriage. The 1991 census documents 500,000 widows in a population of under 10 million!

Many women, as a result of male migration, found themselves abandoned— a kind of pseudo-widowhood. They were left without means of support, and due to the repression of women, poor education, and limited job opportunities, they found few avenues to better their conditions. Many received a pension from their husbands, but as the pay scale was meager during the Salazar years, they were not adequate. It was not until after the revolution that universal pensions for the elderly and widows were instituted, calculated based on the woman's age, length of marriage, husband's occupation, and the number and ages of children. This social security payment, though small, can influence important life decisions such as living independently or remarrying, though remarriage for widows is not socially encouraged.

The plight of the widow with children was particularly serious. It was common for economically disadvantaged women to give away their children to orphanages or more financially stable relatives as a survival strategy. These "adoptions" were done informally, so there is no way to know exactly how many there were. In many cases, living with relatives was a positive development for both sides, as the children were provided with an education, and later maybe an inheritance; and often very strong emotional bonds were formed between the adoptive parents and these children who, particularly the girls, would look after these otherwise childless parents in their old age. Not so long ago, parents looked to their daughters or other female relatives to provide care and shelter in their golden years. Today, the elderly rely more on the government for support and long-term medical care, which is a change from the days of large extended families that cared for the elderly at home. With the increasing "nuclearization" of the Portuguese traditional family structure, where both men and women work outside of the home, the elderly are more likely to be institutionalized for elder care. As a result, the elderly are becoming more and more isolated from society.

There is an unstated, strong social pressure against remarriage for widows both from the culture and the church, though this attitude is becoming outdated. The government pension plays a role in many widow's decisions to remarry, and most still choose not to. Traditional, social stereotypes cast the widow as an undesirable choice, especially for a single man, illustrated in the proverb, "O amor de uma viúva é caldo a referver; nunca nenhum é tão bom como o outro marido." (The love of a widow is like reheated broth, never as good as for the first husband.) Some widows consider marriage for life, even after the death of their husbands. These widows will wear the black mourning clothes (*luto*) for the rest of their lives, a symbol of penance and piety. In the villages where traditions die hard, it is a common sight to see many "black widows" of the older generation. Some equate the length of wearing *luto carregado* with the amount of love or respect for a dead husband, and a widow may even eschew wearing *luto* after a very short time—or altogether—if her husband abused her during their marriage. Again, these customs are changing, and it is generally up to the widows to decide how long they will wear black. Interestingly, this attitude of prolonged mourning has not been equally embraced by male widowers or the culture, as can be seen in the words to the proverb, "Dor de mulher morta dura até a porta." (Grief for a dead wife lasts to the door.) It means that a male widower's grief should end when his wife's coffin is taken out the door of his house, whereas a female widow is expected to grieve for her dead husband for the rest of her life. Male widowers are encouraged to marry again, especially if they have young children in need of a mother, but the women who marry widowers are usually older or "old maids," have children out of wedlock, or some other aspect that marks them by cultural standards as "damaged goods." Men who marry widows are usually themselves widowers, or divorced. Legally, a woman must wait 300 days and a man 180 days to remarry in order to avoid any paternity claims in case of pregnancy.

Changing images and attitudes of widowhood began with the creation of the self-advocacy group Movimento Esperança e Vida (MEV), begun in 1958, which now boasts over 10,000 members. The MEV provides a forum for widows to share their feelings, problems, and increasing involvement in social causes, creating solidarity that transcends class. Discontinuation of many of the costly customs of widowhood, such as lavish cemetery decorations and masses, have provided women with the resources to pay for courses of study at the elder university in Lisbon or for other life-enriching experiences. Stereotyped images of widows as women to be pitied, as somehow incomplete for lack of a husband, are falling away as more and more women enter the workforce and gain independence.

Many families do not attend celebrations of any kind during their period of mourning. Masses are held regularly in the name of the deceased, although the frequency varies according to individual and region. Most common is to hold a mass seven days after the death, after which many services are held monthly and yearly on the anniversary of the death. In some families the dead are remembered in memorial masses for several generations.

GENDER

Historically, gender roles in Portugal have followed traditional lines and division of labor, with men being the breadwinners and women taking charge of the household and raising children. Slow change in these roles picked up speed around 1967 due to a sharp increase in male emigration. Women were left behind while their husbands attempted to start new lives abroad, with the expectations that they would send for their families once they had achieved a certain level of economic stability. Immigration laws being what they were, sometimes the wait was extended for years, and women received money sent home with no possibility of reunion in the new chosen country. In the interim, women became the heads of households.

Despite the fact that women gained new power and responsibility in the absence of their husbands, the court system had not legally recognized their new position. They remained legally dependent on their husbands. In 1976 the new post-revolutionary atmosphere led to some corrections in terms of succession and rights of family in the courts. Divorce was legalized in 1975 after having been banned under the dictatorship. New laws provided for domestic violence protection and a woman's right to property in cases of divorce. As in many other nations, child custody generally favored women. The greater change, however, came in the area of better legal protections, such as non-discrimination in the workplace and professions and equal pay for equal work. Article 68 of the new constitution also created special rights for women in the workplace, allowing maternity leave and guaranteeing a woman's employment during and after pregnancy. It also addressed the right to a profession and civil rights.

At the beginning of the 1970s, women made up 20 percent of the working population; this figure rose to 50 percent by 2002. To maintain a middle-class standard of living today, it is necessary for both parents to work. Economic pressures have forced women into the workforce, where they are now found at all levels of all professions. Whereas they once comprised 80 percent of domestic staff, the figure declined to 58 percent as women's opportunities expanded. As employees, women are a minority in the manufacturing sector but a majority in the agricultural and service sectors. They represent a majority of public administration and public service employees, especially in health and education. At 56 percent, there are more female university students than male, and women receive 65 percent of university degrees. Women have greater influence in the labor market, education, and family than they do in politics. Nevertheless, despite men's domination within political parties, 61 women of 230 representatives were elected in 2005, accounting for 26 percent of parliament. This development is interesting for a patriarchal society given that in the more progressive United States, women held only 16 percent of the seats in Congress in 2007.

Portugal's previous patriarchal society has achieved a more visible balance between the sexes, as evidenced by the growing number of female employers in the last 25 years, from 10 percent to 26 percent. In addition, where previously 22 percent were self-employed, in 2002 the figure had more than doubled to 46 percent. Furthermore, female employees have increased in number from the previous 35 percent to the current 45 percent. While unemployment has never risen above 10 percent in Portugal, the figure for female unemployment is usually 15–20 percent higher than for males. Periods of extreme economic crisis may see women approach the 50 percent unemployment mark, which generally hits hardest young workers in industry and transport, women in domestic service, those with short-term contracts, those with basic educations, or the unskilled. The percentage of women working in agriculture and industry are the highest levels for Europe.

It would be a mistake to assume that the advances in women's employment equity in the workplace would transfer to the home as well; the women's movement is comparatively slow to take hold on the domestic front. Despite entering the labor force, most women are still in charge of their households. In addition to their full time jobs outside the home, women are expected to perform the bulk of housework, childcare, cooking, and caring for the elderly or sick, while men generally are responsible for small maintenance and repairs to the house. Interestingly, the majority of Portuguese women do not resent the additional burden placed on them and do not think it is unfair that they spend 19 hours per week on domestic chores while the men only spend three hours.

Gay, lesbian, bisexual, and transgender individuals have had a difficult time considering Portugal's conservative moral standards that have been influenced by centuries of Catholicism and the nonexistent social debate. It is only in the last decade that homosexuals have begun to openly declare their sexual orientation. The nation attempts to defend the principles of equality espoused by the European Court of Human Rights, but not fervently. The legal system is not keeping up with the changes requested by the rising movement, as discrimination is frequent in both the public and private spheres. Laws that do exist are often not implemented or enforced. Homophobic violence has also risen since 1996 as sexual orientation issue advocates became more vocal.

After the 1974 fall of the dictatorship, some progress was made in broadening the country's rigid views regarding sexual orientation. The major advance, however, came with Portugal's membership in the European Union in 1986. While Portugal may not have adequate laws to protect its gay and lesbian population, the European Court of Human Rights steps in when necessary. In 2001 parliament extended to gay and lesbian couples living together for at least two years the same limited rights of common-law marriage that were granted to heterosexual couples in 1999. Portuguese law does not yet allow same-sex civil marriage. Neither can openly gay men or lesbians serve in the military or police forces.

ILGA Portugal, affiliated with the International Lesbian and Gay Association, was formed in 1995 and recognized by the government in 1996. Pride festivals began in Lisbon in 1997 and have expanded to the cities of Leiria and Porto. Among the major agenda items espoused by the association are equalization of the age of consent (currently 14 for heterosexual relationships but 16 for gays and lesbians), transgender rights, and adoption. It is clear that sexual orientation issues are gaining a stronger public presence and that their advocates are raising their political voices.

EDUCATION

Education in Portugal has its roots in the country's infancy. In the twelfth century, monastic, cathedral, and parish schools existed based on Catholic Church teachings, rote memorization, and deductive reasoning. The University of Coimbra, one of the oldest in the world, was founded in 1290. Education was centralized and dominated by the Catholic Church and public officials. The Inquisition begun in the 1530s centralized education even more in the hands of the Church, mainly the Jesuits.

The beginning of the eighteenth century brought the first girls' schools to Lisbon. The Enlightenment's influence on the Portuguese educational system began with the eighteenth-century reaction against the Church's dominance. With the same swift decisiveness and sense of order he brought to the redesign and rebuilding of Lisbon in the aftermath of the 1755 earthquake, the Marquês de Pombal implemented reforms to overhaul Portugal's educational system and wrench it from the grasp of the Church. These reforms included the expulsion of the Jesuits in 1759, the foundations for public and secular primary and secondary schools, the introduction of vocational training, the creation of departments of mathematics and natural sciences at the University of Coimbra, and the introduction of new taxes to pay for these reforms.

At the beginning of the nineteenth century, higher education was expanded to include an agrarian institute, the creation of polytechnic schools and new medical schools in Lisbon and Porto, and a department of Liberal Arts at the University of Lisbon. Nevertheless, the educational system remained highly elitist, with illiteracy remaining above 80 percent for various reasons. Underdevelopment was a contributing factor, especially in the rural regions, and led to the evasion of compulsory education because even the youngest hands were needed in the fields or at home to contribute toward the family's survival. Additionally, low levels of industrialization did not require much skilled labor. The majority of the population, therefore, did not see much advantage to increased literacy.

The overthrow of the monarchy in 1910 and the creation of the First Republic led to public policies aimed at decreasing the elitism of the educational system via the creation of a Ministry of Public Instruction, new universities in Lisbon and Porto, and new teacher training colleges. A campaign was begun to reduce illiteracy, secularize educational content, and integrate more scientific and empirical methods into the curriculum. Three years of primary school became obligatory and was increased to five years in 1919.

The military's overthrow of the First Republic in 1926 ended most of these reforms. With the exception of Salazar's creation of the Technical University in Lisbon, for the next 30 years educational innovation lagged, illiteracy remained high, and vocational training was almost nonexistent. For many years of his rule, the Liberal Arts at Oporto University was closed, and respected, liberal professors who held teaching positions before the start of the dictatorship lost their posts to unqualified and indifferent government appointees. Compulsory education was reduced to four years, religion was reinserted into the curriculum, and educational content was watered down. Salazar emphasized education from the middle classes up, deliberately neglecting the lower classes. At the start of the dictatorship in 1930, Portugal had an illiteracy rate of 70 percent, which suited Salazar's philosophy just fine. His fear was that literacy of the lower classes could potentially lead to instability; that the utter poverty they faced might lead them to read subversive literature. He was more interested in creating an elite class that he believed could educate and lead the nation. As he put it, "The great problems of the nation are not solved by the rank and file of the people but by trained staffs around which the masses can group themselves."[1] The result of these policies was that by 1960, a full century after Pombal's reforms, illiteracy remained at 40 percent. In the mid-1960s, public education for all children between the ages of 7 and 12 was created under the Caetano dictatorship, considered to be a bit more liberal than the Salazar regime.

The Revolution of 1974 that overthrew the dictatorship disrupted the educational system, as it did other aspects of the regime. For a time after the revolution, faculty and curriculum were highly politicized as varied groups vied for control of the schools and school systems. The constitution approved in 1976 based its educational policies on a foundation of equal opportunities. That is, all citizens have the right of access to and success in their educational pursuits. Education was expected to minimize economic, social, and cultural differences, stimulate democratic participation in a free society, and promote mutual understanding, tolerance, and a spirit of community. This philosophy has succeeded to a certain extent.

From 1974 to 1986, varied reforms were implemented that included the increase of compulsory education from six to nine years and the extension of secondary school to 12 years, including the unification of the first cycle. Several new universities were also created: Universidade de Trás-os-Montes e Alto Douro (Vila Real), Universidade de Aveiro, Universidade da Beira Interior (Covilhã), Universidade do Algarve (Faro), Universidade da Madeira, and Universidade dos Açores.

The post-revolution compulsory education program of Basic Education (currently in place) lasts nine years, divided into three consecutive cycles: The first cycle lasts four years (6 to 10 year olds); the second cycle lasts two years (10 to 12 year olds); and the third cycle lasts three years (12 to 15 year olds). Basic Education is free. Students do not pay entrance or enrollment fees, and they are provided with school insurance. They must purchase books, school materials and meals, and transport, unless they are truly needy. Almost all children go through the school system until they are 15 years old. By 1997, alternative curricula classes were created for pupils in basic education who had records of repeated academic failure and problematic integration into the school community (those in danger of abandoning basic education) and others who had learning difficulties. One goal of this curriculum is to promote the practical application of knowledge to include vocational, artistic, pre-professional, or professional components.

Preschool education is still optional, although it is part of the state educational system. The enrollment availability falls short of the number of applicants. The state recognizes that preschool education plays a significant role in children's social development and positively impacts their future educational performance; thus, expansion of the preschool network has been prioritized.

Secondary education is optional; a student must remain in school until he or she is either 15 years old or has completed nine years of instruction.

Even in the increasingly depopulated rural areas, children are continuing on to the secondary level despite the additional expenses, as books and accessories are not included in public education. For their rural parents who did not migrate to the cities to improve their lifestyles, their children's secondary school attendance is seen as the path of upward mobility. Nevertheless, only 49 percent of youths between the ages of 20 and 24 completed secondary school in 2005 when compared to the European Union average of 72 percent in 2004.

The secondary system is organized in a single cycle covering grades 10–12. The goal is to consolidate and deepen the knowledge acquired in basic education to prepare students for further studies in university or technical school and/or employment. There are two training opportunities: general courses or courses mainly geared towards continued studies and technological courses or courses focusing on working life. Courses are organized into four groups: natural-scientific, arts, socioeconomic, and humanities. Professional courses cover administration, services and commerce, agro-foodstuffs, environment and natural resources, performing arts, graphic arts, civil construction, design and technical drawing, electricity and electronics, hotel trade and tourism, information, communication and documentation, data processing, personal and social services, metallurgy, cultural heritage and arts production, chemistry, textiles, clothing, and shoes.

Access to the university or polytechnic colleges is highly competitive and determined by a combination of school grades and performance on national entrance exams. For certain fields, demand outpaces the availability of spaces so that students must search for an alternative or seek out many of the new private institutions that have lower entry standards than the public system.

The needs of older, nontraditional students have not been adequately addressed. Overall, the educational system has been seriously criticized to the point where the government is trying to rectify some of the more pressing problems. For years, massive under-funding led to high student dropout rates and a decline in the recruitment of teachers, who are underpaid and overworked. In addition, most schools do not have sufficient resources to cover even a decrease in the student population. The declining birthrate has led to some under enrolled and closed schools. In 1992, for example, there was a drop in school enrollments by 50 percent in primary schools and by 80 percent in upper secondary schools. An Organization for Economic Cooperation and Development survey conducted in 2004 found Portuguese students spend less physical hours and years at school than their peers in other countries. These problems have resulted in the loss of a competitive edge in the global employment marketplace.

Despite the current problems in education, and considering the exceptionally high level of illiteracy and educational backwardness that existed until the end of the dictatorship, Portugal has made enormous strides in educational reforms and literacy improvements in only a few decades of democracy. Heightened public awareness of education's value and the government's continued commitment to improvements bodes well for the future of the system.

NOTE

1. António Ferro, *Salazar: Portugal and Her Leader* (London: Faber and Faber Ltd., 1939), 66, as quoted in Tom Gallagher, *Portugal: A Twentieth Century Interpretation* (Manchester, England: Manchester University Press, 1983), 98.

SELECTED READINGS

Alão, Ana Paula. "As Mudanças na Condição Feminina e na Família," and "Do Amor-fidelidade ao Amor-sinceridade." In *Portugal Contemporaneo, 1974–1992. Vol. VI*, edited by António Reis. Lisboa: Publicações Alfa, 1990.

Almeida, João Ferreira de. "Society and Values." In *Modern Portugal*, edited by António Costa Pinto. Palo Alto, CA: The Society for the Promotion of Science and Scholarship, 1998.

Ambrosio, Teresa. "O Sistema Educativo: Ruptura, Estabilização e Desafios Europeus." In *Portugal Contemporaneo. 1974–1992. Vol. VI*, edited by António Reis. Lisboa: Publicações Alfa, 1990.

Barreto, António. "Social Change in Portugal: 1960–2000." In *Contemporary Portugal: Politics, Society and Culture*, edited by António Costa Pinto. Boulder, CO: Social Science Monographs, 2003.

"Education System in Portugal." http://www.shelteroffshore.com/index.php/living/more/education_system_in_portugal/ (accessed April 5, 2006).

Ferreira, Virginia. "Engendering Portugal: Social Change, State Politics, and Women's Social Mobilization." In *Modern Portugal*, edited by António Costa Pinto. Palo Alto, CA: The Society for the Promotion of Science and Scholarship, 1998.

Gallagher, Tom. *Portugal: A Twentieth Century Interpretation*. Manchester, England: Manchester University Press, 1983.

Higgs, David. "Portugal." In *Encyclopedia of Homosexuality*, edited by Wayne R. Dynes. New York: Garland Publishing, 1990.

Neto, Manuel. "Solidão (também) mata . . . não só idosos como jovens." *Diário de Notícias*, December 6, 2004.

Neves, Ceu. "Família e profissão em Portugal. Mulheres trabalham muito e acham normal." *Diário de Notícias*, January 15, 2005.

———. "Menos apoios e cada vez menos crianças." *Diário de Notícias*, November 6, 2005.

"Portugal—History and Background." http://education.stateuniversity.com/pages/1220/Portugal-HISTORY-BACKGROUND.html (accessed June 5, 2007).

Rapp, Linda. http://www.glbtq.com/social-sciences/portugal.html.

Santos, Ana Cristina. "Lesbian, Gay, Bisexual, and Transgendered Rights." www
.eumap.org/journal/features/2002/april02/portugesesexorient.

Sousa, Jesus Maria. "Education Policy in Portugal: Changes and Perspectives." *Education
Policy Analysis Archives*. Vol. 8, No. 5, January 10, 2005. www.epaa.asu.edu/
v8n5.html.

"Thematic Review of the Transition from Initial Education to Working Life—
Portugal." November 1997. http://www.oecd.org (accessed April 5, 2006).

Tovar, Patricia. "Images and Reality of Widowhood in Portugal." *Portuguese Studies
Review*. Fall-Winter, 1997–1998. Volume 6, no. 2.

Viana, Luís Miguel. "Partídos limitam mulheres no acesso aos cargos." *Diário de
Notícias*, May 20, 2005.

Wiarda, Howard J. "The Society and Its Environment." In *Portugal: A Country Study*,
edited by Eric Solsten. Washington, DC: U.S. Government Printing Office,
1994.

4

Leisure Activities and Holidays

THE PORTUGUESE culture is all about social interaction. Enjoying life at work and play, spending time laughing and talking with friends, coworkers, and family is as integral to life as breathing. The Portuguese know how to relax and have fun in the company of others; and if it can be said they have raised leisure to a high art, then the café is their museum.

Neighborhood cafés and pastry shops are frequented throughout the day by loyal workers and patrons, who pass unhurried hours reading the paper, playing cards, chess, or dominoes, or stopping in briefly to have a *bica* (espresso) and a sandwich or pastry on the way to an appointment or shopping, the office, or on the way home from work. Cafés are on every street corner, and almost every village in Portugal has at least one. They are common meeting places for friends to sit and chat, with never any pressure from the owner to drink up and go; and so they linger, reading the newspaper, arguing politics, or just watching the world go by. On rare occasions, in some taverns of the old districts (Alfama and Bairro Alto) of Lisbon, someone may show up in the evening with a guitar and accompany a Fado singer for a spontaneous concert, called *fado vadio*. In the evenings Portuguese couples will go to the corner café to have their after-dinner coffee in public rather than drink at home alone. For the Portuguese, the saying "the more, the merrier" could be a kind of social credo.

During the work week families are content to spend their evenings in front of the television and do most of their socializing on the weekends.

The Portuguese are a hard-working people and take a personal pride in the quality of their work; however, they do not share the frenzied, get-ahead attitude of more industrialized nations. In fact, the European attitude about work and play is in direct contrast to the American Dream and has given rise to the expression, "Americans live to work, Europeans work to live." Although the workday ends later, the pace is more relaxed. Admittedly, Portugal's inclusion in the European Union has accelerated the pace of life, but by and large the society moves at a leisurely stroll; one's job takes second place, with leisure time focused on spending time with friends and family. The lunch "hour" is longer (from 1 p.m. to 3 p.m.), there are frequent breaks, and interaction with customers and coworkers throughout the day is an occasion to connect, however briefly, in a social context. Because the work week is more relaxed and has such a social component built into it, the weekends do not hold the desperate promise of "unwinding" after a stress-filled, hectic week. There is no concept of "TGIF" in Portugal. Weekends are reserved for relaxing close to home, visiting family and friends, playing sports, and watching the world pass by at the neighborhood café.

The Portuguese love to window shop, and although many stores remain open on Sundays in the largest cities, in the suburbs they will be closed. Shopkeepers in such small residential neighborhoods know their neighbors will be strolling by, even though they are closed for the day, and take the opportunity to use the entire floor space and large front window of their shop to artfully display their latest merchandise. In weekly changing compositions, children's clothing and toys, stationery and art supplies, or candies and chocolates cavort playfully across the floors in elaborate and creative arrangements that grab the attention of even the most jaundiced eye, bringing the act of window shopping to new heights.

Families and food go together in Portugal, so it is not surprising to learn that joining together for a meal with the extended family is one of the most favored ways to relax on the weekend. Gatherings are not just about food; the enjoyment comes from gathering with one's family and friends to pass the time telling stories, jokes, and singing. Meals can last for hours, and often do. On a given weekend it is a common sight to see half the tables in a restaurant being pushed together to enable a large family to celebrate a birthday or anniversary.

The Portuguese enjoy being out in public, strolling in the many urban parks and squares. Public gardens are everywhere in the cities; many are centrally located, but some are tucked away in old neighborhoods or private courtyards. Portuguese gardens are complicated compositions of structured, green hedges—meticulously sheared into geometric shapes and arabesques—that border beds of brilliantly colored flowers—that are changed seasonally—with ponds, lakes, or fountains that provide the Portuguese with a lovely backdrop for their socializing. Most residential neighborhoods have their own park, many with elaborate climbing structures for the children and outdoor cafés where their parents can sip a cold beer while they keep an eye on them. Public parks are often settings for weekend children's activities such as puppet shows, magic acts, face painting, and children's theater. Local parks are extensions of the neighborhoods, everyone's own backyard. One is likely to see the same old man on the same park bench at the same time of day for years, feeding the pigeons or tipping his hat to passers-by. The man who sells ice cream from his cart will be in the same spot for years and will pride himself in knowing all his customers' favorite choices.

SPORTS AND SPECTACLES

Spectator sports are popular, and Portuguese everywhere enjoy watching *futebol* (i.e., soccer) most of all. All major towns have a soccer club, and many local parks boast *futebol* fields. During important matches the streets are deserted, as everyone is either at home or in a café glued to the television. Little boys live and breathe the sport, and they can be seen everywhere absent-mindedly practicing fancy footwork with their soccer balls with such ease it almost appears like they are born with some kind of soccer DNA. Not surprisingly, soccer is considered the national sport, with Portugal producing many world-renowned players. While the Portuguese are certainly passionate about the sport, there is rarely the violence that so often mars *futebol* in England and Germany, countries known for their soccer "hooligans." Although the Portuguese possess a certain pride in their illustrious history and particular "terra," they could hardly be described as a nationalistic people, a term so often associated with cultural arrogance. The exception to this rule is any time Portugal is involved in an international soccer tournament. *Futebol* inspires a true national fervor, and hundreds of flags can be seen fluttering on balconies; hordes of cheering, shrieking fans jam their local cafés, voices raised together to sing the national anthem "Heróis do Mar," with a joyful, contagious enthusiasm of national pride!

Bullfighting is popular, especially in the Ribatejo region where the bulls and horses for the sport are bred and trained, but it does not enjoy the passionate following as in Spain. Bullfighting originated during the time of the crusades when the horse was used as an instrument of war. To develop the skills of both horse and rider, Portuguese and Spanish knights went up against the notoriously bad-tempered bulls of Iberia. Unlike in Spain, which celebrates the skills of the toreador on foot, Portuguese bullfighting today remains closer to its roots as a demonstration of equestrian skill and is considered more of an art than sport, a cultural event that celebrates the skill and dexterity of horse and rider. First, the *toureiros* (toreadors) confront the bull on foot with capes. They are really just the warm-up act to the most revered part of the fight, when the *cavaleiros* (horsemen), splendidly clothed in satin, ruffles and tri-corn hat, and skilled in classical dressage, enter on horseback for a demonstration of agility and valor. The bull's horns are sheathed in leather to protect the precious horses. The *cavaleiro* is judged based on grace and style and his ability to work in partnership with the horse as they confront the bull. He is assisted by a team of men on foot with capes, to distract and prepare the bull as the *cavaleiro* thrusts six lances of progressively shorter lengths along the bull's back. The true test of skill is to do so without injuring the horse. The *cavaleiro* is followed by the "*Pega de Cara*," which means grabbing the face, during which about eight men on foot attempt to subdue by sheer force of will and numbers the bleeding and enraged bull. It is this part of the bullfight, unique to Portugal, where machismo runs rampant and provides the culminating thrill toward which all this blood and showmanship has been building. With an arrogant swagger the lead man approaches the bull and challenges, "Toiro, eh toiro." He attempts to grasp the charging bull around its neck while some of his supporters keep him up there and others grab the bull's tail to stop him from charging. The reality is that they are often tossed into the air and trampled by the furious bull to the dismay and glee of the crowd. The bull is then led away to the slaughterhouse or to the breeding pasture, never killed in the ring, as in Spain; public slaughter of the bull has been prohibited since 1799, when the son of the Marquis of Marialva was gored to death before the eyes of the court.

LEISURE IN RURAL AREAS

In the villages, life stays close within the boundaries of home. Work and play are often intertwined in the form of harvesting parties or in the holiday atmosphere that permeates the large weekly or monthly regional markets and fairs. As most peasants do not own cars, many businesses come to the village. On a weekly or biweekly basis, the fish monger drives his truck to the village center, blasts his horn to announce his arrival, and his customers trickle out of their houses to his mobile storefront. The area baker delivers bread in this way six days a week. Not only do villagers get their goods, but through these traveling businesses they can keep abreast of, and pass along, local gossip as well. The traveling knife and scissor sharpener, a charming relic from the past that can still be found meandering along the streets of towns—and even big cities—on his bicycle, tweeting his penny whistle to announce his arrival. His equipment is cleverly rigged to the wheel of his bicycle so that it not only provides his means of transportation, but powers his grinder as well.

Larger rural parishes and towns have a weekly, biweekly, or monthly marketplace where everything from clothing, plastic house wares, to produce and meats are sold. These markets have a wonderful, festive atmosphere with bustling shoppers haggling over the price of a kilo of tomatoes and vendors loudly hawking the merits of their goods. Bartering is a must with many vendors at the market and requires wit, charm, and a sense of humor on both sides of the table. A good-natured sparring is anticipated, and a well-worded and clever insult to lower the asking price on a kilo of dried beans is appreciated and admired, and will often get a quick-witted shopper a better deal than expected. To offer the asking price outright without an argument can sometimes be seen as an insult, and the vendor may refuse to sell vegetables or flowers to such an uncooperative buyer. (Do not try this in the cities, where sophistication prevails!) Neighbors and family members enjoy strolling among the rows of stalls, and at lunchtime the wafting scents of grilled meat and fish tempt shoppers to stop at the outdoor restaurants set up under large tents and linger over a glass of wine and a plate of *sardinhas assadas* (grilled herring). Bakery stalls cover the trays of pastry with cheesecloth to protect them from the honey bees that rise up in little clouds each time the baker shakes them off to offer shoppers their choice, whereupon the bees settle back down to their sweet beds. Old gypsy women, with their long braids and floor-length skirts offer to tell your fortune. (They will give you a tantalizing, damning sample for free: "You have many false friends," but if you want to hear the good stuff or find out who among your friends is false you have to pay!). And everywhere is heard the cry of the Lottery ticket vendors. All over Portugal market day is a giddy mélange of color, noise, scents, and most of all, social connection.

In some countryside regions, villagers gather in the *povo*, or square, where the men sample the wine from each other's cellars and the women gossip and work on their ubiquitous, white cotton, crocheted bedspreads and doilies. Unfortunately, this custom is more frequently replaced by the television, and lazing in the *povo* is mostly reserved for the weekends in the summer when the daily chores are finished. For the aging population of many villages that have watched their young migrate to the cities or emigrate to other European nations in search of improved prospects, the summers are something to look forward to; it is a time when so many emigrants return from abroad to spend their holidays with the family, bringing life, noise, and children back to sleepy, near-empty *aldeias*. On summer weekends the nights are filled with dancing, eating, and drinking as each village celebrates the *romarias* (village patron saint festivals). Families put on their Sunday best and gather for the afternoon meal.

It is at these festivals that many a courtship has its beginnings, and everyone, young and old, enjoys them.

During harvest time some villages have parties when farmers come together to help bring in each other's crops. The cost to rent large harvesting machinery as well as harvesting duties might be shared among several families; and frequently, after the day's hot and dirty work, they will gather to relax and unwind. Grape and olive-gathering, corn-husking, and threshing parties have important social and economic benefits to the villagers and are also an excellent excuse for more eating, drinking, and storytelling. There is singing, bawdy poetry recitations, and lots of flirting. Sadly, like so many of Portugal's best community-oriented traditions, these ways too are becoming less common; as the villages become de-populated, there are fewer and fewer hands to help bring in the crops.

Hunting and shooting are popular pastimes in the country. Pigeon, pheasant, rabbit, and in some places, wild boar, are common targets. Fishing, in all its varied forms (river, lakes, and ocean) is also enjoyed.

In Portugal, vacations are serious business and are, in fact, a matter of state concern. A noteworthy change after the 1974 revolution was the acknowledgment that workers deserved paid leisure time. As a result, all workers receive 13 months of pay for 11 months of work. Not only do laborers receive five weeks of paid vacation each year, they also receive a vacation bonus of an additional month's pay. Most urban dwellers take their vacation weeks all at once to allow an extended stay back home with their families in the countryside. Portugal's long coastline has hundreds of miles of beautiful beaches and is a favorite destination for domestic and foreign travelers. Many families pack up and spend an entire month at a campsite near the beach. The Portuguese are homebodies and prefer to spend their holidays in their own country.

FESTAS AND ROMARIAS

Summer is the season for festivals. They are so numerous that in rural areas it is possible to go to a festa nearly every summer weekend in the surrounding villages. While music, cultural, craft, and dance festivals happen in every part of the country, the majority are rural, religious festivals (romarias) when each village, town, and city celebrates its patron saint with revelry that often lasts for days. In 1973, the sociologist Pierre Sanchis identified 216 romarias (both small and large), 99 of which were for the Virgin Mary, 83 for a saint (14 for Rainha Santa Isabel de Aragon alone), and 29 for Christ, not to mention those in the islands of the Azores and Madeira. Most sanctuaries and romarias can be traced to the Christian Middle Ages, but even those practices were often based on celebrations of even older gods from the Celts and other peoples.

Most villages have a festival committee, comprised of local residents, that spends months organizing the music, games, donations, and other activities for the celebration, including the creation of hundreds of cut, tissue-paper flags that are glued to strings and hung back and forth across the main route of the procession. Festivities and offerings vary from village to village, and what a town is able to arrange by way of entertainment is dependent upon individual resources and any surplus money earned from the previous year's festival. Many villages rely on donations sent back to their village from immigrants in the United States, Europe, and Brazil. Emigrants are expected to, and do, contribute generously to the festa, especially if they have prospered in their lives abroad. The money is used to purchase raffle prizes, decorating supplies, food, and to pay for several nights of musical entertainment. Celebrations vary from small religious affairs to larger, more elaborately organized events with music, feasting, and dancing to huge extravaganzas that go on for days, or, as is the case in Lisbon, for weeks. Until very recently, *festas* were announced by way of smoke signals from fireworks shot off by the committee in the days prior to and during the big day. However, due to the devastating fires that consume thousands of acres of forest each summer across the country, rockets are banned and *festas* are announced by posters. *Festa* is a time when many emigrants return to their homes, and their presence brings much needed life and monetary resources to the village.

The structure of a *romaria* varies from region to region and even from town to town within regions. Much depends on the resources of each *festa* committee, community interest, and which traditions have been preserved; therefore it is difficult to produce a standard model. We must content ourselves with a description of a typical rural *romaria* from the village of Fronhas in the Beira Alta with the disclaimer that it does not represent all *romarias* in the nation. Fronhas is lucky to have a large emigrant population in the United States, France, and Brazil who contribute generously to the festa funds and a dedicated group of residents who have kept old traditions alive where they have been lost elsewhere. Here, on the first day of the *festa* celebrating their patron saint, Nossa Senhora do Livramento, the celebration begins with a morning mass at the chapel, followed by a procession of the statue of the patron saint through the streets with the entire village following behind wearing their Sunday best. The village women drape their best and most colorful bedspreads over the sills of the windows along the procession route. Seen against the backdrop of crisscrossing lines of brightly colored, tissue-paper flags that are produced by the villagers in the months preceding the procession, it is a brilliant kaleidoscopic impression of color, pattern, and texture. Behind the Saint come the village women balancing on their heads large, wooden trays draped with lace cloths that hold the *fogaças*, elaborate meals cooked by the local women to be auctioned off at the end of the procession. Roasted kid or rabbit stewed in wine are perennial favorites and make a special meal along with a good bottle of wine or port, fruit, olives, and a plate of sweet rice pudding decorated with patterns of powdered cinnamon. Here a woman's skill in the kitchen pays off for the whole village: the *fogaças* of well-known local chefs have many bidders and are auctioned off for a good price. It is a matter of pride and reputation for some women that their *fogaça* brought in the highest bid of all. Families bid for their lunches, and for those not lucky enough to win the *fogaça* of choice there is *caldo verde* (kale soup) and fat slices of *broa* (brick oven-baked, whole grain bread) for sale to those from neighboring towns. In the afternoon, a brass band will march through town playing traditional songs after lunch with everyone from the village singing and dancing behind, with periodic stops at several villagers' houses or courtyards where the whole crowd will be invited in to sample the host's own wine. At night there is a dance and people come from miles around to attend. The very young to the very old make merry until they stagger home to their beds in the wee hours of the morning, all to begin again the next day!

As old traditions die out, new ones spring up to take their places. Renaissance fairs can be found all over the country, and Portugal provides an ideal setting for them, with its castles and ruins lending an air of authenticity and drama to the medieval atmosphere. Theme-based festivals—beer, chestnut, 1940s—are also popular.

Fireworks in Portugal are a serious business. They have achieved an amazing level of artistry and are used in every significant celebration. In larger cities they are grand affairs, intricately coordinated to music, lights, and dancers in the foreground. Fireworks even sometimes adorn parade floats. In one elaborately choreographed parade whose theme was sea monsters from the Age of the Discoveries, Chinese dragon-type puppets were carried by 20 or more marchers with attached fireworks that sizzled and popped and shot sparks into the delighted crowds that good-naturedly scrambled and parted like the Red Sea to allow the floats to pass and save themselves from stinging sparks. There is much to be admired here, both for the rockets in the air that explode in dazzling patterns and changing colors as for ones on the ground, that when lit swirl and whiz as painted wooden figures chop wood or hoe an imaginary field. A Portuguese fireworks display is not to be missed for its unusual creativity and fine craftsmanship!

Some larger cities and towns are famous for their extravagant celebrations or significance as pilgrimage destinations. In Matosinhos (near Porto), 300,000 people visited the Bom Jesus sanctuary in a three-day period. Even when the sanctuaries are located away from population centers where access is difficult, they attract a phenomenal number of worshipers. São Bento da Porta Aberta, for example, is secluded in the Gerês Mountain, yet in one morning alone 10,000 celebrants arrived on foot for a festival that lasted five days. The city Tomar, the original seat of the Knights Templar (founded in 1119), is known for its spectacular religious procession of the Tabuleiros, an event so elaborate and time-consuming to organize it happens only every four years. The religious procession of the Tabuleiros comprises 400 young girls in white dresses, each balancing a tray that forms the base for a precarious tower of bread decorated with flowers, ribbons, and sheaves of wheat, topped with a crown and cross or a paper dove to symbolize the Holy Spirit. The towers can weigh up to 30 pounds, and some are as tall as the girls who carry them, so they are accompanied by boys dressed in black and white who help them balance the load. The town is bedecked with intricate paper decorations strung across the main thoroughfares, perhaps a candlelight procession on the final night as the religious statues are returned to their sanctuaries, topped off with a fireworks spectacle. The next day the bread is blessed by the priest and distributed to local families.

Redondo, a town in the Alentejo, is known for its thematically decorated streets during its festa celebration. Neighbors join together to choose a theme based on local history or the regional harvest and create elaborate and detailed scenarios in twisted and cut crepe paper. Common themes include sheep shearing, honey gathering, wine making, and cork harvesting. Cunningly wrought figures, animals, and flowers festoon the narrow roads, and some even include specially constructed fountains and rivers for a dazzling display of color and ingenuity. Nightly concerts in the town square and, of course, fireworks add to the festivities and draw crowds from great distances.

Saint Vincent is the patron saint of Lisbon, although most residents prefer Saint Anthony, who was born in Lisbon in 1195. The city celebrates the Festa dos Santos Populares (São Pedro, São Joao, and Santo António) all through the month of June with outdoor music festivals, folkloric dance competitions, parades, fireworks, and street parties nearly every night. Festa do Santo António begins on the evening of June 12 and continues through the night and the next day. The highlight takes place on June 12 with the Marchas Populares when dozens of communities march along the Avenida da Liberdade with the culminating *arraial* in the Alfama the same night. During the night a great crush of people meander through the narrow streets and staircases of the Old Alfama district (one of the few neighborhoods to survive the earthquake in the eighteenth century, retaining its medieval layout of tiny streets, staircases, and hidden courtyards) to gather along the ramparts of Saint Jorge's castle built high on a hill overlooking the city and the Tejo River to watch the fireworks display. All along the way, folk are invited to stop and have a snack of grilled herring and local wine at one of the tiny impromptu cafés set up in any little corner spot by local residents. The smoky air is redolent with the scents of garlic, grilling meat and fish, and wine. Occasional snatches of the plaintive national music called fado can be heard issuing from one of the closet-sized bars along the winding way, or a few happy revelers may break out in a folk song that will be quickly picked up by the surrounding crowd whose merry, albeit slightly drunken accompaniment, reverberates along the walls and alleyways.

Saint Anthony is also considered the patron saint of love and of lost things, and on this day men and women write letters to him requesting assistance in finding true love. Lovers present each other with little pots of marjoram available for sale on every street corner, with love letters or romantic verses tucked inside. Couples (most commonly those of little means) can apply to be wed in a mass ceremony on Saint Anthony's Day, in the romanesque Sé Cathedral, to be paid for (dress, food, and all) by the government of Lisbon. Children make altars to the saint all month and decorate them with candles and pictures of Santo António. They beg a penny, which in earlier days was used to restore the church of St. António da Sé, destroyed in the earthquake, but now pays for a feast for the little ones. The romarias are an occasion for family and friends to socialize and immerse themselves in cultural and commercial activities via the events and fairs that accompany the celebrations. Beginning in the spring, with the majority occurring in the summer, religious festivities continue into late autumn.

CHRISTMAS AND NEW YEAR

Christmas is a festive time of year. Entire families come together for the big feast of Christmas Eve, where they share the traditional meal of bacalhau e batatas (boiled salted codfish and potatoes). During the season every pastry shop in Portugal bakes the much-loved "Bolo Rei," a special Christmas fruitcake containing a single fava bean. The person who gets the slice containing the bean is the king of the party and has to buy the "Bolo Rei" for the New Year's celebration. Children leave a shoe by the fireplace for Pai Natal (Father Christmas) to fill with small gifts of chocolate, colored pencils, new socks, and coloring books. In the countryside, a large bonfire (*cepo*) is lit in the village square on Christmas Eve, around which people gather to share the holiday spirit. The *cepo*, symbolizing the fires the three Kings lit to keep warm as they traveled to Bethlehem to honor the baby Jesus, is kept burning continuously until *Janeiras* (the Day of the Kings, on January 6). Ashes from the Yule log are believed to provide protection during thunderstorms and times of illness. On the night before, the young people go from door to door to sing about the arrival of the three Kings in Bethlehem. At each house, the inhabitants are expected to give the group an onion, a potato, some kale, or sausage in payment for the entertainment. The youths then return to the *cepo* to create and cook a meal from the collected booty. In the more cosmopolitan areas the Portuguese have adopted the foreign traditions of the Christmas tree, decorating with holly, mistletoe, and lights and exchanging gifts. Every worker receives his Christmas bonus of an extra month's salary at this time to help fund the celebrations.

CARNIVAL, LENT, EASTER, AND CORPUS CHRISTI

Carnaval is the pre-Lenten festival celebrated during the last three days before Ash Wednesday. It is the last opportunity to indulge before the fasting of Lent begins. The celebration begins with Domingo Gordo (Fat Sunday). On this day, like bears going into hibernation, families prepare for a long period of fasting and sacrifice with a feast of their favorite dishes. The three days of Carnaval are a time of parody and practical jokes, dressing up in costume, and playing silly pranks on neighbors. It is all in fun and considered bad form to take any of it personally. As the saying goes, "Pelo Carnaval, ninguem leva à mal." (At Carnaval, no one gets mad.) Celebration lasts through *Terça do Entrudo* (Tuesday) when the King Carnaval performs the *Dança do Folia*, a pagan fertility dance: dressed all in black, hooded and masked, the disguised "King" dances crazily about the village with a large clay jar on his head. While he cavorts about banging on a tambourine or small drum, others try to knock the jar off his head to shatter on the ground. There are costume balls, parties, and dances in the cities. Carnaval ends on Ash Wednesday, and the season of Lent begins, a 40-day period of fasting, during which time no meat is eaten on Fridays and one must give up something important such as a favorite food or activity. Catholics end their fast on Easter, the most important of the Roman Catholic holidays, which celebrates the Resurrection of Christ. In the country, after Easter morning mass the priest passes through the village, stopping at each house to allow the occupants to kiss the cross he carries. Families gather to eat roast spring kid (*cabrito assado*), a meal that represents the coming of the season and new beginnings.

"Dia do Corpo de Deus" (Corpus Christi) is celebrated nationally between May and June. Corpus Christi is the commemoration of the Last Supper and has been a day of religious observance since medieval times. In the Açores, in the city of Ponte Delgada on the island of São Miguel, people make a flower petal carpet three-quarters of a mile long upon which marches a brightly colored procession of high-ranking clergy and red-robed priests, followed by the First Communicants (children who will receive the Eucharist for the first time). The little boys are dressed in dark suits with red capes, and the girls wear white dresses with veils.

FÁTIMA

Although not an official holiday, May 13 and October 13 hold great religious significance for thousands of Portuguese Catholics who travel to Fátima, the most important pilgrimage site in all of Portugal. On May 13, 1917, three shepherd children (Lúcia dos Santos, 10, and her cousins Jacinta, 7, and Francisco Marto, 8) saw an apparition of the Virgin Mary above a tree in a field where they were tending their sheep in the village of Cova da Iria. According to the children, the Virgin told them everyone should pray for peace and recite the rosary. She promised to return to them on the thirteenth day of the following five months. What began as a very private affair with the Virgin appearing to the children became a gathering of the faithful, a throng that increased in alarming numbers with each passing month, all in hope of sharing the vision of the Virgin, bringing with them in addition to their faith increasingly complicated ramifications for the three children, their families, and the village.

Despite initial skepticism by the church the children's story was immediately embraced by the faithful. Today, what devotees accept as the actual events of the apparition come from memoirs written between 1935 and 1941 by Lúcia at the convent of the Sisters of Saint Dorothy, which she entered in 1921. Before this time she did not reveal specifics of the Virgin's messages. After an experience at the convent that convinced her to write about what she had intended to keep secret, and with the encouragement from her spiritual advisor, Lúcia wrote down Mary's message in three parts, which became known as "The Three Secrets."

According to these documents, the Virgin first showed the children a vision of hell. She assured them World War I would soon end, but if people did not stop offending God there would be more war during the pontificate of Pius XI (i.e., World War II). She also said that Francisco and Jacinta would be called soon to heaven, but that Lúcia must stay and do God's work on earth. Second, the Virgin asked for devotion to the Immaculate Heart of Mary to save sinners. She asked for people to pray for the consecration of Russia and the communion of reparation of first Saturdays for six months. She warned of the rise of communist Russia as a world power, and that if Russia was not converted it would spread war and persecute the Church. The third secret was kept under lock and key at the Vatican and was not revealed until 2000, in which the Virgin predicted the attempt on the Pope's life (1987). The apparitions at Fátima were declared worthy of the assent of the faithful in 1930, but were not known outside of Portugal until the early 1940s. Mary's messages began to attract international attention during the horrors of World War II and the post-war period and because the Catholic Church began to use the message of Fátima as an ally in its fight against communism and socialism.

The events of May 13, 1917 had a profound effect on the lives of the three children. Prior to this day, Lúcia had had other religious visions, and when she reported what she had seen to her family they had not believed her. Because of her previous experiences she urged the other children not to speak of it, but the next day little Jacinta told her mother of the beautiful lady they saw in the field. Word spread through the village quickly, and by the second month there were about 50 people from the village waiting alongside the children; by October a crowd of 70,000 had gathered to witness the anticipated final visitation, during which the crowd is said to have witnessed the sun whirling like a wheel of fire and many of the disabled in the crowd were miraculously cured. On May 13, 1946 one-tenth of the population of Portugal, or about 700,000 pilgrims, gathered at the Fátima shrine to give thanks for the end of the war. Today, more than four million people visit the Fátima shrine each year.

Skeptics often suggest after religious visions are reported that the seers involved wished to bring attention to themselves and their families, but it should be noted that these children suffered greatly as a result of speaking of their visions and the resulting attention from the church (in the form of aggressive interrogations) and the faithful (who flocked to the village by the thousands to request help from the children). It is significant that these visions were reported at the time of the First Republic (1910–1926), a period during which the government had been repressing religious expression and trying to reduce the influence of the church. It is very possible that these tensions between the government and the church led to the ambivalence, and in some cases, naked aggression of local priests and government officials. One particularly anti-religious mayor of Ourem, Arturo Santos, imprisoned the children, all under the age of 11, and threatened to boil them alive in oil if they did not admit they had made it all up. Santos had the children brought in for questioning again in August and kept them in jail overnight so they could not be present for the August 13 promised visitation. He questioned each child separately, and even had a pot of hot oil prepared that he showed them. One can only imagine the terror they must have felt, and yet the children insisted they were speaking the truth.

Lúcia especially suffered and was persecuted by her mother and sisters and by the villagers who blamed her for the loss of a favorite priest. The local priest was very popular and at first treated her kindly, but as the church officials became more aggressive and insistent in their interrogations, sending many priests to test, threaten, and harangue the children, they became fearful of *all* church officials, and thus became estranged from their own priest, who, seeing he had lost their trust, became hostile toward them and eventually left to avoid any connection with the events of the village. While Francisco and

Jacinta's parents seemed to be supportive of their children's stories, Lúcia was frequently beaten by her mother and ridiculed by her sisters, who had to be called away from their paying jobs outside the house to take on the burden of Lucia's chores so that she could tend to the hundreds of pilgrims who looked to her as a saint who could intercede on their behalf to the Virgin Mary. As word spread about the visions, the tiny village was overrun with pilgrims. The family's garden was trampled by the crowds that grew ever larger with each additional vision and could not be replanted because it was too near the site. This plunged the family into terrible poverty, and although many pilgrims offered food and money to the children, their parents forbade them to accept any such gifts. When Francisco and Jacinta fell ill from the influenza epidemic, they never fully recovered their strength and died within a year of each other. It was later speculated that their deaths resulted in part because their parents were unable to protect them from the strain of the demands placed on them by the church, government officials, and the never-ending requests of the faithful. So little did Lúcia's family support her that when death threats were made against her life, Lúcia's mother declared it was fine with her, as long as they got the truth out of her first! It is amazing that in spite of these terrifying and arduous experiences the children never wavered from their original statements about their visions. It is partly because of this steadfastness in the face of such aggressive interrogation that Fátima has been given such credibility and status among the faithful.

Fátima is considered by the church to be the most important of the three twentieth-century apparitions, and one of the world's most important visions of Mary. Future sightings in other areas of the world were seen by the seers as extensions of Mary's original message at Fátima, and Fátima became a model, along with La Salette and Lourdes, against which subsequent apparitions were tested for authenticity.

SECULAR HOLIDAYS

Portugal retains bragging rights as the European nation with the oldest established borders and takes this idea of nationhood and independence very seriously. There are several holidays that commemorate Portugal's continual and historical struggles to retain its independence from foreign or repressive regimes. Restoration Day, recognized on December 1, celebrates the restoration of independence from 60 years of Spanish rule in 1640. Another important national holiday, Republic Day, is celebrated on October 5. It honors the establishment of the Portuguese Republic in 1910 and the end of two centuries of monarchical rule. The most important national secular holiday in Portugal has only been celebrated since 1974. Liberation Day, popularly referred to as "25 de Abril" (25 of April) commemorates the military coup that put an end to 48 years of the repressive Salazar-Caetano dictatorship, and it is celebrated with parades and political speeches. Other national holidays are Labor Day on May 1 and Portugal Day on June 10, which marks the anniversary of the death of Luis Camões, considered Portugal's national poet and author of the Lusíadas, an epic poem exalting the heroic voyage of Vasco da Gama to India. It is celebrated with patriotic speeches and parades in Lisbon and in Portuguese communities throughout the world.

SELECTED READINGS

Henderson, Helene, and Sue Ellen Thompson, eds. *Holidays, Festivals, and Celebrations of the World Dictionary.* Detroit, MI: Omnigraphics Inc., 1997.

Sanchis, Pierre. *Arraial: Festa de um Povo, as Romarias Portuguesas.* Lisboa: Pulicações Dom Quixote, 1983.

Zimdars-Swartz, Sandra L. *Encountering Mary: From La Salette to Medjugorje.* Princeton, NJ: Princeton University Press, 1991.

5

Cuisine

PORTUGUESE FOOD evolved mainly from its hard-working peasant culture. It is nourishing, sustaining, and comforting. Recipes are simple to prepare, using few utensils and uncomplicated techniques, and rely on fresh, locally available produce, meats, and fish. Considered to be a "Mediterranean Diet"— high in complex carbohydrates, emphasizing the white meat proteins like chicken, pork, and fish, and high in polyunsaturated fats, with vegetables and legumes providing fiber and using the mono-unsaturated fat of olive oil as a foundation—it is quite a healthy way to eat.

What sets Portuguese cuisine apart from its European cousins, most notably Spain, with which it is so often lumped? It is natural that, with the long Atlantic coastline, Portuguese culture and cuisine would be so heavily influenced by the ocean's gifts. Since the fifteenth century, when the seafaring passions of Prince Henry the Navigator thrust his nation forward to become great explorers and traders in the world, Portugal's cuisine has benefited from the delicious fruits mined from the sea. Prince Henry cast his net to the far corners of the world, and the Portuguese gained a powerful hold on the ocean trade routes and served as the gateway to Europe for the Spice Trade's valuable commodities. The Age of the Discoveries, "Os Descobrimentos," brought home an astounding influx of spices, foods, and cultures from Asia, Latin America, and Africa. From the Orient came tea and the heady spices of clove, cinnamon, curry, and nutmeg. The Americas contributed tropical fruits, corn, tomatoes, peppers, and potatoes. Coffee, originally from Ethiopia, is believed to have been brought to Brazil by Portuguese sailors.

These new discoveries, with their new cultures, ingredients, and cooking techniques, combined with the additional influences of the many peoples who over the centuries had settled throughout Portugal, to create a cuisine unique in Europe. Phoenicians, Turks, and Arabs all made contributions to what is today known as "Portuguese" cooking. The Phoenicians brought wine and olives, and the Arabs introduced wheat, rice, citrus fruit, almonds, sugar, saffron, and salt. In Portugal, meat is braised using the Arab technique of first cooking it in an aromatic liquid, after which it is seared, as compared to the western process that begins with searing. The Moors introduced almond trees to the southern region of the Algarve. The Turkish influence taught the uses of sugar and developed the nation's sweet tooth.

The early peasant cooks were frugal and resourceful. Anything that could be used was: the tops and bottoms of root vegetables and bones (soup), blood (sausage and puddings), guts and organs of animals (sausage casings and tripe [dobrada]). The leafy greens of kale, fennel, and turnips are combined with dried legumes (such as chickpeas, kidney, and pinto beans) to create stews and side dishes that are nourishing and economical. Marinades of wine and garlic flavor the meat with a distinctly Portuguese character. While the primary protein in most dishes is chicken, pork, or fish, creative Portuguese cooks have concocted sumptuous dishes of rabbit stewed with wine, onions, and potatoes; mutton stew (chanfana); and veal (vitela). There are as many ways to prepare the famous dried cod (bacalhau) as there are fish in the sea. Codfish and potatoes could be considered a national dish, along with the popular kale soup, caldo verde, as these dishes are found in all corners of Portugal.

While outside influences and ingredients brought exotic additions and expanded the country's palate as a whole, Portugal is a land of varied landscapes and climates that affect agricultural production and, as such, regional styles and dishes do exist. For example, Minho, the far northwestern coastal area, is said to be the heart of Portuguese peasant cooking where most dishes originated; these were modified from cook to cook as the recipes were passed down and people moved to outlying regions, and today they can be found with regional variations all over the country. It is here that one finds the dense, richly flavored stews like dobrada (tripe), feijoadas (bean stews), caldo verde (kale soup), and the ubiquitous sardinha assada (grilled herring). Minho is also the center of production for Vinho Verde, the popular "green" wine, so named not because of its color, but because it is bottled after only a short fermentation and is still "young." It has a light, crisp flavor and a slight fizz. Being a coastal zone, Minho includes more seafood on its menu than its neighboring province to the east, Trás-os-Montes.

Trás-os-Montes means "beyond the mountains," and it lies in the northeastern corner of Portugal bordered on the north and east by Spain. It is a land of wooded hills, rocky plateaus, and deep valleys. Its steep slopes are crisscrossed by low stone walls to mark the borders of plots of land passed down and divided up into ever-smaller parcels through generations of landowners. Farming the rocky soil is difficult and makes for a hard life. Here, the food must be nourishing and hearty, a sturdy peasant fare that finds many uses for the cured sausage and ham made from the local pigs. The poor soil and harsh weather are ideal for growing the grapes of low acidity that are perfect for making port wine, which is shipped down the Rio Douro to the city of Oporto to ferment in oak casks.

To the south, the Alentejo region in February is a glorious sight to behold! The rolling green fields spread out across the plains like a carpet dotted with blooming trees. During the rest of the year the dry fields are presided over by the magnificent cork oaks, the second most important cash crop of the area. When stripped of their bark every nine years to provide cork for the global market, these trees appear naked and sunburned, revealing their velvety cinnamon-colored under-bark. Beneath these oaks graze the pigs that are used in the region's renowned pork dishes. Most importantly, the Alentejo is the "Bread-basket of Portugal," much like the American Midwest, planted with vast stretches of ocher wheat. Naturally, the bread here is delicious and is included in many regional soups and *açordas* (a cross between a soup and a stew, made by moistening bread to a porridge-like consistency with broth, garlic, and olive oil). Alentejanos enjoy *"açorda de café,"* an afternoon snack of day-old bread crumbled into a bowl, sprinkled with sugar and doused with milky coffee.

The Algarve, the southernmost province, lies beyond a range of mountains cutting it off from the Alentejo. Bordered on two coasts by the Atlantic and Spain to the east, it is here that the Moors had their last stronghold before being expelled from Portugal. Their influence is seen everywhere from the architecture to the local passion for sweets, especially those made with almonds. Almond groves shimmer above emerald green pastures, their fragile white blooms shining in the sun as if caught in a sudden snowstorm. Marzipan is a regional specialty.

In the emerald archipelago of the Açores, cheeses are made from cow's milk and dishes are spicier than on the mainland. Madeira's dishes feature the abundant seafood, locally grown fruits of banana and pineapple, and sugarcane. Madeira's dessert wine is known throughout the world.

The best is saved for last: the fabulous sweets made from egg yolks that range from cakes, custards, tarts, pastries, and creams and fillings found in every region. Most of Portugal's desserts originated in the nation's convents.

The church owned large amounts of land where chickens were raised. With the abundance of eggs, it seems logical that the sisters of the convents would begin to experiment with them and develop an amazing assortment of rich, egg-based treats laced with almonds, sugar, walnuts, and citrus to satisfy the most finicky sweet tooth, or *gulosa*, as the Portuguese call those with an insatiable appetite for sugar and all things rich and delicious. A freshly baked pastry is only minutes away, no matter where you are in the country.

The cuisine of Portugal is not just about food. As in many Mediterranean cultures, Portuguese hospitality centers on food and a willingness to share the abundance of the table. Creating and sharing meals is an important social custom and a matter of pride among the Portuguese, who can be so generous as to appear aggressive. Food is pressed upon the visitor, and it is an insult to refuse this offer of hospitality. Formal dinners can last for hours, with much wine drinking and storytelling between courses; this socializing contributes as essential a part to the meal as the main course. The knowledgeable guest quickly learns to take small portions in order to be served many times; for to take only one helping, no matter how many courses are to follow, is to insult the cook. In the countryside, even a quick visit requires a glass of homemade wine and a dish of olives or a piece of home-baked bread, or if you are lucky, of *broa*, the dense, moist bread found in many peasant villages in Portugal. If a visitor's attention is distracted by conversation, it is possible the cook has slipped away to begin a pot of *caldo verde*, in which case the passing visitor has now become a dinner guest.

The pace of life in Portugal is supported and sustained by the culture's meal schedule. Though the days seem to start earlier and finish later, there are frequent and leisurely breaks throughout to refresh. The Portuguese begin their day with a simple continental-style breakfast, such as bread and cheese and coffee. At mid-morning comes a break for coffee and a pastry (or in the country a wholesome snack such as a sandwich). The typical lunch at about 1 p.m. is hearty and can include several courses such as soup, salad, a meat or fish dish with potatoes and/or rice, followed by fruit and cheese. The hours between 1 p.m. and 3 p.m. are reserved for lunch and siesta, when farmers can nap after their large meal to digest and recharge for the afternoon field work. In the summer, the sun and heat at this hour of the day can be grueling, so it makes sense that the Portuguese use this time to rest in the thick-walled, cool interiors of their homes.

In the cities, stores are increasingly opting to stay open during the lunch period, but many still close between 1 p.m. and 3 p.m. Many workers will return to their homes to eat with the family, and lunch is a relaxed and unhurried affair. A mid-afternoon *lanche* (snack) usually includes an additional boost of espresso and a sandwich or pastry. The urban workday ends at 7 p.m., and workers heading home enjoy a beer or glass of wine at their local café before their dinner meal around 8 p.m. or 9 p.m. Jantar (dinner) is the largest meal of the day. A typical dinner might be meat or fish accompanied by rice, pasta, or potatoes, and then dessert, most commonly fruit. If there is leftover soup from lunch, it would be included. Teenagers, of course, like teenagers the world over, indulge frequently in fast food; but while McDonald's outlets are still found only in large cities and towns, the Portuguese have their own versions of fast food chains with a higher quality of healthier meal choices. Because the Portuguese eat later, they also play later. Cultural events begin between 9 p.m. and 10 p.m., and weekend *festas* in the countryside start even later and can last until dawn.

With the exception of ice cream in the summer and chestnuts in the winter (roasted on street corners and served in paper cones), it is uncommon to see the Portuguese eating on the streets as they go about their business. They prefer to pop into the nearest café to "take a little something," sitting and enjoying a bit of gossip and watching the passers-by if time permits, or standing at the high counter to have a *bica* (espresso) and a fresh, sweet pastry or a cold meat and cheese sandwich, or perhaps a *salgado*, a savory pastry of meat or fish such as *bolos de bacalhau* (deep-fried codfish cakes).

Mention should be made of the importance of wine on the Portuguese table. To the Portuguese, a meal without wine is like a day without sunshine, which is perhaps why the typical diner, on finding his glass empty, will exclaim, "*Estou as escuras!*" ("I'm in the darkness!"), whereupon his glass will be quickly refilled. Not so long ago, the men gathered in the village square in the evening to taste a friend's new wine, share stories of their day, or argue politics, but with the changing demographics of rural life, this social custom is dying fast. Nevertheless, here wine still functions as a kind of social glue, keeping inhabitants connected in camaraderie. In the country, many homes include a wine cellar and peasants make their own wine, and *no* patio is complete without the requisite grape vine. Although this wine is often of questionable quality, when professional Portuguese vintners developed their wines they elevated wine making to an art form; and its production deserves further discussion, especially port wine, for which Portugal is most famous.

PORT WINE PRODUCTION

The Portuguese have been making wine since its introduction by the Romans in the first century B.C., but the production of port, for which Portugal is most renowned, did not begin until the seventeenth century. Portugal, up until that time, had been producing large quantities of wine and shipping it down the Douro River to Porto, to be sold to the Dutch,

British, and throughout Portugal. Even so, most Europeans looked to France for their wine, and Portuguese wine making was not highly developed.

The Douro Valley, possibly the first demarcated wine region in the world, is home to the port vineyards. An inhospitable place, the terrain is mountainous with almost no soil and little rainfall. Of its 618,000 acres, only 82,000 acres are cultivated. The Serra do Marão, the first of a series of mountain ranges that extend to the Spanish border and isolate the region, creates chinook conditions with extremes in temperature that are important in the development of the varieties of grapes used for port: sweltering, dry summers, with temperatures reaching up to 110 degrees Fahrenheit, and freezing winters. This region is one of the few places in Portugal where it snows. Over the past three centuries, the vineyards have been painstakingly carved from the sides of the mountains into steep terraces with back-breaking labor, hand tools, and the frequent use of dynamite. The steep slopes and terracing make it necessary for all the work of ploughing, planting, and harvesting to be done by hand, except on the lowest and gentlest of slopes. The grapes are planted in a rocky soil that was created over a span of 300 years by breaking up the schist rock that formed the steep slopes of the mountains in the valley. In some cases, explosives are needed to create planting holes. Roots descend through cracks in the schist to depths of 40–65 feet to find water. These incredibly difficult conditions speak clearly of the stubborn determination, so much a part of the Portuguese psyche, that caused the Portuguese poet, Miguel Torga, to write, "In this place, man with his bare hands wrings wine from a stone."[1]

The Politics of Port

Politics was instrumental in the history of port and continued to play an important role throughout the wine's development. In 1678, Britain declared war on France and blocked all its ports, creating an immediate wine shortage. As Portugal and England had a close trading partnership since the fourteenth century, the British logically looked to Portugal to provide the wine they could no longer get from France. They soon realized that Portuguese wines were not of the same quality as the French, and they would need to oversee its production to ensure the quality to which they had become accustomed. The Douro Valley, it was found, had the ideal climate to produce grapes of a more intense flavor and deep color, so desired in a quality wine. Wine was shipped down the Douro River for export to England. However, these wines did not travel well, so brandy was added to stop the fermentation process and act as a stabilizer for shipment back to England. This created a sweet, fruity, and strong wine and was the birth of port.

Though this early port was of questionable quality, it was able to maintain a market due to England's constant political turmoil with France. Sales were dependant on England's fragile trading relationship with France, and as such the success and market for port at this time was more by default. In 1703, once again at war with France, the British signed the Methuen Treaty that exchanged British cloth for Portuguese wine. In this way, the port wine industry began to develop quickly, and its expansion was helped along by many British and Scottish wine merchants who set up businesses in Porto. Wine making in the Douro Valley changed rapidly, with vineyards developed, transportation down the Douro river to Porto organized, and the goat-skin storage replaced by oak barrels. Lodges to store the wine were built in Vila Nova de Gaia at the mouth of the Douro.

It is perhaps because of the blood, sweat, and tears necessary to work the vineyards and frustrations with the fickleness of the market that the Portuguese take their business so seriously. In the 1730s it was discovered that some greedy vintners, to economize and stretch their wine, were adding elderberry juice and sugar to the mix, thus creating a sub-standard product that, in turn, caused a drop in the price. The Marquis de Pombal, with the same calm but heavy hand he used to rebuild Lisbon on grande plan after the 1755 earthquake, stepped in to deal with the scandal. He created the Old Wine Company and gave it broad powers to regulate the port wine industry. Not only were production and quality closely controlled, the Company also served to end Britain's monopoly of port wine trade. It was responsible for setting prices and arbitrating disputes. Pombal also demarcated the region of the Douro Valley and had all vineyards and elderberry trees outside of these new boundaries destroyed.

At the turn of the twentieth century, the port industry suffered again due to the political turmoil of King Carlos I's assassination in 1908 and the end of the monarchy a short time later with the abdication of Manuel II in 1910. The new republican governments that followed continued established policies regarding the wine-making trade, and any attempts at change were doomed by strikes, riots, corruption, and constantly changing bureaucrats who did not enforce the law. (There were 49 governments and 60 Ministers of Agriculture in a 16-year span).

The Madeira wine industry had its own problems due to the island's economic dominance by German interests since the late 1800s. When Portugal joined the Allied Forces at the start of World War I, the German holdings were confiscated. With the fall of the Russian Empire and the danger of German submarines, Madeira's exportation of wine was seriously compromised and the island was plunged into devastating poverty. Prohibition in the United States worsened an already dire situation.

Whereas the consequences of World War I devastated Madeira's wine trade and economy, the situation was reversed on the mainland, where the War actually fueled the port wine business for growers and shippers. Because Britain increased taxes on whiskey and other spirits, England once again looked to Portugal and port to fill the gap. Soon, port (cut with lemonade) was commonplace in pubs everywhere, and the port business enjoyed new vigor despite the absence of a Russian market.

In 1927, in reaction to competition from foreign wines and cheap imitation "port" from southern Portugal, the government declared that only wine that was shipped across the bar of the Douro River or from the port of Leixões was entitled to legally bear the label "port wine." The result, when combined with the creation of a warehouse distribution center in Vila Nova de Gaia, was to give an export monopoly to the shippers at the expense of small quintas (estate farms) up in the Douro Valley. This effectively locked the growers into subsistence wages until Portugal joined the European Union and the law was repealed in 1987.

In the 1930s Salazar also intervened in the wine trade to combat falling wine sales, which had become dependent on exports to Brazil's fragile economy. He began to create large, cooperative wineries that were given modern equipment, but the bureaucracy that controlled the cooperatives proved too rigid and cash poor, which resulted in a decrease in the quality of Portuguese wines.

The government still regulates the industry and is solely responsible for declaring a vintage port, the only ones allowed to display the year on the label. This control is limited to port wine and is not extended to general wine making, though demarcation areas for wine production have also been declared by the government. Portugal's inclusion in the European Union and subsequent financial assistance has had a positive effect on the wine industry, allowing new regions to be demarcated, equipment to be updated, new wines to be developed, and old vineyards to be rejuvenated.

Today, the port wine region comprises three areas within the Douro Valley, distinguished by their separate climates. The first and smallest is the Baixo Corgo, which is located closest to the sea and receives the most rain. Its more fertile soil produces the highest yield—50 percent of all port—of the lightest varieties used in ruby and tawny ports. The Cima Corgo, although double in size, allocates only 14 percent of its acreage to grape cultivation. Rainfall is less, and production is about 36 percent of the total, though it is here that most of the high-quality tawny and vintage port is made. Last is the Douro Superior, the largest and most arid area and the least cultivated. It produces only 13 percent of all port.

Port is made from several varieties of grape, with Touriga Nacional recognized as the main varietal which, though low-yielding, contributes its intense color and aroma to the mix. Tinta Roriz is fruity with a high sugar content. Touriga Francesa is used for its "nose," and is flowery and fruity. Tinta Barroca has high sugar and tannin content, and adds structure. Tinta Cão is a light grape grown in the cooler regions, and is added for the fruity and flowery character it brings to the blend.

Production Techniques of Port Wine

Port wine production has been a hand-crafted process from start to finish since grapes were grown in the Douro Valley. Even with the takeover of many famous port houses by multinationals in the 1960s that introduced mechanization to the process, it is generally recognized that the best wines are crushed underfoot in *lagares* (large stone or concrete vats). The harvest begins before the autumn rains and lasts about four weeks. Nearly every resident in the Douro Valley gets involved. The youngest generation helps to fill the men's large baskets that are carried down the steep slopes on their shoulders to the wineries below. The women and older generation are responsible for cutting the vines, with each row checked and picked several times in a harvest, as only the ripest fruit will do. The grapes are placed in the lagares, and the harvest festivities begin. Workers tread knee-deep in grapes, arms linked as they stomp and dance on the grapes underfoot to the beat of traditional folk music, with much singing and drinking by all. Though the workers have toiled in the vineyards since sunrise, festivities can go on long into the night. The stems, seeds, and skin of the grapes rise to the surface of the lagares where they form a crust, which is turned back into the vat with wooden paddles called *macacos* to enhance the color of the wine. In the mechanized process (called autovinification) grape stems and seeds are all crushed together. After the wine reaches the desired color, the seeds and stems must be removed to ensure they do not impart their bitter flavor to the developing wine. In the foot-crushed method, this is not a concern as the feet do not crush the stems and seeds. The crust is skimmed off, and the wine is placed into stainless steel vats to ferment until the level of alcohol reaches 7 percent, at which point brandy is added to stop the fermentation process. The grape spirits increase the alcohol content of the wine to 20 percent. It is then shipped to the port houses down river, by truck, where it is aged in oak casks for several years and finally bottled, where it undergoes a further aging process.

Many of the small quintas have returned to the old ways of foot pressing to produce high-quality port, but autovinification dominates the industry today. The most renowned of the small, family owned port houses are Fonseca/Taylor and the Symington family (Dow, Graham, and Warre). Multinational companies include Cockburn, Croft, Sandeman, and Delaforce.

NOTE

1. As quoted in www.intowine.com.

SELECTED READINGS

Anderson, Jean. *The Food of Portugal.* NYC: HarperCollins, 1994.

Mayson, Richard. "Portugal." In *A Century of Wine: The Story of a Wine Revolution.* Edited by Stephen Brook. London: Mitchell Beazley, 2000, 146.

Modesto, Maria de Lourdes. *Cozinha Tradicional Portuguesa.* Lisbon: Editorial Verbo, 1997.

Ortins, Ana Patuleia. *Portuguese Homestyle Cooking.* Northampton, MA: Interlink Publishing, 2002.

Robertson, Carol. *Portuguese Cooking: The Authentic and Robust Cuisine of Portugal.* Berkeley, CA: North Atlantic Books, 1993.

www.bar-do-binho.com.

www.intowine.com/port.html.

www.portwine.com.

Built in 1160 as a strategic defense post of the Templar Knights, Almourol Castle sits proudly in the middle of the Tejo River. (Courtesy of Rhonda Cunha.)

The restored ramparts of the Castelo dos Mouros wind their way along the mountain in Sintra. Built between the ninth and tenth centuries, from atop this windy perch the Moors could see for miles across the plains far below. (Courtesy of Rhonda Crute.)

Óbidos is a medieval fortified town surrounded by Moorish walls that overlook the lush plains below. Named one of the seven wonders of Portugal, the town is a popular tourist destination. (Courtesy of Rhonda Cunha.)

In post-revolution Portugal, political murals were a common sight along the streets of Lisbon. (Courtesy of Rhonda Cunha.)

The first of May political march, a major holiday in Portugal commemorating workers' struggles, marked its tenth anniversary of democracy in Portugal in 1984. Still a fledgling democracy, the political situation was fragile, plagued by frequent protests and workers' strikes. (Courtesy of Rhonda Cunha.)

In the baking sun of the central plains region, a cemetery dazzles in a blaze of white marble. This ornate cemetery is a mosaic of mementos and memories. (Courtesy of Rhonda Cunha.)

In the winding streets and steep alleyways of the ancient Roman city of Coimbra, ornate doorways and windows can be found around every corner. (Courtesy of Rhonda Cunha.)

The old shopping district in the heart of the Roman city of Coimbra. (Courtesy of Rhonda Cunha.)

Old and new share territory without rancor. With so many historic buildings and ornate facades in an ancient city like Coimbra, it is inevitable that a gas station would share space with such an exalted neighbor. (Courtesy of Rhonda Cunha.)

Fishing boats bob in the harbor at Cascais, a popular resort town on the coast west of Lisbon. (Courtesy of Rhonda Cunha.)

A fisherman stands knee-deep in fish as he unloads his catch on the beach at Praia da Mira. Here, oxen in beautifully carved yokes are used to haul the nets onto the sands. (Courtesy of Rhonda Cunha.)

Women relax in the shade of the povo, or square, gossiping and telling stories as they create knotted fishnets, a craft passed down through the generations in this village. (Courtesy of Rhonda Cunha.)

The open-air marketplace is a weekly tradition all over Portugal. Hawkers sing the praises of their wares and haggling is still practiced in many rural markets. (Courtesy of Rhonda Cunha.)

An old woman protects her head from the noonday sun as she sells fruits and vegetables from her impromptu market stand on a street corner. (Courtesy of Rhonda Cunha.)

A typical village house in the mountains of north-central Portugal. Animals live on the ground floor, under the family's quarters. There is a large veranda for drying grains and beans, and, of course, the mandatory grape arbor. (Courtesy of Rhonda Cunha.)

A rutted road in a sparsely populated village in the Beira Alta region. Villages all over Portugal are emptying as younger generations abandon them for a better life in the cities. (Courtesy of Rhonda Cunha.)

A young shepherd guides his flock along the steep and winding roads that wrap the mountainsides of northern Portugal. (Courtesy of Rhonda Cunha.)

Igreja do Carmo, in the northern city of Oporto, boasts magnificent blue and white tile murals. Tiles are used extensively throughout Portugal to adorn public and private buildings, both inside and out. (Courtesy of Rhonda Cunha.)

The church at Mértola, originally a mosque, was converted in the twelfth century during the Christian Reconquest. (Courtesy of Rhonda Cunha.)

6

Literature

PORTUGUESE LITERATURE has a long tradition of lyric poetry and historical writings, but until recently most of the Portuguese literary tradition has been undervalued or overlooked, due in part to widespread illiteracy until the 1970s, censorship, lack of interest by the literate, and the high cost of small press runs. Such ambivalence and illiteracy caused José Maria de Eça de Queirós, one of Portugal's greatest Realist novelists, to call his own language "the tomb of my mind."[1] For these reasons many of Portugal's best writers wrote in another language to reach a larger audience. The few poets and chroniclers who did receive the recognition they deserved were little known outside the borders of their own country. Portuguese critics in the later part of the nineteenth century and twentieth-century critics abroad have reexamined Portuguese literature and breathed new life into it through better translations and more rigorous research and criticism, enabling Portuguese literature, and especially its lyric poetry, to attain a broader recognition and deeper appreciation on an international level. In fact, Portugal's lyric poetry is considered to be among the very best of European medieval writings.

Lyric poetry was written by all classes of people, from kings to peasants. The tradition has a uniquely Portuguese flavor, which is surprising considering the vast and varied foreign experiences of the country's adventurers as they struck out to explore new lands, oceans, peoples, and opportunities. Influences from other European countries, the Far East, Greece, and Rome contributed their marks, but overriding all outside experiences and styles was every Portuguese citizen's connection to "soil and soul"[2] eloquently expressed in the early *cantigas*, the plays of Gil Vicente, the poetry of Guerra Junqueiro and Antero de Quental, and in the prose of Castelo Branco and Eça de Queirós. Popular and religious themes dominate the works of poets and chroniclers, historians, travelers, and explorers. Regional literature intimately portrays the daily life of peasants, their troubles and humble triumphs. This is prose and poetry born of hardship and toil. It portrays a people who are fatalistic in their outlook, deeply religious, passionate and artistic, and faithful in the face of adversity. They have a remarkable ability to suffer and survive; they accept their place in life and feel there is little they can do to change their situation.

There is a strong national unity and identity bound up in a melancholic persistence of *saudade*, a word that describes an aspect of the Portuguese psyche that is so unique there is no direct equivalent for it in any other language. Essentially, one must be Portuguese to truly understand its meaning and significance in Portuguese culture. Fernando Pessoa, Portugal's national poet, dryly states in one of his poems that only the Portuguese are able to feel *saudades* because they alone have a word to describe it; an explanation as intangible as the feeling it seeks to explain.

More a presence of mind, it is difficult to put into words, so any definition of saudade will be incomplete. If a concrete definition must be tried, however, one could say that *saudade* is a subconscious longing for something that can never be; a heartfelt melancholy for something long past; a haunting, subtle sadness. It has been described as a kind of muted sorrow, a mournful pensiveness, a wail of despair without the savageness of truly deep torment. It is best left to the poets to represent this bittersweet longing that cuts to the heart and leaves a delicious pain. Pessoa describes *saudade* as "a pain that you enjoy, a pleasure from which you suffer." *Saudade* romanticizes the past as a refuge from the hardships of the present and the uncertainties of the future.

Sebastianism, a messianic faith that Portugal's glorious past will be restored, is an example of this longing for a restoration of a glorious past. It is named for King Sebastian, who inherited the throne at the age of three. In 1568, at the age of 14, he assumed the reign from his regent, Cardinal Henrique, and began a disastrous 10-year rule. Indifferent to the affairs of state, stubborn, and poorly educated, he cared only for his religion and warfare. He sought to marry these two interests in a great crusade to Morocco to recover territory lost during his grandfather's reign and spent the next 10 years amassing funds, support, and an enormous army composed of paid mercenaries from Spain, Germany, England, Holland, and the best of Portugal's nobility. All told, there were 15,000 infantry, 1,500 cavalry, 500 ships, and about 9,000 camp followers. Dreaming only of an easy victory and great glory, the young king ignored any displeasing military advice, including reports of an overwhelming Muslim force. In 1578, King Sebastian led his men into an advancing Muslim army of 40,000, suffered a crushing and brutal defeat on the battlefield of Alcazarquivir that resulted in his death and the death of about 8,000 of his army, with thousands more taken as prisoners for ransom. Less than 100 escaped.

In the span of one terrible day, Portugal lost its king, its army was decimated, and a good portion of the nobility was wiped out. Soon the national coffers were emptied to pay the exorbitant ransoms of the prisoners. Sebastian died without heirs, and his body was never recovered. The lack of nobles created a shortage of leaders, and the country fell into chaos. Within two years, through the adroit political maneuvering of Philip II, Spain gained control of Portugal. The Portuguese had suffered not only militarily, economically, and politically, but also spiritually. Sebastianism expressed the people's longing for a return of Portugal's former glory and illustrious past of heroism and great adventure and fueled the public's desire for national independence. The people believed their lost king was not dead, but in hiding, and would return to restore to Portugal all that had been lost. The humiliation of Spanish rule only strengthened the people's need to be delivered in a miraculous and heroic manner.

Portuguese literary tradition is rich in the contemplation of faith, love, and the beauty of the land. Poets and writers speak lovingly and sensitively of their beloved *terra*: Sá de Miranda writes of Minho; the poetry of Diogo Bernades describes his romance for the Rio Lima; the prose of Castelo Branco and the poetry of Teixeira de Pascoaes depict the rugged beauty of the Trás-os-Montes; and Camões writes of the River Mondego. One can drink in the scents and noise and the anguish and joys of the peasantry through the works of Gil Vicente and the lyrics of Junqueiro's *Os Simples*, Trancosos's *Contos e Histórias*. The nineteenth-century historian Teófilo Braga compiled a four-volume collection titled *Canções Populares* that contains thousands of quatrains that give a vivid picture of the Portuguese spirit and the people's connection to religion and the land.

EARLY LITERATURE

Portugal's connection to its glorious past is deeply ingrained in the Portuguese connection to the sea, from which was drawn so much of its wealth, adventure, heartache, and heroism. The rhythmic presence of water flows both thematically and stylistically through all forms of its literary tradition from the poetry of the troubadours to the written and spoken word.

The earliest known Portuguese literature dates back to the twelfth century *cancioneiros* or lyric songbooks, which were a more developed form of oral, poetic tradition written by professional court troubadours, public entertainers, aristocrats, and clerics. The troubadours' songs have several formats, and most can be categorized several ways. *Cantigas de amigo*, which originated in the popular poetry of Portugal and Galicia, use lyrics that are more narrative and descriptive, covering topics such as nature, rural peasant life, and domestic living. Always sung from the female peasant's perspective as perceived by male poets, it is not surprising that interwoven in the fabric of the verse is a clear undertone of the patriarchal social customs. A woman's life is suspended in the absence of male love, as they devote themselves to domestic life while pining for their missing or absent lovers. The lyrics include laments of suffering while awaiting their soldiers' return from the wars and expeditions for the king, often left in doubt as to whether their lovers have been lost or have abandoned them for another. *Cantigas de amor* are songs that are sung from the masculine point of view, and they contain grand, sweeping passions of the man for the woman he loved. Focused on the code of courtly love and infused with the erotic connection between the poet and the object of his desire, the lady was an idealized, superior beauty, unattainable and perfect, to whom the troubadour swore total submission, a patient and humbling vassalage to honor and serve her faithfully, and most importantly because the women were often married, discreetly. The songs develop the relationship between the poet and his love in four stages. First he sighs for her, then he begs for her love, and next he courts her, and last he becomes her lover. The most common theme of Cantigas de Amor describes a delicious agony, bordering on delirium, of impossible love and the lover's inability to translate into words the fine qualities and loveliness of his lady. *Cantigas de escárnio* are satires that use ambiguity, double entendre, and subtleties so that the subject would not be recognizable by a quick reading, but whose identity could be discerned by carefully piecing together the clues. They often satirize the decadent morality of the nobility and clergy. *Cantigas de maldizer* are songs that use direct satire to bluntly and specifically expose the offended subject of the song. They are aggressive, vendetta-like payback for the poet's enemies.

King Dom Dinis (1261–1325) was the most prolific of the troubadours. Considered Portugal's most successful king, Dom Dinis encouraged learning and founded Portugal's first university in 1290. He was a learned scholar, a great statesman, and a sensitive poet, producing 138 known compositions, 76 of *amor*, 52 of *amigo*, and 10 of *maldizer*. Today, the tradition of the troubadours lives on in the Portuguese love of singing and creating poems and songs, often spontaneously. A wonderful extension of the *Cantigas de escárnio* practiced today is the tradition of *cantares ao desafio* or *desgarradas*, which literally translated means "to provoke through a duel." It is indeed a kind of spontaneous verbal duel that starts out innocently enough with the first singer making a personal comment about his opponent, perhaps about his looks, his lack of intelligence, or his mother. (Any Portuguese man will tell you this is just asking for trouble.) The second singer has the opportunity to rebut the comment and throw his own barb. These back-and-forth insults require a great wit, sharp tongue, and ready intelligence, as they must be invented on the spot and are sung in a strict format. It often escalates to the most bruising and hilarious, but good-natured ribbing, loaded with puns and ribald double entendres. The "duels" of talented satirists exhibit a subtle and sophisticated knowledge of the language and are the highlight of any party or festa.

Portuguese prose began with anonymous chronicles of the fourteenth century. The first great chronicler was Fernão Lopes, who was commissioned by King Duarte (1435–38) to compile a record of the House of Aviz. He spent 30 years as the national chronicler, working in the national archives, Torre de Tombo, and traveling wherever necessary to check documents and inscriptions. Scrupulously accurate, he wrote in a charming spontaneous prose. Sixteenth-century chroniclers (such as Gaspar Correia ca. 1495–1565, Diogo do Couto ca. 1543–1616, or Fernão Mendes Pinto ca. 1514–1583) focused on the passage to India and the expansion of the maritime empire.

The first great Portuguese playwright was Gil Vicente (ca. 1470–1536), poet to the Renaissance court of King Manuel I (reign 1495–1521) and goldsmith to Queen Leonor. Believed to be the creator of the monstrance of Belem and numerous devotional plays, farces, and tragicomedies written in a medieval style, Vicente is as important to Portugal culturally as Shakespeare is to England. His innovations helped to modernize Iberian theater, as he was the first to write dramas in the modern Iberian languages: 12 plays in Spanish, 20 in Portuguese, and 16 written in both languages. He also wrote in other Romance languages and in Latin. His *Comédia de Rubena*, considered a great masterpiece, was a significant advance in the construction of the drama and its division into three parts. He was one of the first European playwrights to include stage direction for his actors. He worked during the heyday of theater, which was due in large part to its exploitation by the Portuguese royal court, the richest and most powerful in Europe at that time, who saw the theater's potential to polish the monarchy's image and as a way to present socio-political discourse to the public.

For 30 years all court occasions included one of Vicente's *autos*, which were religious dramas-farces that called upon stereotypical characters to distinguish virtue from vice on stage, with women, the clergy, and courtiers being the butt of his sharp and often ribald satire. Despite their slapstick aspects, the objective was to impart a serious religious moral. His plays give a vivid depiction of the customs, language, and daily life of all classes of people as seen through the eyes of a sympathetic, truly Christian humanist. Both serious and farcical, his plots are simple, peppered liberally with beautifully finished lyrics and spirited dialogue laced with the expressions, word games, and interjections of his time. By the beginning of the sixteenth century the Inquisition put a stop to secular theater, and even Gil Vicente's *autos* were censored.

Francisco Sá de Miranda was Portugal's first Renaissance poet (1481–1558) and was the first to introduce comedy to Portuguese prose. Philosopher, Greek scholar, and meticulous self-editor—his ecologue *Basto* has 12 versions—he lived for many years in Italy and introduced the Italian sonnet forms developed by Petrarch, adapting them to Iberian traditions and styles. Seen as the leader of the new school of poetry, the verse style he introduced revolutionized Portuguese poetry and influenced the rest of the sixteenth century, though it encountered some resistance at first. He is best known for *Cartas de Sá de Miranda* (poetic epistles), *Éclogas*, and *Sátires*. His beloved Minho is celebrated in his pastoral verse and demonstrates his compassion for the plight of the peasantry and their struggle to scratch a living from the earth in the face of social injustice and oppression by the aristocracy and landowners. His work illustrates his nostalgia for a time of rustic simplicity and his desire for a return to traditional morals and values, which he felt had been supplanted during the Discoveries' colonial expansion and exploitation of foreign gold and easy riches. When he died in 1588, he was mourned by all Portuguese poets.

Luís Vaz de Camões (1524–1580) is hailed as Portugal's greatest poet, a literary national treasure. Camões was born poor, and he lived an unlucky life in and out of trouble. Educated at the University of Coimbra, he went to Lisbon and fell in love with one of the Queen's ladies-in-waiting, and for this he was banished to North Africa where he fought as a soldier against the Moors, losing an eye in a skirmish. On his return to Lisbon, he wounded a court official during a quarrel, was imprisoned for a year, and only released on the condition that he leave Portugal and serve the king in India for five years. There he also served in the military and stayed in Goa. Camões left Goa after serving jail time for debts, and went to Macau, and later to Mozambique, dragging his bad luck along with him. He returned to Lisbon in 1570 to find a city devastated by the plague, his old friends dead or scattered. Two years later he wrote what is considered Portugal's national epic, *Os Lusíadas* (1572), a lyric poem of Vasco da Gama's voyage to India embellished with ancient mythology, Portuguese history, and modeled on the *Aenid* of Vergil.

It praises Portugal's past leaders and the nation itself as conquerors over nature. *Os Lusíadas*, whose title alludes to the original inhabitants of Portugal, contains many episodes (1,102 stanzas, and 8,816 verses), with evocative descriptions of the sea in calm and storm, and includes the moving and tragic story of the murder of Inês de Castro. While he was also a playwright, his fame is in lyric poetry of varied styles, including sonnets, songs, pastorals, and metricals. He died a pauper at age 56 and was buried in a public grave. His epic poetry captures the heroic spirit and courageous nature of the Portuguese during the Discoveries, which brought wealth and great glory to the small nation. No writer since has been able to duplicate Camões' depiction of Portugal's illustrious past.

Few women are recognized in the history of Portuguese prose, but one volume stands out as remarkable and gained immediate international recognition. Published anonymously in 1669, *Lettres Portugaises*, published in French, known by the popular title of *Letters from a Portuguese Nun*, was attributed to Mariana Alcoforado, who was considered the most distinguished woman writer before the twentieth century. The original letters, according to the publisher, were written by a Portuguese nun, "Marianne," cloistered in the south of Portugal, to her faithless lover, an officer in Louis XIV's army with whom she began a secret, passionate affair when he was stationed in her town during the wars of the Restoration. When he left her, the abandoned nun declared her undiminished affections in five poignant love letters. Although most scholars now attribute this work to French courtier and diplomat, Gabriel-Joseph Lavergne de Guilleragues, this epistolary masterpiece in which the abandoned nun's anguish is beautifully expressed in passages that contain both rhetorical complexity and psychological contradictions has inspired writers for three centuries, including Elizabeth Barrett-Browning's *Sonnets from the Portuguese* (1850). An instant bestseller in France, its fame spread across Europe, and a clever publisher, seeing the potential for exploiting the popularity of the original, produced a sequel, while others produced the erstwhile lover's epistolary responses to his devoted nun. Surrounded by controversy from the time of their publication until new scholarship in 1926 brought to light previously unexamined evidence of their true authorship, *Letters from a Portuguese Nun* continued in the spotlight of literary criticism well into the twentieth century, most notably serving as the springboard for the controversial *New Portuguese Letters* of 1972, discussed later in this chapter.

The eighteenth century proved to be a dry spell for Portuguese literature, with the exception of Manuel Maria Barbosa du Bocage (1765–1805), considered by some to be among the giants of Portuguese poetry, in the exalted ranks with Camões and Pessoa, Portugal's national literary treasures. Bocage was one of the most popular writers of his generation, known for his love poems that focused on the darker, more desperate side of the emotion—unrequited love, inconsistent lovers, ingratitude—and satirical critiques of government, society, clergy, and the nouveau riche. His outspokenness and bold political critiques, combined with his rakish lifestyle, caused him many problems. Critical of religion during the waning years of the Inquisition and critical of the political system under a monarchy that persecuted anyone suspected of deviating from the status quo, he risked his personal freedom for his art. Some of his work was confiscated by the police and seen as sympathetic to the French revolution, and he was imprisoned for crimes against the monarchy. With the help of influential friends, he was not convicted of these crimes, but almost as soon as he was released he was handed over to the Inquisition for blasphemy and immorality. His fame and popularity brought him a short sentence, but after his experience with the Inquisition's "re-education," he modified his public behaviors and stopped producing his more ribald poetry. It is not clear whether this was from a genuine desire to reform his ways or a result of the repression he experienced at the hands of the Church. He died at the age of 40 from an aneurysm. A six-volume set of his poems was published post-humously, titled *Poesias de Manuel Maria de Barbosa du Bocage* (1853). Bocage introduced Romanticism to Portuguese literature, popular in Europe but unknown in Portugal at the time, and advocated for cultural reform, introducing new ideas and free thinking to Portuguese literature.

THE LIBERAL ERA AND REALISM

Realism returned literary writing to the use of the spoken word. According to the literary critic, João Camilho dos Santos, the writers of the second half of the nineteenth century set the mythical heritage, world vision, and language for their successors in the twentieth century. Modernity in Portuguese literature began with Almeida Garrett (1799–1854) and his *Viagens na Minha Terra* (1846), a critique of the destruction that liberal ideology imposed on Enlightenment values. The Renaissance had begun a separation between the written and spoken word. Garrett used a new narrative form that imitated the unpretentious spontaneity of everyday speech and initiated an interior monologue in modern Portuguese literature, causing the literary language to become national once more and enabling the literate public to relate his work to their own lives.

Liberalism dominated the prose fiction of Garrett, the historian-novelist Alexandre Herculano (1810–1871), Júlio Dinis (1838–1871), Camilo Castelo Branco (1825–1890), and Eça de Queirós (1845–1900) as well as the philosophical and political concerns of Antero de Quental (1824–1891) and the poetry of Cesário Verde (1855–1886). Their writings evoked and recounted the nature of social and economic conflicts or power struggles that developed with the liberal revolution of 1820. These writers rejected the individualistic values of Romanticism and believed that literature had a social function.

Antero de Quental was heavily influenced by Positivism and was the guiding light behind the Generation of 1870, a group of scholars and writers with similar views that included Queirós, Teófilo Braga, Dinis, Jose Ortigão, and Joaquim Martins. Quental lived a turbulent life as a socialist and philosopher. Born in the Açores and educated in Coimbra, he had a great sympathy for the humble peasant. His strong verse reflects a clear vision, agonized strivings, and a serene tranquility. His *Odes Modernas* (1865) reveal Quental's tormented spirit. He committed suicide at 39.

The novel was late in arriving in Portugal, and it was not until the middle of the nineteenth century that this literary form was embraced by Portuguese writers, inspired by the works of Sir Walter Scott, Charles Dickens, Victor Hugo, and William Thackeray. Camilo Castelo Branco, a Bohemian journalist, was Portugal's first successful novelist and most celebrated writer of his time. Due to the attention of serious scholarship, inclusion in school reading lists, and reprints of his work, his place as one of the most widely read Portuguese novelists is secure. Castelo Branco was a prolific writer and by the age of 25 had written plays, poetry, short stories, novels, and comedy. His life was full of melodrama, immorality, and dandyism, and his exploits were well known to the public. In a futile attempt to control his wild ways, he enrolled in a seminary, where he engaged in simultaneous affairs with his landlady and a nun. So much for reform. Perhaps as a result of his own shortcomings, he was the ultimate pessimist and had a darker vision of liberalism than his contemporaries. Castelo Branco sought both commercial success and recognition from his literary contemporaries, and he was plagued by financial concerns most of his life. Not having completed a marketable course of study in university or taken vows at the seminary, he was unable to secure any kind of stable job, but he published often and paid close attention to editorial and public preferences. His novel *Amor de Perdição* (*Doomed Love*), published in 1862 and written while he was in jail on a charge of adultery, was a critical and commercial success, which alleviated his financial woes for a time. His characters were blinded by passion, forgetting their long-term interests and appearing more committed to anarchic and irrational self-destruction than to embracing the new order. To Castelo Branco, love, relationships, and marriage did not lead to peace and happiness but instead to crime, disaster, and tragedy. The individualism of liberalism did not end class conflict but was conditioned by old notions of nobility and superiority. Castelo Branco ended his own life in 1890, during a period of failing health in which he was completely blind and under pressure from perpetual financial problems.

One of the Generation of 1870, Eça de Queirós was the most original novelist, evident in his objective style and narrative talent. A diplomat, he lived abroad much of his life, which enabled him to have a more objective perspective of his homeland, although his penetrating observations of Portuguese society, which showed its problems and limitations, made many readers uncomfortable. His father was a judge and served in two scandalous trials at the time Queirós was in law school; one of those cases involved his friend Camilo Castelo Branco, who, as mentioned above, was accused of adultery, spent time in jail, but was later acquitted. The other involved a wealthy nobleman who was found guilty but had the ruling overturned through his political connections. These experiences fed his growing disillusionment with social immorality and the legal system, but apparently not so profoundly that he was above having his own dalliance with a baroness, which ended suddenly when they were caught red-handed in her bedroom during a party. While studying at the University of Coimbra he befriended Antero de Quental and Teófilo Braga. His realistic social novels dealt with Portuguese society in the late nineteenth century and addressed the backwardness and poverty of the country, with the blame being laid on the clergy and the superstitions of women. Eça de Queirós' satire often criticized the presumption that European values could be imposed on the Portuguese people. His best works include *O Crime de Padre Amaro* (1875), *O Primo Basilio* (1878), and *Os Maias* (1888), a satire of members of Lisbon's high society who blindly followed foreign social trends. Due to translations and adaptations of his work, Eça de Queirós has had a wide audience, both in Portugal and abroad.

Júlio Dinis represented the hope of the liberal period. His work is a bridge between Romanticism and Realism in Portuguese literature. Although they are characteristically romantic, his writings also include a realist's critical attitude toward society. Love is a central theme in all of his novels, and his narrator is clearly not an impartial observer; however, this same narrator is equally capable of injecting a realist's critique of society and politics. Dinis's work weaves significant historical details of nineteenth-century Portugal into the lives of his romantic fictional stories, such as the impact of rural development or the ignorance of both unscrupulous politicians and voters in the election process. In a more optimistic vein, his novels portray marriages that spanned the social classes, emphasizing virtue over education and culture. He denounced the liberal political system as cynical, corrupt, opportunistic, power hungry, and unscrupulous. Despite these vices and limitations of liberalism, Dinis felt that it did allow individuals to pursue fulfillment and more readily find happiness. Three of his four novels are set in the countryside, which for Dinis embodied all that was good and healthy in life. Each of them involves love affairs between couples from conflicting social classes. The happy-ending marriages are symbolic of aspects of the new social order's triumph over prejudice and traditional roles: unions between boss and worker, aristocracy and the bourgeoisie, varying levels of education and different cultures, and urban and rural perspectives. His subjects explore a society in crisis and transition, struggling for some common middle ground. Like so many others in the Portuguese literary canon, namely Quental, Queirós and later, Saramago, Dinis expresses his contempt for the damaging influence of religion, especially on the poor and poorly educated.

LITERATURE UNDER THE FIRST REPUBLIC

Raul Brandão (1867–1930) is credited with the development of the new Portuguese novel. His works are a study in extremes. He wrote plays and obsessive narrative works of a pessimistic nature, about the wretchedness of life and human misery and contemplations on death and God. At the same time he produced works of hope, regaling the beauty of life and nature. Florabela Espanca (1894–1930) produced erotic lyricism, love poetry from a woman's perspective. French Symbolism, which emphasized a retreat into the senses, influenced Portuguese literature via Coimbra's poet Eugénio de Castro (1869–1944). Camilo Pessanha (1867–1926), although publishing only one collecton, *Clépsidra*, was the most important Portuguese symbolist. His emphasis on the musical cadence of language and his mixture of varying states of consciousness helped usher in a modern aesthetic to Portuguese literature and served as inspiration to another of Portugal's greatest poets, Fernando Pessoa.

The writers of the Modernist movement, which began at the turn of the twentieth century, and later, the neo-realist writers, were devoted to the problems of the working class, with most of the fiction set in rural areas. After the 1950s writers began to focus their attention on the problems of the middle class. They still believed in a transformation of man and society. Modernism reached its heights with the works of Fernando Pessoa (1888–1935), Almada Negreiros (1893–1970), Mário de Sá Carneiro (1890–1915), and Miguel Torga (1907–1995), the solitary humanist. Portuguese modernism attacked the bourgeois values of the liberal period, challenged its notions of good taste, and was influenced by Proust, Dostoyevsky, Gide, and psychoanalysis. Modernism emphasized diversity, questioning established ethical and literary values, and innovations in literary technique that avoided conventions and rules.

During his lifetime, the avant-garde poet Pessoa published just one book in Portuguese, *Mensagem* (1924), and though at the time it received only a luke-warm reception, he has come to be recognized as Portugal's most important poet since Camões. *Mensagem* is a valuable and expressive work on the anguish and contradiction of modern man, reflective of Pessoa's conflicted life, which was plagued by depression and alcoholism. Recognized today as one of the greatest twentieth-century writers in the Portuguese language, his work expressed the philosophical, spiritual, and psychological issues of his time. He was well versed in Portuguese literary culture and tradition, but he was equally qualified in rationalism from the English training he received for nine years while living in Durban, South Africa after his mother's second marriage. He returned to Portugal in 1905 to study liberal arts at university, which he abandoned one year later to pursue his studies independently.

The most fascinating aspect of Pessoa's work, and one that has occasioned worldwide interest as his work becomes available through translation, is Pessoa's astounding creativity of expression, writing under more than 72 heteronyms (including the most prolific and respected Álvaro de Campos, Ricardo Reis, and Alberto Caeiro), giving to each a unique personality and characteristic style. As Pessoa explains in a letter to his friend Adolfo Casais Monteiro (1935) describing his heteronyms, "the mental origin of my heteronyms lies in my organic and constant propensity towards depersonalization and simulation."[3] Pessoa writes of how he embraces these various heteronyms, envisions their physical attributes, complete with personal histories and dif-fering linguistic abilities and writing styles. He admits to creating them, yet he is quite separate from them, serving more as a conduit, with each hetero-nym having a kind of autonomy that allows them to interact with each other and for Pessoa to react to them. In the same letter Pessoa writes of the independence of his heteronyms, "I established it all in patterns of reality. I graded the influences, was aware of their friendships, heard within me the discussions and the differing of judgments and in all this it seemed to me that it was I, the creator of everything, who had the least to do with it all."[4] Such was the autonomy of these imagined writers that Álvaro de Campos, the most familiar and unpleasant of the heteronyms, publicly criticized his creator's only published play. Campos took over when Pessoa wanted to write but did not know upon which subject; his work was influenced by the American poet, Walt Whitman. Ricardo Reis, the heteronym who wrote the best poems and essays, lived in Brazil, and wrote a conservative, formalist poetry in the form of the ode, corresponded with Alberto Caeiro during his lifetime and frequently wrote about him after his death. Caeiro was recognized by the other major heteronyms, and by Pessoa himself, as their "master." Pessoa's masterpiece, *The Book of Disquiet*, is attributed to Bernado Soares, who

Pessoa described as a "semi-heteronym" because he was more of a "mutilation of my own personality"[5] than a truly autonomous heteronym. Not published until 1982, *The Book of Disquiet* brought as much international recognition to Soares as to Pessoa himself. Soares wrote with bitterness and contempt on the themes of anonymity, solitude, boredom, and the dream-like nature of existence (apropos coming from a writer who literally existed solely through his own work). The themes in Soares's prose appear in Pessoa's poetry as well, but are expressed with less bitterness. Pessoa's heteronyms "could be interpreted as Pessoa's representation of man's attempt at listening to and expressing the various voices within."[6] Pessoa's poetry and prose gives readers a poignant insight into the elusive nature of personal identity in the twentieth century.[7] As Álvaro de Campos wrote in Pessoa's first contribution to *Presença*, "Fingir é conhecer-ce." (To fake is to know oneself.)

Neo-realism dominated Portuguese literature from the mid-1930s to the beginning of the 1980s. This literary form was heavily influenced by Italy and often stressed social injustice and conflict and class struggle, especially in the post-World War II period. Aquilino Ribeiro (1885–1963) was an early neo-realist who published novels, short stories, and children's books. His work depicts life in Beira with a vocabulary so rich it required a glossary to make it accessible to outsiders. He admired the perseverance and wit of rural and working-class people, and he wrote candidly (for its time) of the physical love between them, which resulted in most of his work being banned after their first printings.

Mario Sá Carneiro is considered one of the great twentieth century writers. Sá Carneiro was born into a wealthy family and traveled the world with his father as a child. In 1911, after dropping out of the law school at University of Coimbra, he moved to Paris to study at the Sorbonne, where he remained most of his short life, with occasional visits to Lisbon. Living in the cultural capital of the world and frequenting literary circles that emphasized modernist ideas such as breaking with the past, experimentation, and rejection of bourgeois conventions, he was able to share with his Portuguese contemporaries literary innovations as they happened. He was a close friend of Pessoa and exchanged letters with him. It was through this exchange that Portuguese modernism was born and through these letters that they developed their aesthetic vision. Together, they were among the founders of *Orpheu*, a journal financed by Sá Carneiro's father, which published some of the crowning achievements of Portuguese literature and marked the beginnings of Modernism in Portugal, though its life span was a short two issues. Sá Carneiro's best work was produced during this period from 1914 to 1916, which was cut short at the height of his career by his suicide in 1916 after emotional and financial crisis.

Neo-realism attracted writers who reacted against the abstract and meta-physical concerns of Pessoa and his followers. They felt the need to deal with political reality rather than focus on aesthetics. Miguel Torga, from the rugged and impoverished northernmost region Trás-os-Montes, wrote of the brevity and harshness of existence and ridiculed sacrifice as a futile gesture. His work *Bichos* (1940) featured animals capable of human emotions trapped in a natural circle of life they had no control over and could not change. The realist view is seen in the works of Ferreira de Castro (1898–1974), José Rodrigues Miguéis (1901–1980), Soeiro Pereira Gomes (1909–1949), and Irene Lisboa (1898–1952), who dealt with women's issues. After 1950, neo-realism began to exhibit more aesthetic sensibilities in the works of Alves Redol (1911–1969).

In 1971 three women writers began a collective writing project that based its format on the seventeenth-century French language epistolary work of supposed author Mariana Alcofobara, *Cartas Portuguesas*, popularly referred to as *Letters from a Portuguese Nun*. Although twentieth-century scholarship has cast doubt on its authorship, it is nevertheless considered an important work of literature. The project was conceived by Maria Isabel Barreno as a reaction against negative public criticism of Maria Teresa Horta's book of poetry, *Minha Senhora de Mim*, which was deemed too sexually explicit and banned within weeks of its publication by state censors. These two "Marias" were joined by Maria Velho da Costa to begin a project with the intention of examining the material and the symbolic lives, both past and present, of Portuguese women. The "Three Marias," as they came to be known, identified Mariana Alcofobara's letters as expressive of the plight of all women who are oppressed and confined. The relationship between the nun and her French lover also served to underline eternal difficulties of communication between the sexes. The authors met each week to share childhood memories and their current attitudes and experiences as wives, mothers, and working women, and a part of their writing adopted the form of written letters to each other about their views, as well as other letters written from the abandoned and lonely perspective of women writing to their husbands who emigrated or their sons who had gone off to fight in the colonial wars in Africa. Written toward the end of Europe's longest surviving dictatorship, whose policies promoted a conservative, patriarchal family model and severely restricted women's socioeconomic position, their published work, *As Novas Cartas Portuguesas* (*The New Portuguese Letters*) created uproar on a national level and was embraced internationally as a rallying cry for the worldwide feminist movement. Disregarding the controversy over the authorship of the original *Cartas Portuguesas*, the authors saw them as a relevant context from which to discuss historical and contemporary women's issues.

As Novas Cartas Portuguesas was cast into the international spotlight by the highly publicized 1972 court case brought against the Three Marias and their publisher by the Caetano regime on charges of pornography and offending public morals. The indecency charge was simply an attempt by the dictatorship to suppress the politically charged and emotionally sensitive references to the unpopular colonial wars and the difficulties faced by Portuguese women, exacerbated by the regime's repressive policies. Feminist movements embraced the cause, and the foreign media put a close watch on the proceedings. It was argued that the book had brought a prestigious light to contemporary Portuguese literature and that it had already crossed national borders and had a worldwide recognition, which contradicted the condemnation by the Portuguese government. With sentencing delayed by a sympathetic judge, the case was interrupted by the military coup in April 1974 and was ultimately dismissed, with the defendants exonerated of all charges. Barreno, Horta, and Velho da Costa each went on to produce bodies of work that have made valuable contributions to Portuguese contemporary women's literature. Velho da Costa received the 2002 Camões Prize, the highest literary honor in the Portuguese-speaking world, given annually to a writer from Portugal, Brazil, or Lusophone Africa, and firmly establishes Velho da Costa as one of the most important authors writing in the Portuguese language today.

Novels have dominated literature since the 1950s, with José Saramago being the best known contemporary writer. Saramago, a poet and dramatist, is best known for his novels, the first of which was published when he was 50 years old. He is the first Portuguese writer to receive the Nobel Prize for literature (1998). Prior to writing fiction, Saramago worked as a journalist for *Diário de Notícias* and as a translator. Many of his novels are allegories on the struggles of ordinary people in complicated political and social times. In his novel, *Levantando do Chão* (*Risen from the Ground*), he writes with great compassion for the peasants of the Alentejo, hard-working, long-suffering people victimized by the hypocrisies of government, the arbitrariness of justice, and the repression and perpetual poverty inflicted upon them by the landowners of the region; people who put their faith in a deceitful Church that Saramago saw as both accomplice and beneficiary of the State and landowners.

His controversial and provocative novel, *O Evangelho Segundo Jesus Cristo* (*The Gospel according to Jesus Christ*), in which a mean-spirited God exploits a human Jesus in order to found a repressive religion that has led to violence and intolerance, was nominated for a European Literature Award. Although it was both a critical and commercial success in Portugal, the Church attacked the work as heresy, and it was removed from competition by conservative members of Parliament. Announcing their decision to withhold the novel from competition on the anniversary of the April 25 Revolution led some to view the decision as a symbolic return to the censorship of the Salazar dictatorship. A disgusted Saramago described the situation to an Italian newspaper as the return of the Inquisition to Portugal. Soon after, he left Portugal to live in the Canary Islands.[8]

Helena Marques (1935–) is one of the most recognized Portuguese writers of the twentieth century. Her strong, independent, older women characters are accomplished and take control of their own destinies, rebelling against a traditional patriarchal society. She grew up in Funchal, Madeira during the Salazar dictatorship and was influenced by her grandfather, a senator of the Portuguese republic before the dictatorship began. Marques worked most of her life as a journalist and moved with her family to Lisbon in 1971, where she worked on a number of newspapers. She began writing novels after retirement from *Diário de Notícias* in 1992, and she has written four novels, the first three considered a trilogy. The books are written from a feminist perspective and document with the passage of time the women characters' development of rights, growing independence, and the attendant problems of the male characters' abilities to acclimate to these changes. Unlike most Portuguese writers, Marques sets several of her novels in the Madeira Islands, a symbolic peripheral geography alluding to the marginalization of women by the patriarchy.[9] In her work, *O Último Cais* (*The Last Harbor*), she portrays a sensitive male character who openly displays his love and devotion to his wife. His greatest ambition is to be a good husband; in creating such a character, Marques challenges the traditional gender roles of nineteenth-century Portugal. The last novel in the trilogy, *Terceiras Pessoas* (*Third Persons*), takes place at the end of the twentieth century and shows the plight of contemporary women, caught between the commitment of family and career. Her female character outgrows her once happy marriage and becomes independent to the point that it causes problems in her marriage. She is a strong, successful career woman, whose domestic life is supported by third persons who run her household, care for her children, and essentially support her career endeavors. Marques's work stresses individual choice in achieving fulfillment and happiness.

Like Marques, Teolinda Gersão (1940–) writes of the disenfranchised state of women and their challenges to the subordinate positions imposed upon them by a patriarchal tradition. She began writing after the suffocating censorship of the Salazar dictatorship ended in the revolution of 1974. Her first novel, *O Silêncio*, was published in 1981.

Since 1974, French literary theory, with its emphasis on linguistic and technical aspects of narrative, has been the biggest influence on Portuguese literature. Young writers draw on experiences of the revolution, social class injustices, and decolonization. Other important writers and poets of the late twentieth century include Herberto Helder, Ana Hatherly, Augusto Abelaira, and Sophia de Mello Breynor Andresen.

ORAL TRADITION

Portuguese folk tales play a central part in the oral tradition. Simple stories that reveal the basic cultural values, beliefs, and customs of the people, folk tales are varied in their presentation and appear as fairy tales, moral stories, fables, anecdotes, and legends. Folk tales can function as an important historical record and, when studied over a period of time, can show changes in the social, political, and religious order. A large part of these stories were initially told by the educated and later adopted and adapted by the common folk. Portuguese storytelling is an art unto itself. At times, seemingly more important than the subject of the story is the way in which it is told. A good storyteller's tale is rich in details of daily life, subtly sardonic, slyly sexual, and can have many branches along which the story develops so that the journey from beginning to end has many twists and turns that make the original theme almost incidental.

The village elders keep the oral tradition in the countryside alive today. It is impressive to see the long memory and profound knowledge the older generation has of family history and events of village life. These stories are all the more precious now in the face of rapid modernization, to record a way of life that is fast disappearing as Portugal barrels forward in the name of progress since the fall of the dictatorship in 1974 and its entrance into the European Union in 1987. Gone are the days when the men gathered in the evening by lantern light in the village squares while their dinners were being prepared, to tell jokes and stories, sing, and discuss politics. With electrification of the countryside, the television has replaced an important aspect of Portuguese oral tradition, and people stay isolated in their homes at night and obtain their news and entertainment from the television. Where there is interest, the older generation has wonderful stories to tell, both fables and actual village history; and they can trace family ties back for generations, no matter how obscure the connection.

NOTES

1. Eugene Keefe et al., *Area Handbook for Portugal* (Washington, DC: U.S. Government Printing Office, 1977), 177.

2. Aubrey Fitz Gerald Bell, "Portuguese Literature," in *Portugal and Brazil: An Introduction*, ed. H. V. Livermore, (Oxford: Oxford University press, 1963), 111.

3. George Monteiro, ed., *The Man Never Was: Essays on Fernando Pessoa* (Providence, RI: Gavea-Brown, 1982), 93–107.

    4. Ibid.

    5. Fernando Pessoa, *The Book of Disquiet*, trans. Richard Zenith (New York: Penguin, 2003).

    6. Isabel Murteira França, *Fernando Pessoa na Intimidade* (Lisbon: Publicações Dom Quixote, 1987).

    7. Ibid.

    8. David Frier, "José Saramago's O Evangelho Segundo Jesus Christo: Outline of a Newer Testament," *The Modern Language Review* Vol. 100, no. 2 (April 2005): 367.

    9. M. Rector and F. M. Clark, eds., "Portuguese Writers," in *Dictionary of Literary Biography* (Detroit, MI: Gale Publishing, 2004), Vol. 287.

SELECTED READINGS

Bell, Aubrey Fitz Gerald. "Portuguese Literature." In *Portugal and Brazil: An Introduction*, edited by H. V. Livermore. Oxford: Oxford University press, 1963.

França, Isabel Murteira. *Fernando Pessoa na Intimidade*. Lisbon: Publicações Dom Quixote, 1987.

Frier, David. "José Saramago's O Evangelho Segundo Jesus Cristo: Outline of a Newer Testament." *The Modern Language Review* Vol. 100, no. 2 (April 2005): 367.

Keefe, Eugene et al. *Area Handbook for Portugal*. Washington, DC: U.S. Government Printing Office, 1977.

Monteiro, George, ed. *The Man Never Was: Essays on Fernando Pessoa*. Providence, RI: Gavea-Brown, 1982.

Pessoa, Fernando. *Obra Poética*. Rio de Janeiro: José Aguilar Editora, 1972.

———. *The Book of Disquiet*. Translated by Richard Zenith. New York: Penguin, 2003.

Rector, M., and F. M. Clark, eds. "Portuguese Writers." In *Dictionary of Literary Biography*. Detroit, MI: Gale Publishing, 2004. Vol. 287. (Appendix 1: Medieval Galician-Portuguese Poetry for the stuff on DonDinis and cantigas de everything.)

Saramago, José. "The 1998 Nobel Lecture." In *World Literature Today*. Vol. 73, no. 1 (Winter 1999).

http://www.instituto-camoes.pt/cvc/literatura.

http://br.geocities.com/edterranova/pessoa.htm.

7

The Media and Cinema

THE MEDIA

Public opinion plays a central role in democratic societies; it expresses the citizens' political will. Therefore, analyzing the varied forms of media presentation and representation is of vital importance. The media functions as a powerful vehicle to inform and influence the way a population perceives the issues of the day. Providing the words and ideas to discuss a particular issue, the media is a key player in the formation of public opinion, especially if the public lacks access to other means of information and contextualization of events. In this manner, the media present themselves as brokers between information and the public, interpretively framing reality by providing coherence and reason, as well as bias.

Television is the primary communication medium used by the vast majority of Portuguese (99.3%) independent of age, sex, economic, or other demographic sectors. It has become the "lareira electrónica," (electronic hearth), replacing the traditional evening gathering place of families. While the Portuguese still spend a considerable amount of time interacting with friends, family, and neighbors, the television has become a ubiquitous fixture in most homes, ever-present in the background—a kind of white noise soundtrack of quotidian life. After television, the Portuguese turn most frequently to radio (82.6%), and newspapers and magazines (77.5%) for their news and entertainment. Let us not forget the café as an important partner in the dissemination and exchange of ideas and information, which in the pre-revolutionary past has served as a greenhouse for the growth and development of radical political thought.

The Media during the Dictatorship

Censorship began with the 1926 military dictatorship, although it was not legally established until the 1933 constitution took effect, which allowed Salazar strict control of the media. The press was heavily censored, with radio and television under government control, and writers who violated the rules were subject to severe sanctions, including seizure of the copies, closure of the publisher for specific periods of time or permanently, fines, or even jail sentences. Even foreign magazines were subjected to censorship before being placed on the newsstands, as were pamphlets and posters. Between 1932 and 1936 the censors curtailed dissenting periodicals on the left as well as the right: integralist, republicans of the Democratic Left and the Liberal Union came under the censor's knife in 1932; monarchists (1933); democratic republicans (1934); independents (1935); and the socialists (1936).

Beginning in 1936 new periodicals could not be created nor could books be circulated without the permission of the General-Directorate of Censure Services (under the Interior Ministry). Any references to suicide, political prisoners, cholera, "hippies," labor strikes, drug abuse, homosexuality, massacres, nudism, floods, yellow fever, hunger, imperialism, rape, pollution, the Portuguese Communist Party, fraud, racism, abortion, mental illness, shanty towns, price increases, or emigration, as well as many other subjects, were also censored. The press was not allowed to print white spaces where censored material might have been cut, a sly maneuver by the government to keep readers ignorant that information had been removed. In order to publish without complications, writers and editors began self-censoring, anticipating what might be cut. The panel of censors, mostly army officers, were permanently installed in newspaper offices. The result was a bland and cautious conformity by the media.

Censorship and repression of opposition groups led to an underground press that can be categorized by subject. Radical Republican Reversalists were especially active from 1926 to 1928, as were Democratic Republicans.

More than 124 individual Anarchist publications were produced between 1886 and 1950. Many were short lived, although some, such as *A Batalha*, had a long life and were well-known mouthpieces of the anarcho-syndicalist General Confederation of Labor. By the time it was closed by the military in 1927 it had legally published 2,556 separate issues. *A Batalha* appeared less regularly after 1927 as a clandestine publication.

The official Portuguese Communist Party (PCP) newspaper, *Avante!*, was integral in strengthening the party's internal organization, expanding the PCP's influence and countering anarchist and *"reviralhista"* (reversalist-Republican) influences. With a clandestine press, the leaders' abilities to implement their analyses improved tremendously. The party was able to communicate with the masses regularly because the press provided a vehicle for party propaganda directed at their enlightenment and organization. While *Avante!* is probably the PCP's best-known publication, a wide array of material rolled off the communist presses prior to 1974. In 1933, *O Militante* became the PCP's theoretical and organizational bulletin, superceding similar publications that appeared sporadically after 1929. The PCP press also printed a number of affiliated publications for various trades and syndicates.

Other publications were heavily influenced by the communists even if they were not actual communist publications. *O Diabo* (1934–1940), for example, became a leading cultural weekly newspaper and included pieces by well-known writers of the time, such as Miguel Torga. Its direction was handled by Manuel Campos Lima, a PCP member. Among the contributors were Álvaro Cunhal, the charismatic leader of the PCP, writing on economics and social problems, Fernando Piteira Santos, Soeiro Pereira Gomes, Manuel da Fonseca, Mário Dionísio, and Alves Redol. Other important publications of this type with PCP influence were *Seara Nova* (1926–1939), *Presença* (1927–1940), *Sol Nascente* (1937–1940), and *Vértice* (1942).

Antifascist Unity publications came from varied oppositionist agglomerations such as Portuguese Popular Front, Movement de Unidade Antifascista, especially active from 1944 to 1947, the Patriotic Front for National Liberation, which published from Algiers, and the National Democratic Movement.

In the 1940s socialist tendencies were especially active in clandestine publishing, but after the formation of Portuguese Socialist Action (ASP) in 1964 the press runs became more numerous because socialists became more active. One of the most important titles was *Portugal Socialista*, which was published in Italy with the support of the Italian Socialist Party.

Critical Catholic press was generally from the progressive (more liberal) Catholic opposition and included the *Cadernos GEDOC* and *BAC*. It became especially active after D. António Ferreira Gomes, Porto's bishop, wrote a critical letter to Salazar in 1958 calling for regime change and shattering the view that the Catholic church was completely supportive of the dictatorship.

Extreme-left publications began in the early 1960s with the splintering of PCP groups more inclined toward Maoism or Trotskyism. Many oppositional publications did not fit into any of the above categories.

In 1958 there were two major newspapers in Lisbon, *Diário de Notícias* and *O Século*. After 1968, restrictions were eased somewhat under the Caetano dictatorship so that some novelists and essayists could be more critical without fear of retribution.

The Liberalization of Media and Communications in Post-Revolutionary Portugal

Dramatic changes followed the 1974–1975 revolution and again during the 1987–1995 Portuguese Social Democrat (PSD) majority rule.

During the post-1974 political chaos, there was a power struggle to control the media. Both the communists and military wanted to maintain censorship to insure Portugal's leftward drift and avoid rightist views, while the socialists and forces to their right wanted a pluralist media without censorship. In 1975 the new press law ended censorship, although the Armed Forces Movement still had the right to intervene for national security reasons. The nationalization of the banks left most of the media—controlled by the banks that were themselves owned by Portugal's top elite families—in the government's hands with the exception of *República* in Lisbon and *O Primeiro de Janeiro* in Porto. Radio and television were also nationalized.

Beginning in the late 1970s and throughout the 1980s European nations saw profound changes in their media sectors. The media status quo in Portugal was first challenged by "pirate" radio stations in the early 1980s that sprang up in a disorderly fashion throughout the nation. A few years later the state monopoly broadcasting system was contested by the spread of new technologies such as video and satellite television.

It was only in the mid-1980s that the government invested in substantial upgrades to its telecommunications infrastructure in Portugal, which was largely ignored during the dictatorship, as a result of Portugal's inclusion in the European Union. A 1987 government study showed that Portugal's telecommunications system was 15 years behind the rest of Western Europe. Fiber optic cable was laid and open markets allowed digital exchanges. As satellite television brought private channels to Portuguese homes from abroad, some argued that there was no longer a reason for Portugal to not have its own private channels.

The 1987 center-right Social Democrat Party (PSD) party program stated that the media could not exercise their formative and informative functions completely unless "they are prepared to defend national identity from the invasion" of foreign media by, for example, stipulating that a certain percentage of programming be nationally produced. During the PSD reign from 1987 to 1995, and with the center-left Socialist Party's (PS) support, the state monopoly in television broadcasting was ended, freeing the media from government control but opening them up to corporate control. The government's pro-business approach led to the privatization of newspapers and the liberalization of radio by allowing the creation of private stations. In 1988, a new radio law was approved; the revision of the constitution in 1989 allowed for private television broadcasting, which was approved in 1990, and the creation of the High Authority for Social Communication as the regulatory enforcement body. In 1995 the incoming Socialist Party inherited a changed media and communications system, but with weak regulatory bodies. Its goal was not to change the system but to improve regulation by making it more efficient.

For the film industry, a 1990 body was created, the National Secretariat for the Audiovisual, to elaborate a comprehensive, coherent policy for cinema and other audiovisual production, leading to increased subsidies to the Portuguese film sector. The monies provided remained insufficient and irregular, however, and the problems of film distribution and exhibition, as well as promotion and marketing, were largely ignored. As a result, Portuguese film production continued to flounder.

Television

The RTP was created in 1955 with regular broadcasts beginning in 1957, at first 1.5 hours per day with one hour on Sunday. It increasingly became an essential instrument of the dictatorial regime's propaganda machine. This was recognized and exploited more by Caetano than it was by Salazar, who was not a great orator and had a phobia of new technologies. In 1958 the television tax was initiated, which at the time was paid by 18,000 television owners. Television production facilities were created in Porto, with televised news programs begun in 1959 and televised advertisements begun in 1962. Only by the end of the 1960s did broadcasts cover the entire nation. (In 1959 they reached 43% of the territory and were received by 32,000 sets.) The second channel, RTP-2, was created in 1968. The offerings on the channels were primarily live variety programs, newscasts, and pop music and theatrical lineups. By the 1960s foreign series became viewer favorites, but news programs made up 20 percent of the offerings. In 1980 RTP began transmitting in color, and in 1992 it launched RTP Internacional via satellite to the more than 200 million Portuguese speakers throughout the world.

Cable began experimentally in 1994 and was fully operational by 1998 with Sport TV, and with Canal Notícias de Lisboa, Canal Parlamento, and Canal Programação TV Cabo in 1999. In 2000, SIC Gold and TV Medicina/TV Saúde (health and medicine channels) were added, followed by SIC Radical, NTV, and TVI Eventos the following year. In 2003, SIC Mulher (women) began. Since then many movie, pay-per-view, and other channels have been added.

Portuguese Radio and Television 1 and 2 are public stations. Channel 2 (launched on January 5, 2004) was reformulated to replace its predecessor,

RTP2, when it faced "a strong crisis of identity, strategy, and organization" because of competition from private cultural channels.

RTP1, Dois [Two], SIC, and TAI are generalist, with content ranging from news to sports and entertainment rather than exclusively cultural, where television is intimately related to public service. SIC, owned by a press company, became the first private television station in Portugal when it began in 1992. Later, other members of the press began additional thematic stations, but all on cable networks. TAI belongs to the Media Capital group, the last generalist station to appear on Portuguese television, although it originally belonged to the Catholic church. The Portuguese consider television to be the most trustworthy communication medium (67.7%), followed by radio (65.7%), newspapers (58.5%), and Internet (21.2%).

Television broadcasts must now have 40 percent Portuguese program content (30% national production and 10% in-house production) created by the studio itself without specificity regarding genre.

Radio

While some claim Rádio Hertz began the first broadcasts in Portugal in 1914, they were not true broadcasts but instead radio telegraphy using Morse code. Regular broadcasts did not begin until 1925 with the amateur station CT1AA.

Rádio Clube Português (RCP) began the first radio broadcasts in Portugal in 1931. Smaller stations that were formed in the 1930s later joined together to form the Emissores Associados de Lisboa in the southern region and the Emissores do Norte Reunidos in the north.

The government created the national radio broadcasting system in 1935 with the founding of Emissora Nacional (EN). The Catholic radio station Emissora Católica Rádio Renascença began regular transmissions in 1937. Rádio Ribatejo commenced broadcasting in 1951. All of these private stations shared the airwaves with the national broadcasting system until the nationalization of radio stations in 1975.

Funds for running the government station came primarily from a tax on all radio receivers, 534,063 at the beginning of 1957 and 1.5 million in 1975. Private stations generated funds through advertising as well as by renting radio time to others. Broadcasts at radio's inception were of concerts, lectures, and entertainment programs. Transistor radios made access to the airwaves affordable for the rural masses and were key to their connection to cultural events and news outside of their local region. Likewise, FM broadcasts increased the quality of the sound and allowed transmission in stereo. The broadening of air space allowed the targeting of programs to smaller groups based on age, social, and cultural differences. Soccer match coverage attracted the largest number of listeners, although radio dramas and entertainment series were also popular. Initially, news broadcasts were closely linked to live readings of the written press. In the 1960s RCP created a news bureau and developed a more radio-friendly style.

Censorship, of course, restricted the type of news that could be broadcast. Sporting matches allowed the most spontaneity and freedom as they were not politically sensitive events. Among the country's most historically significant radio broadcasts were the 1974 airings of the songs "*E Depois do Adeus*" by Paulo Carvalho via ENS (on the night of April 24) and "*Grândola Vila Morena*" by José Afonso on Rádio Renascença (on April 25 at 12:20 a.m.) as a signal to the military that the coup to overthrow the dictatorship had begun.

Three underground radio stations existed during the dictatorship. Rádio Revolução (Revolution Radio), known popularly as Rádio Fantasma (Phantom Radio), was produced by anarchists during the Spanish Civil War. Irregular broadcasts came from Barcelona reporting on the repression in Portugal and providing civil war updates. It was through these foreign broadcasts that listeners in the far reaches of the country could learn about repression in other parts of the nation despite the censorship of national news. Rádio Voz da Liberdade (Voice of Freedom Radio) was created by Patriotic Front for National Liberation (which broadcast from Algiers). It was partially supported by the Algerian government and broadcast twice weekly (later expanded to thrice weekly) via short-wave as well as medium-wave signals. Rádio Portugal Livre (Radio Free Portugal) was created in 1962 by the PCP and broadcast in short wave from Bucharest, Rumania.

Foreign stations also tried to influence the Portuguese by reporting news that the national media censored. Radio Moscow broadcast daily in Portuguese via short wave. It led Emissora Nacional to broadcast its own program countering Moscow's claims of worker repression, national strikes, or world events.

Today there are three radio operators with national coverage: Rádio Difusão Portuguesa, which is publicly owned, Rádio Renascença, which is owned by the Catholic church, and Rádio Comercial, a private station geared toward youth. There are also two privately held regional radio stations, one for the north and one for the south of the country. In addition, there are more than 300 local radio stations (347 in 2006). In 2001, the average Portuguese aged 15 or older listened to 191 minutes of radio per day.

Newspapers

The first Portuguese newspaper, *Gazeta*, began in 1641. In the nineteenth century journalism took a great developmental leap forward because a goal of the Liberal Revolution of 1820 was ending the censorship that dominated earlier periods under the Inquisition and other politically dominant powers.

With the new freedom of expression, the first press law was approved in 1821 and permanently protected under the liberal constitution of 1822.

The longest-running newspaper in Portugal—and second oldest in Europe—is the daily *Açoreano Oriental,* published on São Miguel island in the Açores since 1835. In 1864 the *Diário de Notícias* (Lisbon) introduced classified advertisements that allowed newspapers to be sold at lower prices, thereby increasing circulation. Other important newspapers began operations: *O Comércio do Porto* (1854), *O Primeiro de Janeiro* (1869), *Jornal de Notícias* (1888), *Jornal do Comércio* (1853), and *O Século* (1881). The first three are still published.

The most important achievement of the post-1974 period is the end of censorship. Even before it was verified that the military coup had been successful, the newspapers stopped sending their publications to the censor. An intermediary ad hoc junta was set up by the military for the media and cinema to safeguard national and public security. Control of the media and its content was a major issue until November 25, 1975 because the communists wanted to censor the views of the newspaper editorial boards via the journalists and workers that were affiliated with the PCP. Their goal was to prevent coverage of rightist views in the media which, they dubbed fascist. Today, for example, communists are allowed to communicate their views publicly. However, they wanted to eliminate rightist voices from public debate and exclude them from the marketplace of ideas.

The extreme left and the Communist Party argued that the news that affected the working class needed to be published and could not be decided upon by only an editorial committee without the involvement of the journalists and other workers. They argued that producers as well as consumers should be involved in the decision-making process. On February 8, 1975 a press law was approved that supported this view. It gave journalists freedom of access to information sources, guarantees in their professional career, liberty of publication and distribution, free competition, independence, and the right to participate in editorial decisions. Consumers were given the right to be informed free of monopolistic media control, to have the right of response, and to be informed of the paper's political line or particular bias. This issue developed into a problematic case broadcast internationally as extreme-left workers (typesetters and others) took over the *República* newspaper operations because they believed the views of its editorial board and administration had drifted too close to the views of the Socialist Party.

After the April 25 revolution, many newspaper administrators were replaced because they had collaborated with the dictatorship. In addition, many new newspapers of varied ideological leanings were created. In 1975 a respected, independent, left-leaning weekly (*O Jornal*) was born. (It ended in 1992.) The daily *O Público* was created in 1990 as independent of political or economic influence and quickly gained respect.

Magazines

The Enlightenment in seventeenth-century Portugal saw the birth of magazines in the "encyclopedic" style that increased in number in the early part of the eighteenth century after the liberal victory. These magazines represented themselves as repositories of knowledge and often included "Archives," "Museums," "Encyclopedic Newspapers," or "Libraries" in their titles, along with their area of specialty, such as "history," "sciences," "arts," "education," "literature," or "morality." They were a more simplified version of the *Anais das Ciências, das Artes e das Letras* published by exiled Portuguese liberals in Paris between 1818 and 1822. An example of one of these early periodicals was *O Oculto Instruido*. This journal was a type of synthesis of enlightenment ideas for those that neither had the time nor the inclination to read the books themselves. *Revista Universal Lisbonense* stated in an 1842 prologue that it provided a bit of science for all, while books contained a lot of science for a few. Portugal, of course, had a high level of illiteracy at the time, but for the literate these periodicals were very popular throughout the nation. The larger the variety of subjects in any one issue, the greater its appeal to a broad audience. Many of the articles were often translations of foreign pieces. Examples of these magazines were *O Panorama*, *O Arquivo Popular*, *O Ramalhete*, *O Beija-Flora*, or *O Universo Pitoresco*.

In addition to this genre of publication there were also specialized newspapers for literature, science, or other subjects. A popular format at the time was theatrical newspapers that went beyond covering theatrical listings and also provided societal gossip and dramatic narratives. Political newspapers were also numerous.

Cultural magazines have been quite influential in Portuguese history. *Orpheu*, published in 1915, marked the beginning of Portuguese Modernism and drew from the energies of important authors such as Fernando Pessoa, Mário de Sá Carneiro, and Almada Negreiros. As Modernism waned, *Presença* reenergized the style from its creation in 1927 until it ended 14 years later. It emphasized original and sincere art that explored the psychology of the individual. *Seara Nova* (1921–1979) earned considerable prestige and emphasized the artist's interventionist obligation to society. In addition to becoming a major venue for the intervention of intellectuals in politics and society via writings, it also organized seminars, lectures, and conferences. The review reflected the evolution of ideas during the span of its publication beginning with the liberal republican experience to democratic opposition after the 1926 military coup to Marxist influences.

Gente Nova (1927) was published by young republicans in opposition to the monarchist integralist movement. *Pensamento* (1930) emphasized socialist culture. *Revista de Portugal* (1937) was heavily influenced by neo-realism, a leading style of the 1940s, as was *Sol Nascente* (1937), *Altitude* (1939), and *Vértice* (1942). In the 1930s active resistance to the dictatorship was difficult, so many of these cultural magazines became centers of opposition. Because of the limited circulation of these magazines, they published some articles that could never have made it past the censors in the mainstream press, as the ability to decipher the symbolic meaning was limited mainly to intellectuals. For example, reference to a political march with individuals waving poles without flags was interpreted as the communist flag. During the Spanish Civil War neo-realism in Portugal was often a mask for opposition to the Portuguese government. Neo-realism was reenergized from 1957 to 1961 by the Porto-based *Notícias do Bloqueio*. Surrealist magazines also existed such as *Variante* in 1942 and *Grifo* in the 1970s. There were also poets who launched cultural reviews that did not emphasize the artist's social obligation, such as *Cadernos de Poesia* (1940) and *Aventura* (1950). The individual and humanism were emphasized by *Távola Redonda* (1950) and *Graal* (1956). Humanities reviews were important in the 1960s, such as *Colóquio* (1959) or *Brotéria* (1960). In addition to these more academic or artistic venues, there were the informative cultural newspapers listing performances and articles for more general audiences (*JL* and *Letras e Letras*).

Publishing Today

Portugal has more than 50 publishing houses that market Portuguese authors as well as translations of foreign works. The market is small because a relatively large percentage of Portuguese are still illiterate—5.5 percent in 2006, according to government statistics, compared to 1 percent in the United States and most European Union countries—and the literate are not avid readers. (In 1995 about 50% of Portuguese read books, but most read three books or less per year.) The result is expensive books, with even bestsellers having press runs of only 2,000 to 3,000 copies. In 1995 the general literature publications had press runs averaging 1,752 copies.

CINEMA

The pioneer of Portuguese cinema was Aurélio Paz dos Reis, who presented the first national films in Porto in 1896. Between 1918 and 1924, Porto-based *Invicta Film* created some major silent successes such as *Os Fidalgos da Casa Mourisca* (1920), *Amor de Perdição* (1921), and *O Primo Basílio* (1922). The greatest silent Portuguese film is considered to be Manoel de Oliveira's documentary *Douro, Faina Fluvial* (1931). In 1932 a sound film company and studio was built in Portugal (Tobis). The comedy by Cottineli Telmo, *A Canção de Lisboa* (1933), was the first sound film produced in Portugal. Censorship resulted in low-quality films, as only certain subjects (especially sporting themes or fado) could survive the censor's hatchet. Comedy was a favored genre because the government favored films that might divert people's attentions from their everyday problems and societal ills.

While many may debate whether Salazar's "New State" was fascist, it most certainly qualifies as such in regard to its dissemination of propaganda and emphasis on nationalism—typical components of a fascist state. In 1933 Salazar created the Secretariat for National Propaganda (SPN), which produced approximately 60 films in the 1930s and 1940s with António Lopes Ribeiro being the most important director of the Salazar regime. His *A Revolução de Maio* (1937) is a propaganda classic in the Portuguese style, which paints the dictatorship with a romantic brush via nationalism, putting its main character, maternity nurse Maria Clara on a pedestal as the quintessential Portuguese woman, a role model that supported Salazar's political agenda to preserve the nation's traditional, patriarchal structure. Ribeiro also produced *O Feitiço do Império* (1940), which supported Portuguese colonization and nationalism during World War II.

In the 1950s there were attempts at neo-realist films, but rigorous censorship decimated the film industry, turning it into a wasteland. The Gulbenkian Foundation, taking advantage of reduced censorship under the Caetano regime, stepped in to support Portuguese films, which led to two successes: *O Cerco* (António da Cunha Telles, 1969) and *Uma Abelha na Chuva* (Fernando Lopes, 1968–1971).

Today, the film industry in Portugal remains small and produces mainly short films and documentaries for Portuguese television.Only a few directors, such as Manoel de Oliveira (1997, *Viagem ao Principio do Mundo*) or Paolo Rocha (2000, *A Raiz do Coração*), are known globally for their films.

SELECTED READINGS

60 Anos de Luta. Lisboa: Edições *Avante!*, 1982.

Cádima, Francisco Rui. "Televisão." In de. *Dicionário de História do Estado Novo* Vol. II, edited by Fernando Rosas and J. M. Brandão Brito, 970–972. Venda Nova: Bertrand Editora, 1996.

Cardoso, Abílio, "O Cinema: do Mudo aos anos de Agonia." In *Portugal Contemporaneo* Vol. IV, edited by António Reis. Lisboa: Publicações Alfa, 1989.

Cardoso, Gustavo, Carlos Cunha, Susana Santos, and Tania Cardoso. "The Representation of Terrorist Threat on Portuguese TV and the Euro 2004 Cup." In *Comunicação e Jornalismo na Era da Informação*, edited by Gustavo Cardoso and Rita Espanha. Porto, Portugal: Campo das Letras.

Cruz, Manuel Braga da. "Censura." In *Dicionário de História do Estado Novo*. Vol. I, edited by Fernando Rosas and J. M. Brandão de Brito, 364. Venda Nova: Bertrand Editora, 1996.

Cunha, Carlos A. "Imprensa Comunista." In *Dicionário de História de Portugal*. Vol. VIII, edited by António Barreto and Maria Filomena Monica, 252–253. Lisbon: Livraria Figueirinhas, 2000.

Freire, João. "Imprensa Libertária." In *Dicionário de História do Estado Novo*. Vol. I, edited by Fernando Rosas and J. M. Brandão de Brito, 454–456. Venda Nova: Bertrand Editora, 1996.

Geada, Eduardo. "A Tentativa de um Cinema de Autores." In *Portugal Contemporaneo, 1974–1992*. Vol. V, edited by António Reis, 291–300. Lisboa: Publicações Alfa, 1990.

Gomes, Adelino. "Radio." In *Dicionário de História do Estado Novo*. Vol. II, edited by Fernando Rosas and J. M. Brandão de Brito, 809–810. Venda Nova: Bertrand Editora, 1996.

Gomes, Maria do Carmo, Patrícia Ávila, João Sebastião, and António Firmino da Costa. "Novas Análises dos Níveis de Literacia em Portugal: Comparações Diacrónicas e Internacionais." Paper presented at IV Congresso Português de Sociologia. http://www.aps.pt/cms/docs_prv/docs/DPR462de53172c7d_1.PDF

"Imprensa." http://www.ucs.pt/verfs.php?lang=pt&fscod=328&imprimir=1 (accessed July 11, 2007).

Oliveira, César. "Radios Clandestinos." In *Dicionário de História do Estado Novo*. Vol. II, edited by Fernando Rosas and J. M. Brandão de Brito, 811–812. Venda Nova: Bertrand Editora, 1996.

Oliveira, José. "Livro, Leitura, Literacia." *O Militante*. May/June 1997. No. 228.

Palla, Maria. "A Liberdade de Imprensa Entre o Poder e a Independência." In *Portugal Contemporaneo, 1974–1992*. Vol. VI, edited by António Reis, 271–280. Lisboa: Publicações Alfa, 1990.

Pereira, José Pacheco. "As Primeiras Séries do *Avante!* Clandestino," *Estudos Sobre O Comunismo*, No. 0, 1983.

"Rádio." http://www.ucs.pt/verfs.php?lang=pt&fscod=329&imprimir=1 (accessed July 11, 2007).

Reis, António. "A Televisão: Arma do Poder e Janela para o Mundo." In *Portugal Contemporaneo*. Vol. V, edited by António Reis. Lisboa: Publicações Alfa, 1989.

Rezola, Maria Inácia. "Imprensa Clandestina." In *Dicionário de História do Estado Novo*. Vol. I, edited by Fernando Rosas and J. M. Brandão de Brito, 441–451. Venda Nova: Bertrand Editora, 1996.

Santos, Maria de Lourdes Lima dos. "Sociabilidade, Comunicação, e Aprendizagem." In *Portugal Contemporaneo*. Vol. I, edited by António Reis, 365–388. Lisboa: Publicações Alfa, 1990.

Sousa, Helena. "The Liberalization of media and Communications in Portugal." In *Contemporary Portugal: Dimensions of Economic and Political Change*, edited by Stephen Syrett, 133–151. Aldershot, UK: Ashgate Publishing, 2002.

"Televisão." http://www.ucs.pt/verfs.php?lang=pt&fscod=330&imprimir=1 (accessed July 11, 2007).

Torgal, Luís Reis. "Cinema e Propaganda no Estado Novo: A 'Conversão dos Descrentes.'" In *Revista de Historia das Ideias*. Vol. 18, 277–337, 1996.

Traquina, Nelson, and Warren K. Agee. "Portuguese Audiovisual Policy: Confronting the 90s." *Portuguese Studies Review* Vol. 4, No. 2. Fall-Winter (1995–1996): 62–76.

United Nations Educational, Scientific and Cultural Organization (UNESCO), http://portal.unesco.org/education/en/ev.php-URL_ID=41771&URL_DO =DO_TOPIC&URL_SECTION=201.html.

Wiarda, Howard J. "Government and Politics." In *Portugal: A Country Study*, edited by Eric Solsten. Washington, DC: U.S. Government Printing Office, 1994.

8

Performing Arts

PORTUGUESE MUSIC is part of a larger category of cultural elements that includes food, language, popular mentality, and costume. It is difficult to isolate any one of these items, as they interact with each other and are celebrated jointly. For example, a traditional festival will often be celebrated by individuals dressed in costume, singing and dancing to traditional songs. Music has always had an active and well-developed presence in Portugal while other performing arts, such as dance and theater lagged in development after years of neglect or censorship during the dictatorship.

TRADITIONAL MUSIC

Religious Music

There are few studies of music in Portugal during antiquity prior to the nation being formed. Approximately 20 ancient theaters have been found throughout the nation, and it has been established that Roman theatrical productions were accompanied by music. There is also scant information regarding Christian music in the Iberian Peninsula in the early days. A reference exists in the Mértola church to the first known European church musician, André (525 A.D.), known as the prince of singers. The first religious music references began after the Visigoth occupation in the sixth century, with the first written ceremonies showing up in the eighth and ninth centuries. During the eleventh and twelfth centuries the Cluny order dominated religion in Portugal and unified the liturgy via Gregorian Chant (1080–1150).

During the High Renaissance some works survived, such as those of Vasco Pires, singer and master at Coimbra Cathedral, and the Gregorian melodies of Fernão Gomes. The first well-known name is Pedro do Porto, singer for Capela da Rainha Isabel from 1489 to 1499. Évora became the center of music training from the mid-1500s for 200 years. Mateus de Aranda was the cathedral master from 1528 to 1544 and published two music books in Lisbon in 1533 and 1535. The vocal music at this time was influenced by the Franco-Flemish style. Damião de Gois is the best-known Portuguese Renaissance musician. Most Renaissance music in Portugal was written for keyboard instruments such as the organ or harpsichord. Frei António Carreira (c. 1550/1555–1599) was the first great Portuguese organ composer. José António Carlos de Seixas (1704–1742) wrote important organ compositions (sonatas) in the eighteenth century.

Classical Music

The "elitist" music scene in Portugal was dominated by Italian opera throughout the nineteenth century, which prevented a national style from emerging. Marcos António e Fonseca Portugal (1762–1830) wrote Italian-style operas that were well received and made him the best-known Portuguese composer internationally at the time. From 1820 to 1851 only three of 100 operas performed at the Royal Opera House (São Carlos) were Portuguese operas: *Egilda di Provenza* by Pereira da Costa (1827), *Inês de Castro* (1839) and *O Cerco de Diu* (1841) by Manuel Inocêncio dos Santos. Only in the second half of the nineteenth century were dramaturgical, poetic, or novella pieces from romanticism performed: *Beatriz de Portugal* (1862) and *O Arco de Santana* (1867) by Sá Noranha; *Eurico* (1874) by Miguel Ângelo Pereira; *D. Branca* (1888) by Alfredo Keil; and *Frei Luís de Sousa* (1891) by Freitas Gazul—all of which were heavily influenced by Italian operatic style. National comic opera, on the other hand, was more influenced by French style.

In the classical music scene important individuals during the first two decades of the twentieth century included Father Tomás Borba, Luís de Freitas Branco, Pedro de Freitas Branco, Francisco de Lacerda, and Viana da Mota. Viana da Mota viewed the Italian opera's influence on the elite as problematic and saw the closing of the royal opera houses in Porto and Lisbon as beneficial after the 1910 revolution because it provided the space in which a national style could develop. Luis de Freitas Branco introduced Modernism/Impressionism to Portugal with his 1913 *Paraísos Artificiais* (Artificial Paradises). Frederico de Freitas and Lopes Graça emphasized politonal music in the 1920s like *Humoresca* (1929). Cláudio Carneyro wrote Schoenberg-type atonal compositions in the 1920s. In 1934 Orquesta

Sinfónica da Emissora Nacional, the national public radio's own symphony, was formed by Pedro de Freitas Branco and developed an international reputation for its interpretations of Ravel's works. These artistic developments were limited to Lisbon and Porto, leaving the remainder of the nation culturally disadvantaged from a classical perspective. Given Portugal's weak musical education system, it is not surprising that there were only isolated cases of musical genius such as Viana de Mota, singer Tomás Alcaide, and cellist Guilhermina Suggia, who lived in England for many years. One can also add the pianists Sequeira Costa and Sérgio Varela Cid to the list in the 1950s, and later Maria João Pires, the famous Portuguese concert pianist.

Rui Coelho and Fenando Lopes-Graça were two twentieth-century composers who developed their own styles. Rui Coelho emphasized a nationalist strain and developed historicist themes set in Portuguese scenery, myths, and typical figures with compositions on Portuguese poets, sacred music (Fátima oratório), symphonies, suites, and so forth. He pushed for Portuguese language opera *Soror Mariana*, *Rosas de Todo o Ano*, *Inês de Castro*, *Dom Joao IV*, *Belkiss*, *Entre Giestas* that had the Salazarist nationalistic influence.

Fernando Lopes Graça was influenced by Bartok and integrated Portuguese popular music into his compositions. His first composition was the 1928 *Variações sobre um Tema Popular Português*. His vehement opposition to the dictatorship led not only to a debate with Coelho in the newspaper *República* but also to imprisonment in 1931 and 1936. Other typical compositions were *Sonatas* (1936–1939) and *Danças* (1942–1946) for piano, *Canções Populares Portuguesas* (1939–1946), *Concertos* for piano and orchestra (1940–1942), *Quarteto de Cordas* for string quartet (1936), chamber music, and several books on music study.

The Gulbenkian Foundation provided great support for classical music after its foundation in 1956, especially ballet and non-orchestral music that did not receive as much government funding as orchestral music. In 1957 annual classical music festivals began in Portugal with the "Gulbenkian Festival of Music" (1957–1970) and "Jornadas de Musica de Sintra" (Sintra Music Days). The Gulbenkian festivals ended in 1970 when the foundation opened its own performance facilities in Lisbon and presented programming year round. A negative side effect of the Gulbenkian's creation of its own symphony was that it siphoned off the best talent from other domestic orchestras, such as the national public radio's. However, the Gulbenkian's contributions to Portuguese cultural life had significantly more positive contributions, such as the creation of music schools, the publication of ancient Portuguese music on disc and on paper, the creation of a music library, and the funding of music ethnography research. The foundation was able to maintain a greater independence from the dictatorship in its activities given that it was privately funded. It supported a new generation of composers like Álvaro Cassuto (1938–) *Ensaio Breve no. 1* (1958–) with a 12 tonal approach à la Schoenberg, Jorge Peixinho (1940–) influenced by Stockhausen and Boulez, Filipe Pires (1934–), Constança Capdeville (1937–), Álvaro Salazar (1938–), Cândido Lima (1939–), Emanuel Nunes (1941–), António Vitorino d'Almeida (1940–), the most tonal and neoclassical of all, Joly Braga Santos (1924–1988), a neoclassicist, Fernando Lopes-Graça (1906–1994), and Maria de Lurdes Martins (1926–) who emphasized vanguard music.

Folk Music

The earliest references to folk music are in church documents such as a 525 A.D. letter criticizing the practices, especially dancing that was considered to be obscene. The local troubadour tradition began in Galicia/Portugal and was influenced by Southern French tradition. The first of these was João Soares da Paiva (b. 1140) and the last was Dom Pedro (1285–1354), the count of Barçelos (and son of King Dinis). About 1,100 songs exist written in Galician Portuguese. For most only lyrics are available, without written music, on the subjects of love, friendship, and satire. The cancioneiro sang romances regarding the marvels and enchantments of princes and knights.

By the 1930s popular radio began to overshadow some forms of Portugal's long history of folk culture, such as the canto polifónico (Alentejo) sung by generally male groups, Modas de Terno (Minho), which are generally sung by groups of women, and depiques (cantigas ao desafio, desafios, desgarradas) throughout the continent and even Azores.

The Cante Alentejano, some claim, originates in Gregorian Chant, while others claim Islamic origins. The lyrics generally show resistance to power, injustice, and the maintenance of dignity despite poverty. Misery, work, pain, happiness, sadness, and aging are all themes that make this musical style transcend folk into protest music.

Fado

The national tradition of fado bears special mention because it is Portugal's most culturally definitive folk music, inextricably linked to the soul and psyche of the nation's people. Fado is a mournful, plaintive expression of longing, passions, lost love, and the hardships of life. It is generally performed by one singer (usually a black-clad man or woman) accompanied by a Portuguese guitar (a pear-shaped, 12-string that gives fado its characteristically melancholic sound), a Spanish viola, and a larger bass viola. It is a poignant and stirring melody that, when sung by a talented fadista, cuts right to the heart. Fado music is all about "saudade," that elusive and uniquely Portuguese word that embodies an impossible yearning for that which can never be. It is the lyrical interpretation of life's most tragic suffering; the plaintive musical expression of the tormented soul. The lyrics are lamentations for a better life and regret for love, luck, and lost fortunes. Themes include abandonment, poverty, rejection, misery, worker struggles, and hope for a better future.

From the 1820s until the end of the nineteenth century, fado and bullfighting went hand in hand amid the popular classes in Lisbon. Casas de fado (brothels) were soon also tied to fado. At the time famous fado singers were João Black (João Salustiano Monteiro) and Alfredo Marceneiro who at times sang with him. While some have surmised that fado originated in Arab culture, Ruben Carvalho argues that it could not have for five reasons:

1. It originated in Lisbon and then became implanted in Coimbra rather than with Arab tradition.
2. It did not begin in the south where Arab culture dominated and was not even known where Arabs stayed the longest.
3. No book or author prior to this century made reference to Arab origins.
4. Fado poetry lyrics had nothing in common with Arabic poetic style.
5. No mention is made of Fado in old music manuscripts.[1]

While the radio did threaten many folk styles, in the case of fado it helped to spread its popularity, as did LP records and popular shows. In many ways fado also could be called songs of protest of their time. During the Salazar dictatorship, fado's social themes of poverty and dissatisfaction with life's hardships often led censors to relegate fadistas to fado houses, where the singers were licensed and their repertoires approved by the state. The most famous fado singer was Amália Rodrigues who, with her sensitive phrasing and powerful vocal undulations, was so beloved by her people that three days of national mourning were declared upon her death in 2000. Her funeral procession wound through the streets of Lisbon to the National Pantheon, where her body was laid to rest alongside the kings of Portugal. Other traditional favorites are José Mário Branco and Carlos do Carmo.

The city of Lisbon celebrates its "Grande Noite do Fado" yearly, an event where amateurs can wail out a tune in front of a stadium crowd in a kind of open-mike show that begins in the evening and lasts until dawn. Considered by the younger generation to be old-fashioned, interest in the fado tradition has recently been rekindled by a new generation of fadistas making their mark, from the traditional Camané, Mísia, and Mariza to the "new fado" of Cristina Branco. (The latter two have gained international recognition.) The fado tradition also catapulted guitarist Carlos Paredes and singer/composer José Afonso onto the national/international scene, although the former evolved into original instrumentals and the latter into popular songs of protest.

POPULAR MUSIC

Protest Music

In most cases this style of interventionist music was dominated by the excluded and marginalized of the economy and society. In Coimbra a big shift in contemporary music began in 1956 when José Afonso and Luís Góis recorded Fados de Coimbra that moved the fado form toward the political. This musical style enjoyed a politicized renaissance beginning in the early 1960s following the Coimbra protests of 1962 with José (Zeca) Afonso "Os Vampiros" (The Vampires–1963, banned by the censors) and Adriano Correia de Oliveira "Trova de Vento que Passa." Afonso was the oldest of this generation of singers and the most revolutionary. Until the 1974 revolution, "canto de intervenção" best expressed the reality of Portugal via poetry against the dictatorship and emphasized hope for the future. Artur Paredes and Edmundo Bettencourt revived Coimbra fado with a stylistic change in canto and guitar. The lyrics of Manuel Alegre (a 2006 presidential candidate) were put to music by guitarist António Portugal. Luís Cília was an exiled singer. Other authors, composers, and singers joined the protest scene, including Manuel Freire, José Jorge Letria, Benedicto Garcia Villar, Francisco Naia, José Barata Moura, Tino Flores, José Mário Branco, Sérgio Godinho, and later the singers António Macedo, António Pedro Braga (Apbraga), António Vieira da Silva, Carlos Alberto Moniz, Deniz Cintra, Ermelinda Douarte, Fausto Bordalo Dias, Janita Salomé, José Fanha, Maria do Amparo, Nuno Gomes dos Santos, Pedro Barroso, Samuel, and Vitorino.

Portuguese Pop/Rock Music

José Cid Tavares created in 1956 what is considered to be the first Portuguese rock band ("Os Babies") influenced by American artists. Popular music was especially influenced by trends in France and focused purely on entertainment. Pedro Osório e o Seu Conjunto was formed in 1957. José Cid created a new band, Conjunto do Orfeáo, that initially combined rock and bossa-nova (Brazilian pop influenced by samba) and moved to bossa-jazz when he left the group.

At the beginning of the 1960s the main currents of contemporary music were ballads, rock, pop, and bossa-jazz. Daniel Bacelar was the Ricky Nelson of Portugal and the "Os Conchas" duo was the Everly Brothers. Fernando Conde performed rock in a Chuck Berry style, and Zeca do Rock presented it Elvis-style. Isabel Amora was the first woman "yé-yé" (rock artist) in the French or Italian pop style.

Other pop singers were António Calvário, Madalena Iglésias, Toni de Matos, Artur Garcia, António Mourão, Simone de Oliveira, and Maria de Lurdes

Resende. They were singers of what was labeled "nacional-cançonetismo," a genre that was designed by the Salazar regime to serve its propaganda program. The singers generally had fine voices and sang about desirable societal values: platonic love, God, and romance.

The 1960s influence of The Beatles arrived with The Sheiks. From 1965 to 1967, The Sheiks were the most popular Portuguese musical group and even performed in England. They disbanded in 1968, leaving the style to their competitors The Jets and Ekos were also disbanded in 1969 so their members could fulfill the compulsory military service. The Quinteto Académico was the first "Big Band."

The socio-political turbulence of the 1960s led to the formation of new bands such as Quarteto 1111, Chinchilas, Nomos, Grupo 5, Beatnicks, Filarmónica Fraude, and Objectivo. Quarteto 1111 was the first great pop band that performed not only in Portuguese language, but with a Portuguese cultural emphasis. Its first album (1970) was removed from the market by the regime because it spoke of inequality among man, rural poverty, emigration, the politically exiled, opposition, racism, and colonialism. Quarteto 1111 became the first Portuguese pop band to be censored. Petrus Castro was another such pop band.

Since then other developments in the music scene range from Fado de Alcântara (punk band), to Marco Paulo, UHF, Trovante, Fernando Tordo, Rui Veloso, Salada de Frutas, Sérgio Godinho, José Afonso, Dulce Pontes, Shila, Carlos Paredes, and Madredeus.

Portugal has many annual music festivals, from the August Jazz Festival of the Gulbenkian Art Center to numerous classical concert festivals and series. The first rock festival was held in Vilar de Mouros in 1971 and included Elton John, Manfred Mann, and the most important Portuguese bands. The Cascais Jazz festival began in 1971, and later in 1974 the first festival of Música Portuguesa was held in Lisbon emphasizing canto livre (protest music). There are also Woodstock-style rock festivals, such as the Sud-Oeste of the Alentejo. The most famous festival is the yearly Festa do Avante! (sponsored by the Portuguese Communist Party) that generally includes music from all the categories discussed here as well as the latest contemporary pop artists of the day.

DANCE

Folk Dance

Some dances, such as Lundum, are common to several regions of the nation. There are also regional dances such as Fofa, Corridinho, and Chama-Rita (Azores), or the Saias, Chacota, Oitavado, Zabel Macau, Sarambeque, Arropia,

Canário, Chegança, Filhote, Vilão, Viloa, Xotiça, Judiaria, Gitana, Charola, Cativa, Chuleta or Vira (continent). Some of these popular dances even accompanied religious processions until the religious authorities banned them for being too pagan. The fact that complaints were still found in religious edicts of the fifteenth century meant dancing persisted in religious ceremonies despite church opposition. In the second half of the Middle Ages, dance became associated with theater after it was purged from religious ceremonies. Some dances probably originated in Spain, such as Seguidilhas of Vila Real de Santo António and Barrancos, the Fandango of Ribatejo and other regions, the Escalhão of Beira Baixa, and the Penso of Alto Minho, as well as the danças dos pauliteiros (trás-os-montes), a colorful and boisterous dance performed by men in dashing costumes who spin and clash/battle with pairs of sticks in rhythm to the music.

The theatrical folk dance group "Verde Gaio" was created in 1940 with support from the National Propaganda office to dance a "national modern" style that was "national stylized folklore."

Today most councils have at least one local folk dancing group, many of which incorporate aspects of regional livelihoods. Costumes of each regional troupe will often represent typical daily work clothes as well as wedding outfits and elite costume. The dancers might also carry some kind of product or symbol of the work done in the region, such as fishing nets, wine jugs, cork, and carpentry or wool-making tools. The women in the dance troupes from the coastal region of Figueira da Foz, where vast salt fields stretch across the marshes, dance with wide wooden trays of salt balanced on their heads. The more formal costumes of *ranchos* (dance troupes) from the Minho region are perhaps the most famous. These richly decorated costumes boast sumptuous layers of red and gold on the skirts, heavily embroidered aprons with colorful flowers, and lacy white blouses all bedecked with a small fortune in ropes of glittering gold necklaces and filigreed earrings. Folkloric dancing is always the much-anticipated highlight of any festival, and many Portuguese ranchos compete and exhibit around the country and in international dance festivals and competitions. Portuguese immigrant communities around the world form their own ranchos (adult as well as children's troupes) at their local community centers as a way of preserving both folkloric dancing and traditional music from their homeland.

Ballet

Only after 1960 was a professional ballet troupe possible, a dance form previously the purview of amateurs, and even then it was generally supported by the Gulbenkian Foundation. The Centro Português do Bailado depended on subsidies from the Gulbenkian until it was folded into Grupo Gulbenkian de Bailado in 1965. In 1975 the company changed its name to Ballet Gulbenkian and became well-defined and stable by 1985.

The national ballet company, Companhia Nacional do Bailado, was created in 1977, which led the government to discontinue its support for "Verde Gaio." Until the mid-1980s, these two repertory companies were the most active, performing dance tours throughout Portugal and abroad.

Modern Dance

In 1979 two new groups were formed as alternatives to Ballet Gulbenkian. One was the Grupo Experimental de Dança de Jazz which in 1984 was renamed the Companhia de Dança de Lisboa. The other was the Dança Grupo in Trafaria.

In the 1990s a diverse artistic panorama of quality dance began (New Portuguese Dance), expanded, and consolidated in Portugal. Most of the earlier work focused on movements from classical ballet and modern dance. In the 1990s the New Dance generation (Paula Massana, Margarida Bettencourt, Madalena Victorino, João Fiadeiro, Vera Mantero, Francisco Camacho, Paulo Ribeiro, Clara Andermatt, Rui Nunes, and Olga Roriz) altered the pattern by emphasizing ideas and concepts and subjecting movements to their own personal visions. When this generation began its studies in Portugal, the few official dance schools and colleges that existed mostly adhered to a conventional curriculum without teaching modern techniques like Cunningham methods. Openings at the two repertory companies were filled by the best students from the official schools that focused on the traditional techniques. A second generation (Joana Providencia, Amélia Bentes, Aldara Bizarro, José Laginha) often presented their work alongside the first generation. Independent venues have been attracted to the works of Sílvia Real, Filipa Francisco (dancer)/Bruno Cochat (choreographer), Aldara Bizarro, João Galante/Teresa Prima, Paulo Henrique, Amélia Bentes, or Peter Michael Dietz. As the government fulfills European Union directives to distribute funds beyond the metropolis, municipalities see the value of cultural activities as an avenue toward distinction and increased tourism. Artists themselves have returned to their local regions or moved from the metropolis because it has become easier to get support beyond Lisbon.

THEATER

Plays

Portugal's famous playwright, Gil Vicente (c. 1465–1536), wrote Auto da India (1509) and many other works that are considered a transition between the theatrical styles of the Middle Ages and the Renaissance.

The 1820 liberal revolution and the termination of almost 300 years of censorship freed up the theater. The repertory in Lisbon at the time was primarily tragedies based on ancient national history, such as *Zaira* (1804) by Padre José Agostinho de Macedo, *A Destruição de Jerusalém* (1817) by Manuel Caetano Pimenta de Aguiar, or *D. Maria Teles* (1804) by Luís França Amaral, and the varied *Inêses de Castro* of Joaquim José Sabino, Sebastião Davier Botelho, and others. There were also monotonous, allegorical dramas that praised the governing officials (written by the likes of Francisco Joaquim Bingre, Nuno Pato Moniz, and José Procópio Monteiro). Another genre included the jesting farces, *O Doutor Sovina* by Manuel Rodrigues Maia, *O Enredador* by Fernando Vermuel, and *Manuel Mendes Inxúndia* by António Xavier Ferreira de Azevedo (all 1812), *Astúcias de Zanguizarra* (1819) by Ricardo José Fortuna, and *O Verdadeiro Heroísmo ou o Anel de Ferro* (1821) by Fernando José de Queirós. There were also pre-romantic pieces by João Baptista Gomes, *Nova Castro* (1806), and António Xavier Ferreira de Azevedo, *A Sensibilidade no Crime*. Being an underdeveloped art form, there were also many lower-quality works.

Almeida Garrett argued for a radical restructuring of the profession as well as the creation of good theaters. In 1836 a proposal was made to reorganize by creating the Inspecção-Geral dos Teatros e Espectáculos Nacionais and the General Conservatory of Dramatic Arts (Dramatics School, Music School, and Dance School) with first prizes given for theatrical works. Garrett emphasized the need to write dramatic pieces rather than merely translate foreign plays. True to his word he wrote *Um Auto de Gil Vicente* and *Filipa de Vilhena* (1840) and *Alfagem de Santarém* and *Frei Luís de Sousa* (1843). The inauguration of the national theater with historical dramas was, counter to Garrett's criticisms, followed by 10 years of similar productions.

The product of the first half of the romantic theatrical period was dominated by "drama de actualidade" (a replacement of historical dramas and passion melodramas with dramas that dealt with more contemporary issues). One strong influence on playwrights of this period was the Saldanha uprising of the early 1850s, which brought to the surface social and economic issues such as socialist ideas and the proliferation of worker associations. In 1854 the first of these dramas appeared: *O Homem de Ouro* (The Man of Gold) by Mendes Leal, *Um Quadro da Vida* (A Painting of Life) by Biester, and *Odio de Raça* (Hate of Race) by Gomes de Amorim. The following year led to *Cinismo, Cepticismo, e Crença* (Cynicism, Skepticism, and Belief) and *Dois Mundos* (Two Worlds) by César de Lacerda and *Poesia ou Dinheiro?* (Poetry or Money?) by Camilo. Alfredo Hogan most wrote on these subjects. The general themes involved the punishment of vice and the reward of virtue centering on wealthy or politically powerful characters who have fallen into vice or corruption. Many pieces in this genre were written through 1870.

During the dictatorship there was a paucity of theatrical work due to state and self censorship and because the government limited funding to accepted projects. Between 1926 and 1958 theater suffered the effects of limited government funding, especially in the 1920s and 1930s when Salazar was balancing budgets. Consequently, dramatic writing and theater lacked the quality that was found in fiction and poetry during this period. Neo-realism and the debates surrounding it added to the problems because the focus was on narrative (i.e., description), rather than on theater (i.e., creativity). Of the neo-realists only Alves Redol attempted theatrical writing through *Maria Emília* (1946), *Forja* (1948), and *O Menino dos Olhos Verdes* (1950), meaning he had to confront censorship. Romeu Correia was a bit more creative than writing strict neo-realist descriptions. José Régio and Miguel Torga followed their own path in a poetic style. João Pedro de Andrade's works are less well known.

Theater became more active in the post-war period. Luiz Francisco Rebello, a historian of theater, wrote several pieces, and Teatro Nacional staged traditional pieces from home and abroad. Independent theaters and university groups practiced experimental settings and new pieces in addition to the traditional.

In 1958 the theater was peripheral and not very active, but by 1974 the situation had changed, and Portuguese theater garnered occasional international recognition. Into the early 1960s theater was especially affected by calculated censorship, insufficient funding, and a concentration mainly in Lisbon. Brecht and Sartre, for example, were automatically censored, as were plays with social or political connotations, insinuations of homosexual relationships, or works that demystified religious beliefs or historical figures. To circumvent the censors, playwrights had to use double entendres and coded images (a pole with no flag might symbolize the Communist party, for example). Many of the pieces were farces or comedies translated from French, Spanish, and sometimes English. Nevertheless, some actors/actresses did manage to achieve success: Laura Alves, Raul Solnado, Ivone Silva, and José Viana. The most important playwrights were wholly or partially censored: Bernardo Santarena, Luís de Sttau Monteiro, Romeu Correia, Alves Redol, Prista Monteiro, Costa Ferreira, Luiz Francisco Rebello, Manuel Granjeio Crespo, Augusto Sobral, Jaime Salazar Sampaio, Miguel Barbosa, Miguel Franco, Jaime Gralheiro, and others. Meanwhile, attendance at the theater and cinemas declined. Independent theater at the universities presented new alternatives for theater goers. In Lisbon the new companies opened their doors: A Comuna (1972), which presented political productions, and Cornucopia (1973), which focused on classical productions.

After 1974 theaters began performing previously forbidden works by Brecht, Peter Weiss, and others. The Cornucopia produced high-quality tragic-dramas and comedy. In the 1980s many theaters faced economic difficulties from declining attendance. According to the Ministry of Culture, in 2000 there were 130 theater groups throughout the country, with 22 receiving governmental support.

Musical Revues

These were truly popular theater, but mainly for the upper-middle classes in the urban areas, especially Lisbon. The revue began in Paris in the nineteenth century satirizing events, customs, and public figures. In Portugal it began at the end of the same century, and was at times censored because of its critical satire. The production was generally divided into two or three parts with various scenes each, often accompanied by song and dance. These flashy revues served up an abundance of light, color, feathers, and chorus. The satire was often targeted at public figures (generally politicians, stars, and sports figures), family life, relationships between husband and wife and mother-in-law, homosexuality, fashion, economic life, customs. It was the only political theater consistently presented and allowed by the government.

NOTE

1. Ruben de Carvalho, *As Músicas do Fado* (Porto: Campo das Letras, 1994), 37.

SELECTED READINGS

Brito, Manuel Carlos de, and Luisa Cymbron. *História da Música Portuguesa*. Lisboa: Universidade Aberta, 1992.

Câmara, José Bettencourt da. *O Essencial sobre a Música Tradicional Portuguesa*. Lisboa: Imprensa Nacional, 2001.

Cardoso, Miguel Esteves. *Escrítica Pop: Um Quarto da quarta década do Rock, 1980–1982*. Lisbon: Assírio & Alvim, 2003.

Carvalho, Ruben de. *As Músicas do Fado*. Porto: Campo das Letras, 1994.

Fazenda, Maria José, ed. *Present Movements: Aspects of Independent Dance in Portugal*. Lisboa: Edições Cotovia, 1997.

Raposo, Eduardo M. Canto de. *Intervenção: 1960–1974*. Lisbon: Público, 2007.

Reis, António, ed. *Portugal Contemporaneo, 1974–1992* Vols. I–VI. Lisboa: Publicações Alfa, 1990.

Sasportes, José, and António Pinto Ribeiro. *História da Dança*. Lisboa: Imprensa Nacional, 1991.

9

Architecture and Art

Portugal's treasure trove of buildings, monuments, and churches, like most other European countries, reads like a survey course of the history of architecture, with notable examples spanning the centuries from prehistoric ruins through contemporary masterpieces. Period architecture in Portugal generally follows prescribed stylistic formats found in other parts of Europe, so a discussion of period characteristics would be redundant and can be found in any architectural survey book. This chapter instead focuses on a few noteworthy examples of each period and discusses significant Portuguese contributions to the field of architecture.

Portugal suffered invasions from all sides over the ages, and each group— Celts, Visigoths, Phoenicians, Romans, Moors, Spanish—left their mark in some way on the architecture of the country. Évora, a small city in the Alentejo, provides an historical panorama of many architectural influences throughout Portugal's history. Here, one can see a Roman temple, Moorish gardens and patios, medieval walls and cathedrals, Gothic doorways, and Manuelino window details.

In a young country such as the United States, where the oldest standing structures are just over 200 years old and are revered for their historical significance, it can be inconceivable that examples of ancient Roman palaces could be so abundant that many ruins can be found undeveloped and unexplored in an ordinary farmer's fields far removed from any university's team of archaeologists. Twenty years ago it was still possible to happen upon handwritten signs directing the lucky traveler to a lonely field on the outskirts of a village where he would find the low walls that mark the site of a Roman household with a curling piece of cork casually thrown over a section of mosaic to protect it from the elements. In fact, there are so many such examples scattered throughout Portugal that available research dollars cannot possibly be stretched far enough to excavate them all, and so it remains for the fortuitous explorer to stumble upon these hidden gems and imagine and marvel at the potential riches that lie just a foot or two beneath his feet.

This vision could be further enhanced with a visit to Europe's most highly acclaimed Roman ruin, Conímbriga (first to fifth century A.D.), 16 kilometers from Coimbra. First settled in the Iron Age by Celts, it was the Romans who turned it into a prosperous city in the first century A.D. It was destroyed during the barbarian invasions in 468 A.D., at which time the population abandoned the city and removed to Coimbra. The main excavation is an opulent villa with its own bathing complex, a sophisticated heating system, ornamental pools, and colonnaded gardens. The site has been in excavation for decades, revealing bit by fantastic bit the elaborate layout of a typical aristocratic dwelling decorated with intricate mosaics of figures and geometric patterns, pillars, fountains, and baths. The present excavations are extensive and yet it is estimated that only 10 percent of the site has been uncovered.

The Romans emphasized urban civilization and built the infrastructure—roads, aqueducts, baths, temples, forums, fortifications—to support its cities, strategic zones, mines, and commercial interests. Rather than building with local materials such as stone, as their predecessors had done, they made their own supplies, such as stucco, reinforced walls, standardized brick sizes, roof tiles, and vaulting, for their varied projects. The three-floor crypt that currently lies under the Machado de Castro museum in Coimbra is a fine example of their vaulted chambers, built to create a broad enough plaza in hilly terrain for their needs. Roman cities when built from scratch generally followed a similar urban plan, with the forum at the center and a hexagonal city layout. Beja, in southern Portugal, is a good model but hardly the only one; Roman ruins are abundant throughout the nation.

Moorish Influence (711 A.D.–1249 A.D.)

The Moors slowly began making inroads into southern Portugal in the eighth century and ruled the area as far north as the Mondego River (Coimbra) for about 500 years. Like the Romans, the Moors were an urban society organized in such a way that a constant flow of trade and ideas passed through its territories. They left their mark on everything from the language to agricultural methods. The Moors introduced an Arab style of architecture that still dominates housing in the southern regions of the Alentejo and Algarve. Wide, rectangular chimneys rise high against the sides of the low, blocky farmhouses, elegantly simple with their smooth expanses of thick, whitewashed walls that reflect the heat and light in a blinding display punctuated by the colorful outlines of windows and doors in red, blue, green, and yellow that seem to glow in the white-hot glare of the summer sun. Walls are constructed of thick stone to insulate the interiors from the scorching heat that sizzles across the wide plains. The Moors left their mark on landscape architecture as well, introducing water as a prominent feature of planned gardens. Urban centers displaying Arab influence include the southern cities of Mértola and Silves, while Lisbon was the largest with a population of 25,000. Although no Moorish building remains intact today, the vestiges of Arab style such as wrought iron work, horseshoe-shaped arches, and patios may still be seen in many cities and towns of Portugal, especially in the Alfama and Mouraria sections of Lisbon's downtown, with their winding streets and steep staircases enclosing hidden courtyards and flashes of jewel-like gardens.

The Portuguese Christian "liberators" were rural, feudal, and doctrinaire in their views, which explains why so few Moorish religious monuments remain: mosques were generally torn down and replaced by Christian cathedrals. The Aljama church in Mértola, although modified over time, remains the most important Moslem religious monument in Portugal. While few mosques survived the period when all things Moorish were purged from the last strongholds, their influence was deeply embedded in the basic structure and form of southern architecture.

The Romanesque (c. 1100–1230)

The Romanesque period began under King Afonso I, who encouraged the Benedictine, Augustinian, and Cistercian orders to practice in the nation. These orders brought with them French Romanesque influences, reflected in Portugal's first cathedrals. The same Benedictine influence as seen in Spain's Santiago de la Compostela was integrated into the Braga and Porto cathedrals built from the eleventh to twelfth centuries. The cathedrals of Lisbon, Coimbra, and Évora were begun later in the 1140s and exemplify the Romanesque style with their large entrances, ponderously thick walls, and heavy, squat forms. Over the next two centuries Romanesque style would especially dominate religious buildings of the North (Entre Douro and Minho) during the slow reconquest. Pillories, another Roman invention, became prominent in the eleventh century and were in continued use for 500 years. They can still be found in the centers of many towns. In the more southern regions there are only four Romanesque churches, Torres Vedras,

Lisboa and Évora (Sé), and Monsaraz. Even as the Gothic style began to take hold in the south, the north stubbornly adhered to Romanesque. The Sé Cathedral of Lisbon was built in 1150 to commemorate the defeat of the Moors on the same spot where a mosque once stood.

Gothic (c. 1200–1450)

The Gothic style dominates in areas where Romanesque did not, mostly south of Leiria. One of the first Gothic monuments is the twelfth-century Mosteiro de Santa Maria de Alcobaça begun in 1178. The abbey and cloisters with their soaring lightness and clean simplicity stand as one of Europe's finest examples of Cistercian architecture. The late-Gothic Monastery of Santa Maria de Vitória in Batalha (a UNESCO world heritage site) was worked on by Portuguese, French, and Irish architects for over two centuries, reflecting the changing stylistic sensibilities of this long construction process. A massive structure that presides in all its lacy finery over a wide flat plain, it showcases the architectural styles from Gothic to Manuelino to Renaissance.

Manuelino Style (c. 1490–1540)

Portugal's most original contribution to the history of architecture is the Manuelino style. Stylistically unique to Portugal, the Manuelino period, named for Dom Manuel (1491–1521), reflects Portugal's deep and abiding connection to the sea and the glory and wealth of the Age of the Discoveries. Manuelino style mixes symbols of Christianity (the cross of the Order of Christ, the religious/military order that was the principle financier of the explorations) with ornate motifs of ropes, coral, nautical symbols, armillary spheres (a nautical device that was King Manuel's personal symbol), shells, and fantastical sea creatures that encrust the surfaces of monuments like barnacles. Portuguese kings were well aware of the dangers inherent in the maritime expeditions and grateful for the immense wealth flowing into their coffers. Fervent prayers were whispered and divine bargains were struck for the safe return of the daring sea explorers and the successful outcome of their ambitious and dangerous undertakings. Many extravagant monuments were erected as repayment for the seemingly endless supply of riches; the spices, gold, and precious stones that flowed like water through the monarchs' hands and inspired them in a kind of delirious fever to erect extravagant and enormous palaces, churches, and monasteries and to embellish every surface. Convento do Cristo in Tomar, ancient seat of the Knights Templar and begun in the Romanesque period (1160), boasts an ornate window in Manuelino style, and the enormous Mosteiro dos Jerónimos in Belem (1501–1580), perhaps the largest and most extravagant in this style, was worked on by a succession of architects from Manuelino style to Renaissance.

Renaissance and Mannerism (c. 1520–1650)

Igreja de São Vicente da Fora (1582–1627), dedicated to the patron saint of the city of Lisbon, was originally a twelfth-century convent. A more somber and formal style, Mannerism coincided with the years of Spanish rule and the heyday of the Inquisition.

Baroque (1717–1755)

The opulence of the Baroque style in Portugal was funded by the gold, precious gems, and exotic woods that began to arrive from the Portuguese colonization of Brazil. When the gold dried up, so too ended the extravagance of the monarchy in Portugal. In Lisbon there are many fine examples of the Baroque style, such as the church of Santa Engrácia (now the Panteão Nacional), which began construction in 1682 but was not completed until 1966.

The sixteenth-century Madre de Deus Church, which now houses the national tile museum, is a beautiful example of the Baroque style. The walls of its main church were completely covered in blue and white tiles at the end of the seventeenth century. Expanded and reconstructed through the ages, it includes many architectural styles with its renaissance cloister, post-earthquake rococo decorations in the main chapel, and a revival Manuelino facade added in the renovations of the 1800s modeled after the discovery of an old portal and a painting from the sixteenth century. Among its treasures is a priceless tile wall mural depicting a panoramic view of Lisbon prior to the 1755 earthquake.

Igreja de São Roque hides a sumptuously ornate interior behind an austere facade. Inside, the chapels are decorated with a dizzying profusion of precious stones, gilding, marble, gold, and silver. Not infrequently, this fervor of religious faith and unimaginable wealth was expressed in grotesque abuses of wealth and power and produced such projects as the Convent and Royal Palace at Mafra, which, in its cost of human life, time, and national wealth squandered, stands as a monument, albeit an impressively ostentatious one, to the excesses and self-glorification of the monarchy. Built by João V as fulfillment of a promise in return for a male heir, it is dedicated to St. Anthony. What started out as a modest plan to house 13 friars spun out of control with the influx of Brazilian gold to cover almost four square kilometers. Construction began in 1717 and continued until 1750. Twenty thousand workers toiled here, presided over by 7,000 soldiers, and in the final years of construction between 45,000 and 50,000 laborers and craftsmen worked on the behemoth that had 4,500 windows and doors, 300 cells, and 880 halls and rooms. It is known for its beautiful and extensive library, which rivals the library at the University of Coimbra, and for the world's largest set of carillon bells. This is all well and good, but the extravagances of the king bankrupted the economy.

For all the investment in time, lives, and funds, it was seldom used by the royal family and was ultimately abandoned by João VI at the time of the French invasion when he fled with the royal family to Brazil in 1807. José Saramago writes of the excesses of the Mafra project in his novel *Memorial do Convento* (*Balthazar and Blimunda* in translation).

A brief flirtation with the Rococo style produced such cotton-candy confections as the Palace at Queluz, a small-scale version of Versailles complete with ornate structured gardens, painted ceilings, gilding on every curlicue and flourish, and a canal lined with painted tile.

Pombalino (1755–1860)

In the aftermath of the devastating earthquake and accompanying tsunami of 1755 that destroyed most of Lisbon and threw the city into chaos, one man kept his cool and lifted the city back up through the ashes. The Marquis of Pombal was the chief minister of Dom João I. He seized the opportunity (and plenty of political power) to organize the reconstruction of Lisbon with a grand grid-like plan along the lines of Paris, with wide boulevards radiating out from the commercial center, in a simple style that was inexpensive and easy to reproduce on a massive scale.

Ninteenth-Century Building

In the early part of the century the building of monuments skidded to a stop, due in part to a decree in 1834 that dissolved the religious orders. When building began again toward the end of the century it drew on all past styles, using more iron and steel and reflecting Portugal's growing industrialization. Art Nouveau was enthusiastically embraced, and many fine examples can be found in shops and cafes in major cities.

Estado Novo and Modernism (1890–1940)

Portugal barely got a glimpse of modernism before the establishment of the Estado Novo, and Salazar's ideas of an official state architectural style of a stripped-down, Soviet-style monumental classicism became architectural policy. Blank-faced and ugly apartment complexes and dull public buildings were the order of the day. "Salazar's architectural legacy is more in the realm of city planning, with the creation of new boulevards on a Pombalesque scale around the capitol."[1] The political repression and economic control of the New State kept Portugal in historic isolation and put an end to any modernist experimentation.One positive effect of the Salazar years on the development of architecture is that in delaying the arrival of modernism to Portugal, architects could see the deleterious effects of some of those aesthetics and the problems of modern urban planning implemented in other parts of Europe.

With this hindsight they could bypass those mistakes, effectively skipping over the problems without having to see them implemented in Portugal.[2] Modernist architecture of the time frequently disregarded the way people lived in space and espoused the arrogant assumption that architects could reinvent a better way to live. Urbanization was believed to be a miracle cure for society's ills and would provide for a better life, but the commercialization of urban centers marginalized the poor and drove them out of downtown areas. The idea prevailed that nothing from the past was worth keeping and all must be made new (German zeitgeist). The result of many of the modernist experiments resulted in an alienation of the very people for whom those spaces were intended. Fortunately for the Portuguese, by the time modernism arrived in Portugal it was already transformed.

Interestingly, while modernism and its inherent problems were evolving outside of Portugal, the Sindicato Nacional dos Arquitectos (SNA), under the leadership of Keil do Amaral, conducted research on the morphology of Portuguese cities and towns in an attempt to identify a solid historical base upon which to build a new modernist style of architecture. The SNA's findings ran counter to the Estado Novo's ideals, which imposed a "national" architectural style of classicism based on pseudo-historical claims. Its research identified certain themes that emerged in vernacular environments. They found that the shaping of towns followed an organic formation with no imposed geometry upon the layout. Preexisting topography ordered new interventions, and the structural format of the buildings conformed to materials and techniques. Homes and villages acquired additions and extensions over time as a natural outgrowth, rather than tearing down the old and building new. The belief was that a process of modernization could be firmly built upon a deep understanding of historical circumstances of built life. Modernist Portuguese architecture could raise the new on a foundation of deeply rooted principles of order.[3] This experimentation with historical basis and contemporary attitudes and materials/techniques led to a sympathetic style that respects the complexities of the sites and their histories. This awareness of the way architecture and community develop and evolve together was forward-thinking and sensitive to the way people live and use public and private spaces.

After 1974 most new construction focused on apartments because Salazar's regime had not kept up with housing demand. Only in the 1980s did construction again focus on office and commercial building using a third-sector architecture of metal grillwork and pre-fabricated concrete.

Contemporary Architecture

Regional styles of vernacular architecture exist and are closely related to the building materials and techniques at hand as well as the regions' historical influences. However, it can be said that there are consistencies throughout Portuguese vernacular architecture that cross regional boundaries.

Portuguese contemporary architecture is characterized by its whitewashed exteriors, few windows, flat walls, horizontal emphasis, its close connection to the earth, and reductive detailing. Common themes include smooth abstract surfaces, luminous white volumes, and extended spaces. Interplay between site and structure is important. Buildings either melded into the local context (1982 to 1986 apartments in Lisbon's Bairro Alto, Álvaro Siza Vieira's 1996 Chiado project) or were enhanced by integrating the new while maintaining the old structures (mercado de Campo de Ourique of Santa Rita by Alberto Oliveira and Rosário Venade). Concrete, brick, granite, stucco, and glass are the materials most widely used. Steel, due to its cost, and wood, due to its scarcity, are less used.[4]

The failure of all but a few Portuguese architects to make an international impact is related to historic and economic reasons: local industry is more focused on small, craft-based enterprises that lack critical mass for development overseas, low productivity, imports that are limited by cost, and very little timber building. The European Union has been doing much to educate and train construction-industry labor forces, and much has changed over the last 30 years.[5]

Escola do Porto (School of Architecture) began in the 1950s and produced many of the country's leading architects. The work of Fernando Távora (1923) respects traditional values and the notion that architecture is "work made by man for man." Távora was responsible for the sense of unity and identity of the Porto School. His informal conversational style of conducting classes contradicted the rigid academic approach of traditional Portuguese universities. His notable works include Mercado da Vila da Feira (1952–1959), the house on Rua Nova in Guimarães for which he was awarded the Europa Nostra Award, and the Santa Marinha Pousada, also in Guimarães.[6]

Álvaro Siza Vieira (1923), considered the greatest living Portuguese architect, studied under Távora at the Faculty of Architecture in Oporto and was instrumental in bringing contemporary Portuguese architecture to the attention of the international community. His work has been exhibited nationally and internationally, and he has won distinction and prizes from all over the world. For Siza, site is an important consideration, and the new must be considered carefully in regard to its context. The reconstruction of the Chiado district in Lisbon in 1996 is a good example of this. In 1988, fire devastated the historic Chiado shopping district in Lisbon, burning out the insides and leaving only the facades. Siza preserved the facades while updating the interiors, creating a startling yet surprisingly harmonious transition from outside to inside. His important contributions are Casa de Chá da Boa Nova,

Matosinhos (1958–1963), the Faculty of Architecture in Oporto, and the Portuguese Pavillion at Expo 98.[7]

The work of Eduardo Souto de Moura (1952) contrasts with the idea of harmonious interaction between a building and its site. His work instead seeks to impose a new order on the topography. To Souto de Moura the site is a mere tool for the architect. Like Siza, Souto de Moura has brought international acclaim to the field of Portuguese architecture through his important commissions, both abroad and at home, and from numerous prizes won. Siza and Moura have both used mooning windows that jut out of the structure's body like eyes and a wraparound framing on entire buildings like a picture frame.[8]

Other important contributors to the field are Tomás Taveira (Lisbon Amoreiras shopping center in the 1980s); João Carrilho da Graça and Nuno Teotónio Pereira; and Arsénio Cordeiro, Sheppard Cruz, Nunes de Almeida (Torre do Tombo, the Lisbon National Archives built in 1982). Nunes de Almeida's neo-modernist style can also be seen in the Lisbon Lloyd's Bank building built from 1986 to 1987.

Architecture and Society

The appreciation of how architecture and society must coexist in harmony and the findings of the SNA research have endured and can be seen in the way the redevelopment of the east Lisbon docks area for Expo98 has transformed the area into a vibrant and thriving community. Expo98 is a good example of short-term and long-term urban planning at its best. The proposed theme for the 1998 World Exposition was "The Oceans, a Heritage for the Future" and dealt with issues such as how to make rational use of the ocean's resources. When Portugal won the bid for the exposition in 1992, urban planners embraced the theme and extended it to include the river and green spaces. They chose the challenging polluted and industrialized section of the riverfront in East Lisbon, an area that was occupied by fuel depots, container warehouses, slaughterhouses, and sewer and waste treatment plants as the site for Expo98. This rundown area was becoming increasingly abandoned as industrial firms moved their businesses to other locations. Urban planners recognized that this urban and environmental renewal project was a unique opportunity to return a non-functioning, polluting, and hazardous industrial space back to the people and the city of Lisbon. They created a vibrant area to not only celebrate the World's Fair from May to September of 1998, but to become a permanent new neighborhood for Lisbon of combined business and residential spaces. Taking a lesson from the disastrous Seville Expo92, which, six years after it closed as a world's fair was still not fully occupied, and while looking to short-term goals of creating an exciting world's fair, planners never lost sight of the bigger and more important goal of how the space would function in the long term, after the Fair's last visitor had returned home. A forward-looking undertaking of huge dimension, the Expo98 committee applied novel concepts with regard to urban solutions for the future, and their relation to environmental issues in particular. The area is served by the new 17-kilometer Vasco da Gama Bridge that spans the Tejo River, the longest bridge in Europe, an engineering marvel that required the calculation of the earth's curvature; a magnificent train station, designed by Spanish architect Santiago Calatrava, whose glass and steel canopy arches over the platforms like a fragile and lacy cross between a Gothic cathedral's flying buttresses and the enormous exoskeleton of some prehistoric insect; a bus terminal, and metro station that not only facilitated the transport of the expected crowds, but ensured later residents easy access to public transportation around Lisbon, thus cementing the success of future residential neighborhoods that sprang up all around the area. Included on the site between the transportation center and the riverfront is the multiple award-winning, three-tiered Vasco da Gama shopping center, built in the image of a huge sailing vessel whose prow points proudly toward the river, acknowledging Portugal's debt to the sea, with the water theme echoed throughout in the interior design. Upscale shops, fine restaurants, and open-air decks that frequently boast live music have made this a popular gathering spot for the local and not-so-local population.[9]

Ten years later, construction continues as more of the long-range plan is implemented. Tall residential apartment towers turn their prow-like faces toward the river, the marina is undergoing expansion, and city government is slated for eventual relocation to the area. The attention that the high quality of Portuguese architecture garnered beginning in the 1980s has led to an explosion of interest in the field, and the number of architecture schools and corresponding number of students has led to a dilution of training and quality that threatens the advances made in the field in the late-twentieth century. In 1975 there were only two schools of architecture. By 1990 that number had jumped to eight, serving 3,400 students. By 2000, there were 20 schools educating 9,000 students. While this influx of new students has the potential to rejuvenate the field, the concern is that many of these students are superficially trained in schools lacking quality teaching and thorough courses. The top competition winners are still those of the previous generation of Portuguese architects. In the post-Expo98 era, architecture needs to be connected to the social and cultural environment with collaboration between architects, urban planners, sociologists, and economists to avoid the problems of urban and suburban sprawl.[10]

Community

In both village and city, the Portuguese live in close proximity to each other. In urban areas, the vast majority live in large apartment condominium complexes organized around small green spaces. Built in the countryside surrounding large urban centers like Lisbon and Porto, new cities have developed seemingly overnight to accommodate the influx of urban migration, with a younger rural population seeking to escape the economic and social limitations of village life, or immigrants from the former Portuguese colonies in Africa, or from Brazil. One might assume these large "dormitory" cities would breed a certain alienation since to an outsider they seem at first glance to be just a place to rest one's head at the end of a long work day. However, even this "slap 'em up fast" style of development takes into account the way the Portuguese live and play, and public spaces are included in all areas of new building.

A typical urban/suburban housing development integrates residential, commercial, and green spaces. In many apartment condominium complexes the street level is occupied by all manner of commercial business: restaurants, banks, small groceries, pastry shops, shoe repair, small-scale auto maintenance, clothing boutiques, furniture, real estate sales, and cafés. Most of these businesses are small enough that they take up no more space than a one or two-car garage. Each apartment block, typically housing three apartments on each floor, usually has its own committee to collect maintenance fees and determine how the money is to be spent on improvements. Local government is responsible for the upkeep of public spaces and services such as waste removal and road maintenance.

A social people by nature, Portuguese housing supports and reinforces this aspect of the culture, and, respectively, community loyalty and patronage help to maintain and keep areas businesses vital and prosperous. While hypermarkets like Continente and Pão-de-Açúcar are making inroads in retail, tempting those with their own cars to purchase in quantity at discount prices, most Portuguese continue to do their household shopping on a daily basis, at small neighborhood stores and groceries. Since small and medium-sized groceries dot most street corners, commuters are likely to pass at least one or two stores on their way home from the bus or train stop.

The integration of retail and residential serves to nurture and support the sense of community, so often lacking in the isolated suburban landscape of the United States. There is a comfortable stability that is created when people and businesses are intertwined in such a way. Cafés and pastry shops function as a kind of neighborhood social center. Here residents can get a dose of local gossip along with their coffee and pastry. During important soccer matches, cafés are crowded with local men who come to drink beer and watch the game with their neighbors. A comparable planning experiment can be seen in the development of communities in the United States such as Seaside, Florida that based its scheme on a similar awareness of traditional American vernacular architecture and how America's old neighborhood planning supported a sense of community.

The proximity of one's home to shopping lends itself to customer loyalty. Worker retention allows both customer and worker to become "neighbors." Daily shopping is frequently an occasion for socializing, and in most town shops people are known to each other and therefore are expected to exchange pleasantries with the shopkeeper or other customers. It would be considered very bad manners to simply enter a neighborhood store, pay for the goods, and leave without at least some personal exchange with the attending shop assistant. This is, of course, less common in large urban centers like Lisbon.

Most neighborhoods have their own green spaces with sporting areas and gardens. Large, centralized public parks are abundant in nearly all large towns and cities, for the Portuguese dearly love a garden. Lush gardens with a pond or other water feature and meandering paths provide an idyllic backdrop for community residents to relax and enjoy fine weather, strolling along in their Sunday best on the weekend, to see and be seen. Families often bring blankets and little grills to picnic and soak up the sun. Children run everywhere, a band might play marching tunes in the gazebo, and ice cream carts and peanut vendors are around every turn in the path. Not to be forgotten is the mandatory soccer field, as necessary a part of urban planning as schools and roads. A Portuguese child is taught to kick a soccer ball nearly as soon as he is weaned from the breast, and the sport is followed with a nationwide passion that borders on fanaticism. Every town and city of a significant population has its own team that is supported ferociously by the locals. Even in what appears to be impersonal dormitory cities the sense of neighborhood and community exist directly because of this mixture of commercial and residential living.

Vernacular Architecture

Temperatures seldom drop below freezing in Portugal. Winters are short, but can seem interminable as the dampness creeps into the masonry until it seems that one's very skin and bones have been invaded by the damp. This is especially true in the north of the country. Winter can be brutal in the mountains once the daily rains of winter settle in. Night comes early, and the isolated villages are frequently shrouded in heavy gray mists during the day. The damp seems to permeate everything, but because the winter season is so short the Portuguese prefer to tough it out, and simply add a few more blankets to the bed and huddle patiently around the wood cooking stove in the kitchen or the *brazeira* (a round foot warmer filled with embers) at night, roasting chestnuts on the embers of the fire while they watch TV or read the newspaper. The houses are built more to ward off the scorching heat of the long summer than to keep winter's chill at bay. There is no insulation, and only new constructions completed during the last 15 years or so have central heating. Many emigrants accustomed to central heating in their northern adopted countries install wood-fired heating systems when building their retirement homes in rural Portugal. New building materials are cast cement and cement brick covered in smooth cement, stucco, and plaster (inside walls). Very old villages are built from the local stone and may be covered with stucco. Ceilings are high and floors are laid with stone or tile, as is much of the kitchen. These materials keep the interiors cool and comfortable even during the hottest part of the day. In the far north, the roofs are steeply pitched and houses are made of the local granite or schist. Most frequently, the houses are covered in a skin of stucco or cement and painted white or pastel candy colors. A quaint and beautifully preserved relic of northern traditional architecture is that of the mountainside village of Piódão, in the rugged Beira Alta region north of Coimbra. Here, the houses cling to the slopes wearing their dark schist suits in somber gravity, broken only by the incongruously cheerful bright blue paint that accents every window and door in the village. Too steep for streets, narrow staircases wind between the homes and tiny courtyards up and down the mountainside. At the foot of the village in the only open flat area squats a lovely seventeenth-century church that was renovated in the late 1800s, a splash of pure white against a stern backdrop.

A traditional northern village home is built like a mini-compound around a courtyard commonly separated from the street by high walls or fences. The ground-floor rooms built against the perimeter walls are reserved for the animals and store rooms. The compound is often spread with *estrume* (straw or groundcover) gathered in the forest. As this is broken down it is gathered and stored in large piles to compost, to be used later to fertilize the fields, and the floor is spread with fresh material. Villagers commonly now pave these spaces with concrete, as it is easier to keep clean. Farmers who have very large inner courtyards will often host the harvest festivities for the village. Having the animals on the ground floor helps insulate the family quarters above from the chills of winter.

The second floor is where the family lives. There is usually some kind of large patio where the family eats and spends most of its time in fine weather, the men mending their fishing nets, the women preparing vegetables, making brooms from broom straw, or crocheting white cotton into coverlets, curtains, and tablecloths. There is usually a veranda that faces the street, but most family life happens on the patio or else publicly in the square. The kitchen will be small, with a wood cooking stove, a small refrigerator, and a sink. Portuguese peasant cooking is simply prepared using few specialized tools so there is not a lot of space required for storage. There is a shelf to store the terra cotta jugs that hold the cold, clear water from the community *fonte*, or spring. A small dining room is used during the winter months. Many homes also have a summer kitchen in the cool dark rooms beyond the animal stalls.

While nearly all villages now have running water to each home, this was not universal until as late as the 1980s in some regions, and women visited the *fonte* daily to retrieve water for cooking, drinking, and bathing. The women and girls use a *rodilha* (a hard stuffed dough nut of cloth or straw, or in a pinch, a twisted dishtowel) to help balance the heavy jugs on their heads as they stroll home with a graceful, swaying stride over the rutted and rocky roads, giving an outsider the impression the jars are empty. Though it is safe to drink the piped-in water, most farmers prefer the taste of spring water from the *fonte*. Laundry was washed at a communal basin near the *fonte* or in the river if one lived nearby, though today most homes are equipped with a washing machine. In central and northern Portugal farmers usually have a small garden plot adjoining their homes, but as land is divided and passed from one generation to the next, plots get smaller and can be scattered all over the village.

The Moorish influence on southern architecture is evident in the long, low, whitewashed buildings, horseshoe-shaped windows and doors, and the wide flat chimneys. Gardens and water elements are vestiges of the Moorish influences.

Construction

Much of new construction in the suburbs and countryside is being done by returning emigrants who save most of their working lives to build a home to return to once they retire, and its style of architecture is often influenced by the country from which they are returning. A careful observer can drive through the countryside and easily guess in which country each of the residents of these homes has worked or is currently working. The most striking aspect of these emigrants' homes is the sheer size of them, much bigger than the modest, often tiny homes that cluster around a central square to make a village. Often, these modern monstrosities mar the simple lines and unassuming nature of the typical village and stand out embarrassingly like a prom dress at a barbecue. They serve more to boast of the financial status of the owners, alluding to a life of luxury that often masks years and years of squalid and cramped living conditions in their adopted home so that every penny can be saved and poured into their retirement home. These show houses are large and sprawling affairs with great marble-lined courtyards and many large bedrooms. They commonly have a summer kitchen off the storerooms in the basement, where the temperature is cooler during the summer months. They stand empty for much of the year and are usually only visited during the summer vacations when the emigrants return to their beloved homeland.

ART

Painting and Sculpture

Human habitation in Portugal can be traced back at least 20,000 years to the Paleolithic caves used by hunters and gatherers, an example being the Cave of Escoural in Montemor-o-Novo in the South (25,000 B.C. to 13,000 B.C.). The world's largest collection of open-air paleolithic rock art can be found in the valley of the Rio Côa near the Spanish border, discovered by researchers in 1989 who went to the valley to study the environmental impact of a proposed dam in the region. Upon their discovery, the project was halted due to international outcry, and the valley was designated a World UNESCO Heritage site. Archeologists have discovered petroglyphs depicting horses, cattle, and ibex dating from 10,000 to 40,000 years ago. Some of the finest examples of the art and tombs of ancient civilizations in Portugal are in the most remote and inaccessible places; perhaps this very inability to get to them has been their salvation for today's more appreciative audiences.

As discussed, beginning in the second century the Romans made lasting contributions to the architecture and infrastructure of Portugal, as did the Moors beginning in the eighth century, who influenced architectural style as well as introduced tiles to the country, which the Portuguese later embraced with great enthusiasm and took tile decoration to a high art of amazing accomplishment.

Manuscript illumination was an important part of twelfth-century cultural activity at the monasteries in Coimbra, Lorvão, and Alcobaça and reached its peak in the sixteenth century with the 62-volume Leitura Nova (1504–1552), on which the most important illuminators collaborated.[11]

But it is with the initiation of the Gothic style in Portugal that we see the rise of great Portuguese painters and sculptors whose works adorn the altars, chapels, and burial tombs of the religious monuments being constructed all over the country. Prior to the thirteenth century, religious monuments were simply adorned, fortified really, rather than vehicles for surface embellishment as they later became in the Gothic, Late Gothic (Manuelino), and especially during the Baroque, where anything that could be nailed down was carved, gilded, and embedded with precious stones. The Discoveries also served to introduce exotic styles from the colonies in China, India, Africa, and Brazil, and their influences can be seen in the decorative arts of wood and ivory carving, furniture, china, textile arts, and painted screens.

The Mosteiro de Santa Maria at Alcobaça is one of the first Gothic monuments in Portugal and houses what are considered the greatest fourteenth-century sculptures in Portugal, including the beautifully sculpted tombs of Inês de Castro and King Pedro I, who lie foot to foot so they will rise to gaze upon each other on judgment day (and whose tragic love story is told elsewhere in this book).

Another early work of distinction is the polyptych of Saint Vincent by Nuno Gonçalves (1450–1491). Court painter to Afonso V, he was highly regarded in his time and was said to have initiated the Renaissance in Portuguese painting.[12] In the first half of the sixteenth century Flemish painting was a source of inspiration to the Portuguese artists Vasco Fernandes (Grão Vasco), the leading painter in the north, and Gaspar Vaz in Viseu; and Jorge Amado in Lisbon, whose large workshop produced many famous painters, most notably, Garcia Fernandes, Cristóvão de Figueiredo, and Gregorio Lopes. Lopes' paintings document the luxury of Portuguese life of the time with architectural details and rich textiles. The painters distinguished themselves by their skill in portraiture, brilliant color, and sentimental realism.[13]

The Manuelino style of architecture and sculpture developed at this time (late gothic) and was used to embellish gothic buildings in a fantastic ornamentation of twisted ropes, religious and nautical symbols, and flora and fauna of the sea. Some of the most outstanding examples of Manuelino sculpture include the spectacular window of the Convento de Cristo in Tomar, Torre de Belem, and the Monastery of the Jerónimos, both in Lisbon.

From the time of the accession of King Sebastião (1572) until the reign of João V royal patronage of the arts dried up, although religious patronage continued. Uneducated and backward, Sebastião had no love of the arts and cared only for war and his fantasy of a grand crusade to Morocco. His foolish single-mindedness and subsequent death on the battlefield left the country without royal heirs or noblemen to take his place, threw the country into turmoil, and ultimately allowed the Spanish to annex Portugal for 60 years. João V's reign reaped the benefits of the colonization of Brazil, and he used the gold and precious gems coming from the new colony to fund his colossal project at Mafra, where Italian Baroque painters dominated. Soon, however, the Portuguese artists began to win commissions. So great was the undertaking at Mafra that a school of sculpture was founded there to produce the quantity of sculpture and stone carving needed for the project. José de Almeida (1700–1769) was a baroque sculptor trained in Rome and was the leading Portuguese sculptor of the mid-eighteenth century. He was the first sculptor with the technical ability to work in stone; up to this time stone sculpture was imported and Portuguese artists preferred wood or clay.[14] He also worked on the decoration of state coaches.[15] As modest as this sounds, royal coaches were not simply vehicles of transportation for the well-heeled. These were so elaborately embellished with flamboyantly carved figures one would be hard-pressed to spot the living royal riding within. More accurately, they were rolling galleries of gilded sculpture and ostentatious symbols of wealth. Almeida was the master of Joaquim Machado de Castro (1731–1822), who was assistant to Alesandro Giusti at Mafra. Machado de Castro was commissioned to design the enormous equestrian statue of Jose I (1775), in celebration of the rebuilding of Lisbon after the 1755 earthquake. Machado de Castro's statue, three times life-size, which still stands today in the Praça de Comércio, was cast from 37 tons of bronze and was a technical accomplishment for its time. Machado de Castro produced a large body of religious sculpture in stone, terra cotta, and wood and also created tombs and creches, in addition to writing on theories of sculpture.[16]

In the eighteenth century there was a Portuguese Academy of Fine Arts in Rome, but by 1836 academies had been established in Lisbon and Oporto. In 1872, António Soares Reis (1847–1889) created what is considered a great masterpiece of late nineteenth- century Portuguese sculpture. His work, *The Exile*, sought to represent the melancholy sentiment of *saudade* and was revolutionary for its time with its combination of realistic representation, classical form, and romantic sentiment. The subject of harsh conservative criticism when it was exhibited in 1874 at the Salon of the Oporto Academy, Soares Reis found a more appreciative audience for his sculpture in Madrid, where *The Exile* won a gold medal in 1881. Soares Reis accepted a teaching post at the Oporto Academy at that time, but his attempts to reform the teaching system met with hostility from his colleagues there. This treatment by his critics and other professional disappointments are believed to have led to his suicide in 1889.[17]

One of Soares Reis's students, António Teixeira Lopes (1866–1942), had better luck with the critics, and his work was widely exhibited and appreciated, despite rejecting the old formula. His sculptures on the theme of motherhood showed profound expressive emotion, and he was known for his sensitive sculpting of busts.[18] Rafael Bordalo Pinheiro (1846–1905), a political cartoonist, ceramist, sculptor, and illustrator, is one of Portugal's best-known popular artists. He launched the journal *A Lanterna Mágica* in 1874, and its success earned him a contract to work in Brazil on *O Mosquito* and *Psit!!!*. He settled there from 1874 to 1879, but missing the bohemian artistic and literary life of Portugal, he returned to his homeland. The numerous death threats he received thanks to his insightful political satire may have had some impact on his decision as well. He founded the Caldas da Rainha ceramics factory in 1884, which is still today the center of Portugal's ceramics industry, where he designed and produced many stunning examples of art nouveau tiles and tableware still in production today. Examples of his cabbage-leaf dinnerware, especially soup tureens, are present in thousands of Portuguese homes, and the satirical cartoons and figurines of Zé Povinho (an everyman peasant created by Bordalo Pinheiro who mocked the rich, powerful, and political elites of his time) are instantly recognizable to nearly all Portuguese today and helped Bordalo Pinheiro earn a beloved and esteemed place in the hearts of the Portuguese people. From 1900 to 1906, Bordalo Pinheiro, in collaboration with his son, published *A Paródia*, a treasure trove of articles and illustrations of every aspect of Portuguese social life at the turn of the century and a valuable archive for sociologists and historians.[19]

Contemporary Art

José Soubral de Almada Negreiros (1893–1970) is the most recognized name of twentieth-century artists in Portugal. His prolific body of work spans the century, and his popularity stems in part from his passionate embrace of modernism and his understanding of the importance of modernization. A self-taught artist of every media in the arts, he produced paintings, drawings, poetry, literature and theory, novels, plays, graphic arts (posters, advertisements, magazine covers), and interior decoration. He also danced, choreographed, and designed ballet, stained glass windows, ceramic tile murals, and tapestry cartoons.[20] His most important projects were the frescoes he created in Lisbon for the Gare Marítima de Alcantara (1943–1945) and the Gare Marítima da Rocha (1946–1948). He came to the attention of Fernando Pessoa with his caricatures and was an active supporter of the Futurists movement. He contributed to Pessoa's *Orpheu* (1915) and organized a Futurists evening in which the painter/writer[21] Guilherme Santa-Rita (1889–1918) participated.

Santa-Rita, a monarchist, studied art on a fellowship at the Academie de Beaux Arts in Paris from 1910 to 1912 but lost the position after a falling out with the Portuguese ambassador, a republican. Upon his return to Lisbon he had significant influence with the Futurists and, like Negreiros, had his drawings published in *Orpheu*. Of his body of work, only two paintings survive, the rest, by his request, having been destroyed after his death by his family.[22]

Santa-Rita was a contemporary of Amadeo de Souza-Cardosa (1887–1918), a painter and draughtsman, whose style was influenced by Modigliani, a friend and fellow exhibitor in Paris (1911). He produced drawings in a linear and decorative style with medieval and heraldic references. His introduction to Cubism (1912–1913) influenced the structure of his work, and his acquaintance with the Delaunays influenced the importance of color. He explored abstraction briefly, but the landscapes of 1914 show a leaning towards Expressionism in their use of color and gesture. Souza-Cardosa returned to Portugal at the outbreak of World War I, where he worked mostly in isolation with only occasional interaction with the Futurists. He experimented in all the modern movements but did not consider himself a Futurist; his careful drawings do not reflect the Futurist's love of speed and movement. His last paintings, dated 1917, are bright, complex compositions incorporating letters, numbers, trompe l'oeil, sand, and collage. His death, along with Santa-Rita's of the same year, marks the end of the first phase of Portuguese modernism.[23]

Maria-Elena Vieira da Silva (1908–1992) is considered the finest Portuguese abstract painter. Born in Lisbon, she moved with her mother to Paris at the age of 18, where she was influenced by the paintings of Matisse and Cezanne. The checkered tablecloths of the Bonnard paintings she saw displayed in the Galerie Petit influenced her later work; these paintings, with their checks and diamonds so reminiscent of Portuguese tile work, combined with receding and shifting planes, anxious, shrinking spaces, dramatic structure, and a greyish palette give Vieira da Silva's work a distinctive style. She worked and exhibited with her husband (the Hungarian painter, Arpad Szenes). In 1940 they moved to Brazil, where Vieira da Silva saw the work of the painter Joaquin Torres Garcia of Uruguay, whose paintings had an essential influence on her later work. Before and during World War II Vieira da Silva's subject matter became increasingly political. Vieira da Silva was one of the most celebrated painters in post-war Paris. From 1970 many of her works were realized as tapestries. Her beautiful tile murals are installed at the Cidade Universitária metro station.[24]

Paula Rego (1935) is another Portuguese artist to have achieved an international reputation. Rego has lived in London since 1951, but was born in Lisbon and grew up under the Salazar dictatorship. She trained at the Slade School of Fine Art, London, from 1952 to 1956, where she met and married the English painter Victor Willing (1928–88), and with whom she lived in Portugal from 1957 to 1963. Rego returned to London in 1975. She has credited the work of Dubuffet, Picasso, Walt Disney, Gilray, and magazine illustrations by turn-of-the-century caricaturists as major influences. She first won acclaim in Portugal with semi-abstract paintings that exhibited a satiric wit, with violent or political subject matter such as *Salazar Vomiting the Homeland* (1960). Her characters often take the form of animals for satirical effect.[25] Her narrative works show a talent for story-telling, if somewhat unsettling in their choice of subjects, which often draw from the dark underbellies of fairy tales and fables with their incongruous pairings of situations and objects. Her paintings, drawings, and etchings deal with themes of domination, fear, grief, and sexuality. There is a sinister atmosphere in her paintings, a sense of ambiguousness and uncertainty that implies to the viewer that what is presented is not the whole story.

For a crash course in contemporary Portuguese painting take a ride on the Lisbon Metro, where gigantic tile murals by the country's most renowned painters and sculptors can be seen on most every stop. The project was initiated in 1959 when the Metropolitan of Lisbon commissioned Maria Keil to design tiles for 11 stations of the newly built subway. As lines were expanded and stations added in the late 1980s and again in the 1990s, each was assigned to an individual artist or artist team. Accordingly, each station has its own distinct personality, and when seen as a whole they comprise one of the most interesting collections of art in Portugal, a kind of underground museum. In addition to Vieira da Silva, many of the artists whose work is discussed below are included in the Metro's varied collection of tile murals. It is commendable that each of the directors of the Metropolitano de Lisboa at the time of the expansions committed funds (even under budget restraints) to a program that placed such importance not only on improving infrastructure but creating an engaging visual experience for the commuters who use the system. Thanks to their vision and the talent of the commissioned artists, the daily commute begins and ends in a burst of light, color, and pattern.

Júlio Pomar (1926) is a painter, printmaker, and poet. Since the 1940s Pomar has chosen to work in a series based on particular themes or formal problems. His paintings from the 1940s are based on the themes of poverty and work. In the 1960s his work was inspired by compositional elements of Ingres and Matisse. In the late 1970s he produced drawings and collaged canvases with erotic themes. Literary figures became the focus in his later paintings, with subjects such as Edgar Allan Poe and Fernando Pessoa. Pomar's work shows a sense of humor and irony. In 1956 he was one of the founder-members of Gravura, the Portuguese cooperative for graphic artists.[26] Pomar's graphic line drawings can be found in the tile murals of the Alto dos Moinhos station of the Lisbon Metro and are fine examples of his precise but gestural style.

Joaquim Rodrigo (1912–1997) was a painter and engineer. After an initial phase of geometric abstraction he turned to narrative figurative work in the 1960s. His paintings of this time reflect his combined personal experiences with contemporary social and political events. His work of the late 1960s onward features small, figurative motifs used like a symbolic pictorial language, arranged in monochromatic fields of earth-toned colors, in a primitive style that is influenced by the "dreamings" paintings of indigenous Aboriginal peoples of Australia and the spontaneous nature of children's drawings. His beautiful tile mural can be seen in the Oriente metro station outside of Lisbon.[27]

Júlio Resende (1917) is a painter, printmaker, and illustrator. His paintings from the 1940's are based on the themes of work and poverty. Along with other students from ESBA Oporto, he organized independent exhibitions in major Portuguese cities. Formally, his work at this time was influenced by Cezanne, but after a trip in 1945 to Madrid where he saw the work of Goya, his paintings became more expressionistic. After a stint studying in Paris, where he learned fresco technique, he moved to the Alentejo, where he founded the International Mission of Art (1953–1958), which offered workshops to connect professional artists with regional traditions. He took a teaching post at the ESBA Oporto in 1958. The paintings of the 1960s were more fluid, and by the 1970s gestural mark-making and light became more important than the figurative elements. Resende designed several stage sets and illustrated books, and his gestural sprawling animal murals can be seen in Jardim Zoológico Metro stop, site of the Lisbon zoo.[28]

Helena Almeida (1934) studied painting at the Escola Superior de Belas Artes in Lisbon (ESBAL). Her diverse body of work often combines aspects of painting, drawing, installation, printmaking, and sculpture, all with the common denominator of photography. Her large-scale, mixed-media photographic portraits have had a strong influence on Portugal's younger generation of artists.[29]

Eduardo Nery (1938) studied painting at ESBAL. During a trip to Paris in 1959 to visit galleries and museums he was influenced by the paintings of Soulanges and Hartung. An exhibition of paintings he had following his trip to Paris at the galleries at the Diário da Notícias resulted in an invitation to work with Jean Lurçat, who launched a renewed interest in contemporary tapestry. This initiated Nery into an international career as a tapestry artist, and his work was represented in the second, third, and fourth Lausanne Bienal. Nery combined his knowledge of the textile field with the design elements of Op Art. He created innovative works that played with vibrant color and shifting space, which he explored not only through tapestry medium but also in his designs for tile murals, mosaic, and large pavements. In the 1970s his work focused on abstract landscapes and photography. From the 1980s on he worked on art in urban spaces and architecture. His playful tile murals of deconstructed eighteenth-century figures can be seen in the Campo Grande metro station.[30]

Miguel Branco (1963) studied painting at ESBAL. His first works exhibited in 1988 were small, terracotta figures depicting everyday, mundane kinds of behaviors (scratching genitals, smoking, and so forth) that were elevated to an iconic significance by their isolation in iron boxes with focused lighting. His later paintings were small, thematically based or serialized oil paintings on wood or canvas that usually featured a single animal or household object drawn from life or photographs. The subject is decontextualized, lacking any narrative, dramatically lit, and with an ambiguous union between subject and ground created by color or brush marks.[31]

Pedro Cabrita Reis (1956) is a sculptor and installation artist who began to make objects out of found materials in the early 1980s, mixing found objects with wood, copper, glass, and piping. In the early 1990s he created gallery installations that explored the concept of the house as a symbol of a human presence. In this context ordinary, domestic objects act as a symbolic presence within an exposed exterior of pipes and struts. Later, Cabrita Reis began to make temporary installations of site-specific works. In his series *Blind Cities*, he created cupboards or sealed units made out of cardboard and wood, imitating the organic construction of a shanty town, and in this way even the materials begin to function as symbols. His latest work is more refined and abstract.[32]

Pedro Proença (1962) draws from literature, mythology, and contemporary culture to create his large-scale installations of exquisite pen-and-ink line drawings. Compilations of many disparate images and strange juxtapositions meander across the surface in comic strip-like compositions of metamorphosing human, vegetal, and animal forms. Classical figurative references and precise botanical illustrations combine with imaginary objects and bizarre organic/machine-like inventions to create an intriguing narrative of picture, symbols, and words.[33]

Other notable artists include Rui Chafres, Nadir Afonso, José de Guimarães, Manuel Cargaleiros, Martins Correia, Francisco Simões, Querubim Lapa, and Jorge Barradas.

Tile Art

No discussion of the art and architecture of Portugal would be complete without a particular emphasis on the country's love affair with tile, which so creatively melds both areas. Tile in Portugal transcended its utilitarian purpose and became instead a canvas for storytelling and architectural embellishment on an epic scale, and it is a continually evolving media embraced by the country's finest contemporary painters.

Any visitor to Portugal can see instantly by its evidence on nearly every edifice in most large cities and its presence in the interiors of nearly every home no matter how humble that tile is the single most popular form of decoration in the country. This art form has been embraced so enthusiastically and used so exuberantly by the Portuguese that Lisbon's Prussian ambassador wrote in 1845, "The azulejo is part of Portugal's physiognomy."[34] Indeed, it is! It is a common sight to see building after building in a city block covered in swathes of richly decorated tile, creating a dizzying and undulating wall of color and pattern. Bridges and large expanses of walls along city streets are covered in painted tile or cut tile laid out in geometric formations that allude to their Moorish origins.

The azulejo as a decorative element can be justified on a practical level that must surely appeal to the Portuguese sense of thrift and practicality. Tiles are easy to clean; they are a deterrent to fire; they reflect the blistering heat of the summer sun; and are impervious to the driving rain and damp of winter. They require little maintenance to upkeep, and when a change is desired they can be removed without significant modification to the structure of the building they decorate.

History

Tiles were introduced to the Iberian peninsula by Moors from North Africa, and most agree that the Portuguese word for tile, *azulejo*, has Arab origins. However, there are as many theories about which Arab word it is derived from as there are tiles in Portugal.

Tiles first appeared in Portugal in the Middle Ages and were used primarily as flooring. They were a more sanitary and durable replacement for the hard, dirt-packed floors in most medieval buildings. Because of the skill and labor required to produce them, tiles were expensive and, therefore, also functioned as important symbols of class and wealth. Limited to the colors of the clay from which they were produced, floor tiles were laid out in intricate and undulating patterns of contrasting light and dark. They were glazed with a shiny, lead glaze colored with oxides of copper (green and black) and iron (yellow). Today it is hard to imagine, looking at the dull surfaces worn by time, but in their day, with their glazed shiny surfaces intact, they must have made a stunning impact when viewed over the large expanse of floors in the cathedrals and royal palaces where they were most commonly used.

Tile design was initially limited to a few basic fabrication techniques. The simplest method was to cut slabs of clay into a variety of shapes that fit together to form larger patterns. This application is particularly effective when used in large spaces. Two-color inlay tiles are made by stamping an impression into the tile surface and then filling in the depressed areas with a contrasting liquified clay, called slip. When firm, the surface is scraped level to reveal a contrasting design. Less durable and practical for floors is the relief method (surface is built up and modeled) and line-impressed (an image is incised into the surface of the mold and the resulting press of clay reveals a raised line drawing).

Later, in the sixteenth-century, tiles were coated with a tin-based glaze, resulting in a pure white surface that was painted with a thin over-glaze colored with oxides. This technique of over-painting gives the effect of a water-color and allows a skillful painter the ability to work with intricate detail and subtle expressions of light and shadow, texture, and expression. It is these expressive tiles, most commonly painted in varying tones of cobalt blue, for which Portugal is most famous. Although the style of blue-and-white painted tile originated in the Netherlands, it was the Portuguese artisan who raised this kind of tile painting to such a fine art and used it in such a grand scale.

The occupying Moors imported tile to Portugal from the Moorish cities of Granada, Seville, and Valencia. These tiles were geometric in design, with tessellated shapes and arabesques, adhering to Sunni religious doctrine that prohibited the depiction of living things. These tiles were fabricated in the cuerda seca (dry cord) technique: line drawings are painted directly on the tile with a mixture of linseed oil and manganese, which acts as a resist when the tile is coated with glaze. This produces a jewel-like tile with brilliantly colored patterns outlined in a dark burgundy brown line. Tiles were also produced using the raised-line technique, with flat areas filled in with brightly colored glazes.

Tiles began to be manufactured in Portugal from the mid-sixteenth century onwards and were influenced by France, Italy, the Netherlands, as well as non-European nations. By the end of the century Portuguese craftsmen had developed their own tile characteristics. The ceramics were made in small workshops, and individual artisans were inspired by textiles imported from India and other exotic places in the Portuguese colonies. Tiles were tin-glazed (majolica, or faience), providing a clean white surface on which to paint floral compositions and religious scenes in brilliant tones of cobalt, burgundy, green, and yellow. While tiles were popular in decorating buildings all over Europe, the Portuguese truly embraced tile's function as a decorative element. They used tile indoors, as was the established custom in Europe, and on the facades of factories, schools, and houses and other public buildings. By the seventeenth and eighteenth centuries Lisbon, Porto, and Coimbra were pouring out tiles for the country's needs as well as for export. Blue-and-white majolica tiles became the new fashion, drawing inspiration from Chinese porcelain and its beautiful cobalt blue decorations, all the rage in Europe. When Dutch blue-and-white imports threatened the Portuguese tile industry, they were banned. In high demand, the designs were copied and produced with such skill it is nearly impossible to tell the difference between Portuguese and Dutch tiles after the beginning of the eighteenth century.[35] The best examples can be seen in many of Lisbon's churches and the surrounding palaces and villas, including Palácio de Queluz, Marquês da Fronteira, the Convents of Madre de Deus, and São Vincente da Fora).

The great wealth pouring into the country from colonial Brazil and India during the reign of Joao V enabled Portuguese royalty and aristocracy to embrace the costly art form with great passion. Europe's largest panels of intricately detailed painted tiles are found in Portugal, decorating palaces and church walls with scenes from the Bible or documenting Portugal's illustrious naval conquests and explorations throughout the world. The São Bento railway station in Oporto by Jorge Colaço (1868–1942), with its narrative historical panels, is a fine example of the stunning effect of blue-and-white story panels applied on a large scale.

Allegorical and mythological themes were popular subjects of the time, as were landscapes and hunt scenes. During the second half of the century, after the earthquake of 1755, polychrome tiles were once again in fashion and began to be used by the merchant and professional classes. Here the tile was used on a more intimate scale. Panels that are purely decorative in design, with rococo flowers and flowing patterns, were often shaped and bordered with faux architectural scroll work, columns, and finials, especially around doors and windows.

Before the nineteenth century, the primary purpose of art was as a means to religious devotion; its purpose was to instruct and inspire the faithful. Many people were illiterate, and the Bible stories depicted in church paintings and tiles served not only to uplift the spirit but to educate the people and serve as dramatic, moral reminders of Church teachings. They also demonstrated the riches of the monarchy and other noble benefactors of the Church. The tin-glazed, blue-and-white tile painting technique adapted from the Dutch was a perfect vehicle to illustrate the magnificence of religious dogma. The best panels in churches all over the country are on such a large scale that they literally envelop the viewer in the spirit of the composition.

Changing tastes in fashion and styles of living have caused the removal and subsequent loss of a great many antique tiles. Old tiles were replaced by new tiles with contemporary designs, and in some cases removed altogether to make way for wallpaper, which was all the rage in the eighteenth and nineteenth centuries. Rapid urbanization and industrialization is the cultural culprit of the twentieth century. Fortunately, Portugal was slow to industrialize, and urban expansion was relatively slow. This was good news for the preservation of Portugal's azulejos, and there remain hundreds of examples of tile in their original locations, mostly in churches, palaces, and private homes of the aristocracy. There is today a clear appreciation of the importance of Portugal's rich tile heritage, and efforts are made everywhere to protect and restore these treasures. A charming aspect of early restoration efforts to the hundreds of blue-and-white story panels that decorate so many of Portugal's churches is the replacement of single missing tiles with a tile of similar coloring, but without pictorial relevance to the composition being restored. The result is akin to the effect created when a quilt is patched with a new piece of a similarly colored fabric of a different pattern.

In the twentieth century, Modernism, with its love of bare cement, glass, and steel, has pushed the use of tile in new construction to the sidelines. With the exception of a few noteworthy projects, such as the Metropolitan subway stations, tile was relegated to the indoors (primarily to the kitchen and bath). It is only recently, within the past 30 years or so, that tile in Portugal is enjoying a renaissance of sorts.

The appreciation for and skill in using tile on a monumental scale continues today in many public works in Portugal. Among the most wonderful are the renovations of and expansions to the Metropolitan subway system in Lisbon, begun in 1959 when painter Maria Keil was commissioned to design tiles for 11 stations. Considering the poor economic conditions of the time, this was an impressive commitment by the Metropolitan's commission to improve the quality of life for the public using what is often a dark and dreary method of transport. Maria Keil's modern, geometric tile compositions can be easily read by the rushing commuter as shifting panels of contrasting light and dark and changing spatial relationships.

When the Metro was again expanding in the late 1980s, the Metropolitan commissioned well-known contemporary artists (Sá Nogueira, Júlio Pomar, Júlio Resende, Manuel Cargaleiro, and Maria Helena Vieira da Silva) to each design a station. With each expansion comes more original tile art by Portugal's best artists. Portuguese engineers no longer view tile as merely a covering for existing walls; the latest stations to be designed integrate the architecture/ structure of the underground stations so seamlessly to the tile art, one cannot stand without the other.

Querubim Lapa, Jorge Barradas, Eduardo Nery, Resende, and Maria Manuela Madureira all made important contributions to the field, with sumptuous flowing glazes, abstracted figurative compositions, and modernist reliefs elevating the tile from a decorative device to a more revered position in the art world.

Calçadas-Sidewalk Design

The Calçadas of Portugal are an art form in their own right, and like tile they appeal to the Portuguese love of highly decorated surfaces. In a sense they are an extension of the tile tradition applied to a horizontal surface. Any large flat surface can serve as a canvas to be decorated, and the wide open spaces of public squares and pedestrian walkways of the largest cities and towns provide a great opportunity to show off the skills of Portuguese stonemasons. Small limestone blocks of blue and white are set by hand in designs of caravels, armillary spheres, crosses, stars, animals, and waves, as well as abstract patterns. These beautiful displays of public art can be seen all over Portugal, concentrated in the larger cities' sidewalks and squares and on the patios of Portugal's palaces and monuments. At Parque das Nações (formerly Expo98), 220,000 square meters of white stone, 180,000 square meters in granite cobblestone, and 130,000 square meters in concrete pavers were used to surface the pedestrian plazas in the fairgrounds.[36] In keeping with the theme of the seas and the Discoveries the pavements are covered with enormous fantastical sea monsters that allude to the superstitions of ancient mariners best seen from above. Huge expanses of decorated pavement in front of the Oceanário (the world's second-largest aquarium tank) attest to the patience and fine craftsmanship of these Portuguese artisans. The sidewalk designs have a practical value as well as an aesthetic one. When subterranean repairs becomes necessary, the blocks are simply popped out, excavations are performed as necessary, and the designs are reset, leaving no trace of the work done, unlike the ugly patches that frequently accumulate on roads and sidewalks as a result of renovations to areas that have been paved with asphalt or cement.

Crafts

Like the cuisine of Portugal, the type of crafts produced throughout the country is dictated largely by regionally available materials, although some crafts traditions such as ceramics, textile arts, and basketry can be found in various forms throughout the country and the islands. Cheerful painted furniture is made in the Alentejo; baskets of reed, straw, wood, and cork are found in country markets all over the nation. Craftsmen from the Beira Baixa and Beira Alta regions are skilled artisans of wrought iron. Even utilitarian objects are embellished, and the carved ox yokes from Minho are decorated with motifs of flowers and patterns also seen in the embroidery of the region. Intricate translucent flowers made from fish scales can be found in the Açores, red-rimmed leather boots in Madeira.

Functional ceramic pottery is made in nearly every corner of the country, from unglazed water jugs called *cantaras* sold in country markets and fairs to elegant decorative ware painted with reproductions of seventeenth-century imagery. Figurines from Redondo and Estremóz depict scenes of daily peasant life: visits to the village dentist, the butcher, fishmonger, lacemakers, weddings, marching bands. Stylized clay roosters decorated with patterns and flowers are found all over Portugal, but their origin is rooted in a legend from Barcelos in the north. It tells the story of a fourteenth- or sixteenth- century pilgrim who, in the process of passing through Barcelos on the way to Santiago da Compostela, was falsely accused of a crime for which the punishment was death. When he was brought before the judge he emphatically proclaimed his innocence. While he was speaking, the judge's dinner was brought out, a roasted rooster. The pilgrim declared that the rooster would affirm his innocence by standing up and crowing, which it promptly did. Needless to say, the pilgrim was released and the image of the cock became a symbol of Barcelos, and by extension, Portugal.

São Pedro do Corval is a major center for folk pottery in the Alentejo. Not so long ago all the ceramics made in the region were wheel thrown; however, the majority of ceramics produced today in this area are ram-pressed or slipcast. One can still find charming scenes of daily life and fanciful flora and fauna hand painted on these mass-produced plates and bowls from the Alentejo region.

Textile traditions flourish in various forms all over the country. Bobbin lace is produced in the coastal areas of Peniche and the Algarve, needlework carpets are stitched in Arraiolos, and traditional and contemporary tapestries are made in Portalegre. The embroidered silk wall hangings and coverlets of Castelo Branco display amazing artistry and craftsmanship. Crocheted bedspreads, tablecloths, and doilies of white cotton cord are seen in all parts of the country and is a craft that nearly every Portuguese girl learns at her mother's side.

Embroidered "lenços dos namorados" (lover's handkerchiefs) are a charming and old-fashioned tradition from Minho and were embroidered by young girls who, when of a marriageable age, offered them like Valentines to a potential suitor as a declaration of her love. Used also as mementos of affection and fidelity, the delicate squares of white linen were embroidered with symbolic motifs and declarations of love by women and offered to their sweethearts as they went off to sea or other lands. They were worked on in a girl's spare time and used as part of her Sunday best until she offered it to the one she loved, who would then wear it around his neck or on the pocket of his suit. The combined symbols were arranged in an original composition and demonstrated the sincerity of the embroiderer's feelings and her skill with the needle.

Maria José dos Santos (Maria "Barraca" b. 1933) is a contemporary folk artist who uses traditional embroidered tapestry techniques to create intimate scenes depicting stories from the life of Santa Barbara, combining words and pictures reminiscent of the painted religious visions of the American folk artist, the Reverend Howard Finster.

The Alentejo is the world's largest producer of cork for export to wine-producing nations. Recent developments in plastic corks have created a need to develop new uses for cork to keep the industry thriving. The Portuguese have risen to this challenge with a growing industry in cork-based textiles, flooring material, and even clothing. One can now find shirts, handbags, hats, and umbrellas for sale in most tourist boutiques, and the resulting textile is surprisingly supple and smooth.

NOTES

1. Timothy Brittain-Catlin, "Material Encounters: For Reasons of History, There Is an Especially Intimate Relationship Between Materials and Portuguese Architecture that Still Encourages Notions of a Regional Identity," *The Architectural Review* (July 2004), www.findarticles.com/p/articles/mi_m3575/is_1289_216/ai_ (accessed December 6, 2005).

2. Robert Levit, "Modern Architecture Redux: Portugal," *The Journal of the International Institute* Vol. 4, No. 3, www.umich.edu/~iinet/journal/vol4no3/levit.html (accessed December 6, 2005).

3. Ibid.

4. Brittain-Catlin, op. cit.

5. Ibid.

6. Michel Toussaint, "Fernando Tavora," *Editorial Blau*, www.cidadevirtual.pt/blau/tavora.html (accessed December 6, 2005).

7. Pedro Vieira de Almeida, "Álvaro Siza Vieira," *Editorial Blau* (July 1995), www.cidadevirtual.pt/blau/siza.html (accessed December 6, 2005).

8. Hans Van Dijk, "Eduardo Souto Moura," *Archis* (December 1994), www.cidadevirtual.pt/blau/moura.html (accessed December 6, 2005).

9. www.ParquedasNacoes.pt (accessed August 15, 2009).

10. Fátima Fernandes and Michele Cannatà, *Contemporary Architecture in Portugal, 1991–2001* (Porto: Portugal: Edicoes ASA, 2001).

11. José-Augusto França, et al., "Portugal," in *Grove Art Online, Oxford Art Online*, http://0-www.oxfordartonline.com.library.dowling.edu/subscriber/article/grove/art/T068860pg3 (accessed October 8, 2009).

12. Dagoberto L. Markl, "Gonçalves, Nuno," in *Grove Art Online, Oxford Art Online*, http://0-www.oxfordartonline.com.library.dowling.edu/subscriber/article/grove/art/T033155 (accessed October 8, 2009).

13. José-Augusto França, et al., op. cit.

14. José Fernandes Pereira, "Almeida, José de," in *Grove Art Online, Oxford Art Online*, http://0-www.oxfordartonline.com.library.dowling.edu/subscriber/article/grove/art/T001969 (accessed October 8, 2009).

15. John Bury, "Almeida, José de," in *The Oxford Companion to Western Art*, ed. Hugh Brigstocke, Oxford Art Online, http://0-www.oxfordartonline.com.library.dowling.edu/subscriber/article/opr/t118/e46 (accessed October 8, 2009).

16. John Bury, "Machado de Castro, Joaquím," in *The Oxford Companion to Western Art*, ed. Hugh Brigstocke, Oxford Art Online, http://0-www.oxfordartonline.com.library.dowling.edu/subscriber/article/opr/t118/e1547 (accessed October 8, 2009).

17. "Soares dos Reis, Antonio," in *The Oxford Companion to Western Art*, ed. Hugh Brigstocke, Oxford Art Online, http://0-www.oxfordartonline.com.library.dowling.edu/subscriber/article/opr/t118/e2465 (accessed October 8, 2009).

18. Lucília Verdelho da Costa, "Teixeira Lopes, António," in *Grove Art Online, Oxford Art Online*, http://0-www.oxfordartonline.com.library.dowling.edu/subscriber/article/grove/art/T083654 (accessed October 8, 2009).

19. José-Augusto França, "Bordalo Pinheiro," in *Grove Art Online, Oxford Art Online*, http://0-www.oxfordartonline.com.library.dowling.edu/subscriber/article/grove/art/T010062 (accessed October 8, 2009).

20. Ana Filipa Candeias, "José de Almada Negreiros," www.camjap.gulbenkian.pt/l2/ar%7BD2B27546-03B0-4185-A5F8-0B5ACC3E203C%7D/c%7B6c27466d-35db-466c-ae6c-d58f9a23789e%7D/m1/T1.aspx (accessed October 8, 2009).

21. Ruth Rosengarten, "Almada Negreiros," in *Grove Art Online, Oxford Art Online*, http://0-www.oxfordartonline.com.library.dowling.edu/subscriber/article/grove/art/T001950 (accessed October 8, 2009).

22. Ruth Rosengarten, "Santa-Rita," in *Grove Art Online, Oxford Art Online*, http://0-www.oxfordartonline.com.library.dowling.edu/subscriber/article/grove/art/T075859 (accessed October 8, 2009).

23. Ibid.

24. Gisela Rosenthal, *Vieira da Silva* (Lisbon: Taschen, 1998).

25. John McEwan, "Rego, Paula," in *Grove Art Online, Oxford Art Online*, http://0-www.oxfordartonline.com.library.dowling.edu/subscriber/article/grove/art/T071172 (accessed October 8, 2009).

26. Ruth Rosengarten, "Pomar, Júlio," in *Grove Art Online, Oxford Art Online*, http://0-www.oxfordartonline.com.library.dowling.edu/subscriber/article/grove/art/T068548 (accessed October 8, 2009).

27. Ruth Rosengarten, "Rodrigo, Joaquim," in *Grove Art Online, Oxford Art Online*, http://0-www.oxfordartonline.com.library.dowling.edu/subscriber/article/grove/art/T072601 (accessed October 8, 2009).

28. Ruth Rosengarten, "Resende, Júlio," in *Grove Art Online, Oxford Art Online*, http://0-www.oxfordartonline.com.library.dowling.edu/subscriber/article/grove/art/T071582 (accessed October 8, 2009).

29. Maria Almeida Lima, "Helena Almeida," www.camjap.gulbenkian.pt/l2/ar{D2B27546-03B0-4185-A5F8-0B5ACC3E203C}/c{8dad63ff-8354-451d-8d26-780a2d4b17bb}/m1/T1.aspx (accessed October 8, 2009).

30. Maria Almeida Lima, "Eduardo Nery," www.camjap.gulbenkian.pt/l2/ar{D2B27546-03B0-4185-A5F8-0B5ACC3E203C}/c{98f17e25-e97c-4a95-bf30-c039d02b2603}/m1/T1.aspx (accessed October 8, 2009).

31. Nuno Faria, "Miguel Branco," www.camjap.gulbenkian.pt/l2/ar{D2B27546-03B0-4185-A5F8-0B5ACC3E203C}/c{e66308ff-0aae-4564-84de-e37b81745b97}/m1/T1.aspx (accessed October 8, 2009).

32. Catherine M. Grant, "Cabrita Reis, Pedro," in *Grove Art Online, Oxford Art Online*, http://0-www.oxfordartonline.com.library.dowling.edu/subscriber/article/grove/art/T097550 (accessed October 8, 2009).

33. Ana Vasconcelos E. Melo, "Pedro Proença," www.camjap.gulbenkian.pt/l2/ar{D2B27546-03B0-4185-A5F8-0B5ACC3E203C}/c{56bf3c2f-8e4a-4f5e-8a5d-68b7a6af9758}/m1/T1.aspx (accessed October 8, 2009).

34. Joao Castel-Branco Pereira, *Portuguese Tiles from the National Museum of Azulejo, Lisbon* (London: Zwemmer Publishers Ltd., 1995), 39.

35. Noel Riley, *Tile Art: A History of Decorative Ceramic Tiles* (Secaucus, NJ: Quintet Publishing Ltd., 1987).

36. www.parquedasnacoes.pt (accessed August 15, 2009).

SELECTED READINGS

Almeida, Pedro Vieira de. "Álvaro Siza Vieira." *Editorial Blau*. www.cidadevirtual.pt/blau/siza.html (accessed December 6, 2005).

Brittain-Catlin, Timothy. "Material Encounters: For Reasons of History, There Is an Especially Intimate Relationship Between Materials and Portuguese Architecture that Still Encourages Notions of a Regional Identity." *The Architectural Review* (July 2004). www.findarticles.com/p/articles/mi_m3575/is_1289_216/ai_ (accessed December 6, 2005).

Bury, John Bernard. *The Oxford Companion to Western Art* (accessed August 15, 2009).

Fernandes, Fátima, and Michele Cannatà. *Contemporary Architecture in Portugal, 1991–2001.* Porto, Portugal: Edições ASA, 2001.

Fernandes, José Manuel. *Arquitectura Portuguesa: uma Síntese.* Lisbon: Imprensa Nacional, 2000.

"Fernando Tavora." www.cidadevirtual.pt/blau/tavora.html (accessed December 6, 2005).

Grove Art on Line (accessed August 15, 2009).

Katz, Peter. "The Architecture of Community." *The New Urbanism: Toward an Architecture of Community.* New York: McGraw-Hill, 1994.

Levit, Robert. "Modern Architecture Redux: Portugal." *The Journal of the International Institute.* http://www.umich.edu/~iinet/journal/vol4no3/levit.html (accessed December 6, 2005).

Pereira, Paulo. *2000 Anos de Arte em Portugal.* Lisboa: Temas e Debates, 1999.

Pereira, Joao Castel-Branco. *Arte Metropolitano de Lisboa.* Lisbon: Metropolitano de Lisboa, n.d.

———. *Portuguese Tiles from the national Museum of Azulejo, Lisbon.* London: Zwemmer Publishers Ltd., 1995.

Riley, Noel. *Tile Art: A History of Decorative Ceramic Tiles.* Secaucus, NJ: Quintet Publishing Ltd., 1987.

Rosenthal, Gisela. *Vieira da Silva.* Lisbon: Taschen, 1998.

Toussaint, Michel. "Fernando Tavora." *Editorial Blau.* www.cidadevirtual.pt/blau/tavora.html (accessed December 6, 2005).

Van Dijk, Hans. "Eduardo Souto Moura." *Archis* (December 1994). *Editorial Blau,* www.cidadevirtual.pt/blau/moura.html (accessed December 6, 2005).

www.amadorabd.com.

www.camjap.gulbenkian.org.

www.metrolisboa.pt.

www.parquedasnacoes.pt.

Glossary

açorda de café: An Alentejano afternoon snack of day-old bread crumbled into a bowl, sprinkled with sugar, and doused with milky coffee.

açordas: A cross between a soup and a stew, made by moistening bread to a porridge-like consistency with broth, garlic, and olive oil.

agua pé: A weak table wine produced by peasants for their own consumption.

aldeia: Village.

Armed Forces Movement: The military group of mid-level officers that overthrew the Portuguese dictatorship on April 25, 1974, and was influential in politics via its constitutional role in the Council of the Revolution during the democratic consolidation period.

arraial: Festival.

bacalhau e batatas: Traditional Christmas eve meal of boiled salted codfish and potatoes.

bica: Expresso coffee.

Bolo Rei: Christmas fruitcake containing a single fava bean and a tiny toy.

bolos de bacalhau: Deep-fried codfish cakes.

brazeira: A large, round, family-style foot warmer in which embers are placed.

broa: The dense, moist cornbread found in nearly every peasant village in Portugal.

cabeça de nabo: Turnip.

caldo verde: Kale soup.

cancioneiros: Lyric songbooks dating back to the twelfth century that were a more developed form of oral, poetic tradition written by professional court troubadours, public entertainers, aristocrats, and clerics.

cántaras: Clay water jugs.

cantigas de amigo: Friend songs.

cantigas de amor: Love songs.

cantigas de escárnio: Mocking songs.

cantigas de maldizer: Curse songs.

canto de intervenção: Songs of protest that originated in Coimbra in the 1960s.

canto livre: Songs of protest, especially beginning in the 1960s.

cavaleiros: Horsemen, also gentlemen, which often designates the men's restroom.

cepo: Tree stump and the name of the bonfire lit for Christmas festivities.

chanfana: A traditional dish of stewed mutton either served with roasted potatoes or over-boiled potatoes.

comadre and/or compadre: Godparents, which in Portugal represents a special tie with the child's parents, almost like a brother or sister.

Council of the Revolution: Military oversight group created in the 1976 constitution to preserve the conquests of the Portuguese revolution via judicial review powers.

desafios: A form of spontaneous satire sung by a duet.

Descobrimentos: Portuguese global sea-faring discoveries during the age of exploration in the fifteenth and sixteenth centuries.

desgarradas or cantares ao desafio: Spontaneous singing, back-and-forth duel.

dobrada: Tripe, which is cleansed and bleached cow stomach. A traditional dish of the same name consists of tripe stewed with white beans.

drama de actualidade: Theatrical dramas of the early 1899s that dealt with contemporary issues.

Enlightenment: An eighteenth-century philosophical movement rejecting traditional ideas and favoring rationalism.

escudo: Portuguese monetary currency until the Euro was adopted. The escudo disappeared in February 2002.

Estado Novo: Salazar's corporatist "New State."

"Estou na escura!": "I'm in the darkness!" A typical exclamation at mealtime if the diner finds that his wine glass is empty and needs refilling.

estrume: Straw or groundcover used underfoot in courtyards and animal stables that is composted and then used as fertilizer.

Fado: Portugal's national music with its plaintive and melancholic songs of lost love and life's hardships.

Fado vadio: A spontaneous outburst of Fado sung by amateurs at taverns in the traditional regions of Lisbon.

feijoadas: Bean stews.

festa: Festival.

fogaças: Meals made as offerings to a particular saint and/or to contribute toward the support of religious festivities. They are auctioned during the festival after being paraded in the religious procession.

fonte: Natural spring.

futebol: Soccer.

graças a Deus: Thanks be to God.

gulosa(o): Sweet tooth.

Integralism: The Lusitanian Integralist movement founded in 1910 that sought the restoration of the Portuguese monarchy and emphasized God, family, and other traditional concepts.

Jacobin: An extremist group advocating egalitarian democracy and engaging in terrorist activity (influenced by the group active during the French revolution).

jantar: Dinner.

lagares: Large stone or concrete vats where grapes are pressed for their juice. Lagares are also used for crushing olives to produce olive oil.

lanche: Mid-afternoon snack.

lareira: Fireplace.

lareira electrónica: In the past, gathering around the hearth contributed towards communication and socialization as people told stories, sang, and conversed while warming themselves. Television has replaced the traditional hearth and is at times referred to as the "lareira electrónica."

latifundios: Large, landed estates typical of southern Portugal.

lenços de namorados: Lover's handkerchiefs.

Lisboetas: Residents of Lisbon.

Lusitania: Roman name for the region known as Portugal. Today the Portuguese frequently use the word to refer to themselves. For example, Luso-American refers to a Portuguese living in the United States.

luto: Mourning, which for women after the loss of their husbands often means the wearing of black clothes for the rest of their lives.

macacos: Wooden paddles used to turn grape stems, seeds, and skin back into the vat during the port wine pressing process. Also the word for "monkey."

Manuelino: Portugal's most original contribution to the history of architecture. The style mixed symbols of Christianity with ornate motifs that encrust surfaces of monuments like barnacles.

Marquis de Pombal: Ruled from 1750 to 1777 during the reign of King José I and played an important role in rebuilding Lisbon after the devastating earthquake/tsunami of 1755 that destroyed most of the capital.

Methuen Treaty: The 1703 trade agreement with England that facilitated exports of wine and imports of woolen textiles.

minifundios: Small, intensively cultivated, subsistence peasant land-holdings dominant in central and northern Portugal.

nacional-cançonetismo: A musical pop genre designed by the regime as propaganda that emphasized "good" values of society, platonic love, God, and romance.

Onde é sua terra?: Where is your home? (Meaning "What village are you from?")

Pai Natal: Father Christmas (Santa Claus).

pega de Cara: Grabbing of the bull's face during a bullfight.

Pombalino: Of or relating to the Marquis of Pombal reign, chief minister of Dom João I. In architecture the Pombalino style lasted from 1755 to 1860.

povo: Village square.

quinta: Estate farm.

ranchos: Portuguese folkloric dance troupes.

Republicanism: The belief in representative democracy.

retornados: Portuguese settlers (approximately 650,000) expelled from ex-African colonies in 1975.

Reviralhista: Reversals, as in one who wants to reverse a regime to the previous regime.

Rio: River.

rodilha: A hard, stuffed doughnut of cloth or straw used to help balance the loads on women's heads.

romaria: Religious festival.

ruínas: Ruins, such as Roman ruins.

salgado: Savory pastry of meat or fish, such as "bolos de bacalhau."

sardinha assada: Grilled herring.

saudade: A sense of unremitting nostalgia and impossible yearnings for the past while faced with an intolerable present and uncertain future.

Sebastianism: A messianic faith that the lost king Sebastião (1557–1578) will return to redeem the country and return it to its past prosperity and glory.

se Deus quiser: God willing.

serra: Mountain.

tabuleira: Wooden tray, often used to carry bread or fish.

terra: Land (also as in "home" or "place").

toureiros: Toreadors.

Vinho Verde: The popular "green" wine so named not because of its color, but because it is bottled after only a short fermentation and is still "young." It has a light, crisp flavor and a slight fizz.

vitela: Veal.

Bibliography

60 Anos de Luta. Lisboa: Edições *Avante!*, 1982.

Almeida, Pedro Vieira de. "Álvaro Siza Vieira." Editorial Blau. www.cidadevirtual.pt/blau/siza.html (accessed December 6, 2005).

Ambrosio, Teresa. "O Sistema Educativo: Ruptura, Estabilização e Desafios Europeus." In *Portugal Contemporaneo*. 1974–1992, Vol. VI, edited by António Reis. Lisboa: Publicações Alfa, 1990.

Anderson, Jean. *The Food of Portugal*. NYC: HarperCollins, 1994.

António Reis, ed. *Portugal Contemporaneo*, Vol. I–IV. Lisboa: Publicações Alfa, 1989–1990.

Barreto, António and Maria Filomena Monica, eds. *Dicionário de História de Portugal*, Vol. VIII. Lisbon: Livraria Figueirinhas, 2000.

Brittain-Catlin, Timothy. "Material Encounters: For Reasons of History, There Is an Especially Intimate Relationship Between Materials and Portuguese Architecture that Still Encourages Notions of a Regional Identity." *The Architectural Review* (July 2004). www.findarticles.com/p/articles/mi_m3575/is_1289_216/ai_ (accessed December 6, 2005).

Brito, Manuel Carlos de and Luisa Cymbron. *História da Música Portuguesa*. Lisboa: Universidade Aberta, 1992.

Bruneau, Thomas C. *Politics and Nationhood*. New York: Praeger Press, 1984.

br.geocities.com/edterranova/pessoa.htm.

Bury, John Bernard. *The Oxford Companion to Western Art*. www.oxfordartonline.com (accessed August 15, 2009).

Calafate, Pedro, ed. *História do Pensamento Filosófico Português: Volume 1–Idade Média.* Lisbon: Editorial Caminho, 1999.

———. *História do Pensamento Filosófico Português: Volume II–Renascimento e Contra-Reforma.* Lisbon: Circulo de Leitores, 2002.

———. *História do Pensamento Filosófico Português: Volume 5–O Século XX–Tomo 1.* Lisbon: Editorial Caminho, 2000.

———. *História do Pensamento Filosófico Português: Volume 5–O Século XX–Tomo 2.* Lisbon: Editorial Caminho, 2000.

Câmara, José Bettencourt da. *O Essencial sobre a Música Tradicional Portuguesa.* Lisboa: Imprensa Nacional, 2001.

Cardoso, Gustavo, Carlos Cunha, Susana Santos, and Tania Cardoso. "The Representation of Terrorist Threat on Portuguese TV and the Euro 2004 Cup." In *Comunicação e Jornalismo na Era da Informação*, edited by Gustavo Cardoso and Rita Espanha. Porto, Portugal: Campo das Letras.

Cardoso, Miguel Esteves. *Escrítica Pop: Um Quarto da quarta década do Rock, 1980–1982.* Lisbon: Assírio & Alvim, 2003.

Carvalho, Ruben de. *As Músicas do Fad.* Porto: Campo das Letras, 1994.

Costa Pinto, António, ed. *Modern Portugal.* Palo Alto, CA: The Society for the Promotion of Science and Scholarship, 1998.

———. *Contemporary Portugal: Politics, Society and Culture.* Boulder, CO: Social Science Monographs, 2003.

"Education System in Portugal." http://www.shelteroffshore.com/index.php/living/more/education_system_in_portugal/ (accessed April 5, 2006).

Fazenda, Maria José, ed. *Present Movements: Aspects of Independent Dance in Portugal.* Lisboa: Edições Cotovia, 1997.

Fernandes, Fátima, and Michele Cannatà. *Contemporary Architecture in Portugal, 1991–2001.* Porto, Portugal: Edições ASA, 2001.

Fernandes, José Manuel. *Arquitectura Portuguesa: uma Síntese.* Lisbon: Imprensa Nacional, 2000.

"Fernando Tavora." www.cidadevirtual.pt/blau/tavora.html (accessed December 6, 2005).

França, Isabel Murteira. *Fernando Pessoa na Intimidade.* Lisbon: Publicações Dom Quixote, 1987.

Frier, David. "José Saramago's O Evangelho Segundo Jesus Christo: Outline of a Newer Testament." *The Modern Language Review*, Vol. 100, No. 2 (April 2005): 367.

Gallagher, Tom. *Portugal: A Twentieth Century Interpretation.* Manchester, England: Manchester University Press, 1983, 98.

Gomes, Maria do Carmo, Patrícia Ávila, João Sebastião, and António Firmino da Costa. "Novas Análises dos Níveis de Literacia em Portugal: Comparações Diacrónicas e Internacionais." Paper presented at IV Congresso Português de Sociologia. http://www.aps.pt/cms/docs_prv/docs/DPR462de53172c7d_1.PDF.

Graham, Lawrence S., and Harry M. Makler, eds. *Contemporary Portugal.* Austin: University of Texas Press, 1979.

Henderson, Helene, and Sue Ellen Thompson, eds. *Holidays, Festivals, and Celebrations of the World Dictionary.* Detroit, MI: Omnigraphics Inc., 1997.

Higgs, David. "Portugal." *Encyclopedia of Homosexuality.* Edited by Wayne R. Dynes. New York: Garland Publishing, 1990.

"Imprensa." http://www.ucs.pt/verfs.php?lang=pt&fscod=328&imprimir=1\ (accessed July 11, 2007).

Katz, Peter. "The Architecture of Community." *The New Urbanism: Toward an Architecture of Community.* New York: McGraw-Hill, 1994.

Keefe, Eugene et al. *Area Handbook for Portugal.* Washington, DC: U.S. Government Printing Office, 1977.

Levit, Robert. "Modern Architecture Redux: Portugal." *The Journal of the International Institute.* http://www.umich.edu/~iinet/journal/vol4no3/levit.html (accessed December 6, 2005).

Livermore, H. V., ed. *Portugal and Brazil: An Introduction.* Oxford: Oxford University Press, 1963.

Mayson, Richard. "Portugal." In *A Century of Wine: The Story of a Wine Revolution,* edited by Stephen Brook, 146. London: Mitchell Beazley, 2000.

Manuel, Paul Christopher. *The Challenges of Democratic Consolidation: Political, Economic, and Military Issues, 1976–1991.* Westport, CT: Praeger, 1996.

Modesto, Maria de Lourdes. *Cozinha Tradicional Portuguesa.* Lisbon: Editorial Verbo, 1997.

Monteiro, George, ed. *The Man Never Was: Essays on Fernando Pessoa.* Providence, RI: Gavea-Brown, 1982.

Neves, Ceu. "Família e profissão em Portugal. Mulheres trabalham muito e acham normal." *Diário de Notícias,* January 15, 2005.

———. "Menos apoios e cada vez menos crianças." *Diário de Notícias,* November 6, 2005.

Neto, Manuel. "Solidão (também) mata ... não só idosos como jovens." *Diário de Notícias,* December 6, 2004.

Oliveira, José. "Livro, Leitura, Literacia." *O Militante* No. 228 (May/June 1997).

Oliveira Marques, A. H. de. *History of Portugal,* 2 Vols. New York: Columbia University Press, 1972.

Ortins, Ana Patuleia. *Portuguese Homestyle Cooking.* Northampton, MA: Interlink Publishing, 2002.

Pais, José Machado, Manuel Vilaverde Cabral, and Jorge Vala, eds. *Religião e Bioética.* Lisbon: Imprensa de Ciências Sociais, 2001.

Payne, Stanley G. *Spain and Portugal,* 2 Vols. Madison: University of Wisconsin Press, 1973.

Pereira, Joao Castel-Branco. *Arte Metropolitano de Lisboa.* Lisbon: Metropolitano de Lisboa, n.d.

———. *Portuguese Tiles from the National Museum of Azulejo, Lisbon.* London: Zwemmer Publishers Ltd., 1995.

Pereira, José Pacheco. "As Primeiras Séries do *Avante!* Clandestino," *Estudos Sobre O Comunismo,* No. 0, 1983.

Pereira, Paulo. *2000 Anos de Arte em Portugal*. Lisboa: Temas e Debates, 1999.

Pessoa, Fernando. *Obra Poética*. Rio de Janeiro: José Aguilar Editora, 1972.

———. *The Book of Disquiet*, Translated by Richard Zenith. New York: Penguin, 2003.

"Portugal—History & Background." http://education.stateuniversity.com/pages/1220/Portugal-HISTORY-BACKGROUND.html (accessed June 5, 2007).

"Rádio." http://www.ucs.pt/verfs.php?lang=pt&fscod=329&imprimir=1 (accessed July 11, 2007).

Raposo, Eduardo M. *Canto de Intervenção: 1960–1974*. Lisbon: Público, 2007.

Rapp, Linda. www.glbtq.com/social-sciences/portugal.html.

Rector, M., and F. M. Clark, eds. "Portuguese Writers." In *Dictionary of Literary Biography*, Vol. 287. Detroit, MI: Gale Publishing, 2004.

Riley, Noel. *Tile Art: A History of Decorative Ceramic Tiles*. Secaucus, NJ: Quintet Publishing Ltd., 1987.

Robertson, Carol. *Portuguese Cooking: The Authentic and Robust Cuisine of Portugal*. Berkeley, CA: North Atlantic Books, 1993.

Rosas, Fernando, and J. M. Brandão de Brito. *Dicionário de História do Estado Novo*, Vol. I and Vol. II. Venda Nova: Bertrand Editora, 1996.

Rosenthal, Gisela. *Vieira da Silva*. Lisbon: Taschen, 1998.

Sanchis, Pierre. *Arraial: Festa de um Povo, as Romarias Portuguesas*. Lisboa: Pulicações Dom Quixote, 1983.

Santos, Ana Cristina. "Lesbian, Gay, Bisexual, and Transgendered Rights." www.eumap.org/journal/features/2002/april02/portugesesexorient.

Sasportes, José, and António Pinto Ribeiro. *História da Dança*. Lisboa: Imprensa Nacional, 1991.

Saramago, José. "The 1998 Nobel Lecture." *World Literature Today*, Vol. 73, No. 1 (Winter 1999).

Solsten, Eric, ed. *Portugal: A Country Study*. Washington, DC: U.S. Government Printing Office, 1994.

Sousa, Jesus Maria. "Education Policy in Portugal: Changes and Perspectives." *Education Policy Analysis Archives*, Vol. 8, No. 5 (January 10, 2005). www.epaa.asu.edu/v8n5.html.

Syrett, Stephen, ed. *Contemporary Portugal: Dimensions of Economic and Political Change*. Aldershot, UK: Ashgate Publishing, 2002.

"Televisão," http://www.ucs.pt/verfs.php?lang=pt&fscod=330&imprimir=1 (accessed July 11, 2007).

"Thematic Review of the Transition from Initial Education to Working Life—Portugal." November 1997. http://www.oecd.org (accessed April 5, 2006).

Torgal, Luís Reis. "Cinema e Propaganda no Estado Novo: A 'Conversão dos Descrentes.'" *Revista de Historia das Ideias*, Vol. 18 (1996): 277–337.

Toussaint, Michel. "Fernando Tavora." Editorial Blau. www.cidadevirtual.pt/blau/tavora.html (accessed December 6, 2005).

Tovar, Patricia. "Images and Reality of Widowhood in Portugal." *Portuguese Studies Review*, Vol. 6, No. 2 (Fall-Winter, 1997–1998).

Traquina, Nelson, and Warren K. Agee. "Portuguese Audiovisual Policy: Confronting the 90s." *Portuguese Studies Review*, Vol. 4, No. 2 (Fall-Winter, 1995–1996): 62–76.

United Nations Educational, Scientific and Cultural Organization (UNESCO). http://portal.unesco.org/education/en/ev.php-URL_ID=41771&URL_DO=DO _TOPIC&URL_SECTION=201.html.

Van Dijk, Hans. "Eduardo Souto Moura." *Archis* (December 1994). Editorial Blau. www.cidadevirtual.pt/blau/moura.html (accessed December 6, 2005).

Viana, Luís Miguel. "Partídos limitam mulheres no acesso aos cargos." *Diário de Notícias*, May 20, 2005.

Wheeler, Douglas L. *Historical Dictionary of Portugal.* Lanham, MD: Scarecrow Press, 1993.

www.amadorabd.com.

www.bar-do-binho.com.

www.camjap.gulbenkian.org.

www.instituto-camoes.pt/cvc/literatura.

www.intowine.com/port.html.

www.metrolisboa.pt.

www.parquedasnacoes.pt.

www.portwine.com.

Zimdars-Swartz, Sandra L. *Encountering Mary: From La Salette to Medjugorje.* Princeton, NJ: Princeton University Press, 1991.

Index

About the Authors

CARLOS A. CUNHA, Ph.D., is Executive Chair of the Faculty and Chair of the Political Science Department at Dowling College in Oakdale, New York. He is also a research associate in the Centro de Investigação de Estudos Sociológicos (CIES) at Lisbon University Institute (Instituto Superior de Ciências do Trabalho e das Empresas—ISCTE/IUL). He wrote *The Portuguese Communist Party's Strategy for Power, 1921–1986* (Garland, 1992) and has published numerous articles, book chapters, and reviews on various aspects of Portuguese politics, specializing on the use of new media in the nation as well as the Portuguese Communist Party.

RHONDA CUNHA has been an artist and educator for 25 years. She holds a BFA in Sculpture from the University of Massachusetts/Amherst and an MFA in Fibers from Cranbrook Academy of Art. She is currently pursuing an MS in Literacy Education at Dowling College. She was Fulbright Lecturer in Textile Design and Fibers at UFSM/Rio Grande de Sul (Brazil) and has exhibited her artwork throughout the United States and in Portugal and Brazil.